Genderblindness in American Society

Genderblindness in American Society

The Rhetoric of a System of Social Control of Women

Lucy J. Miller

LEXINGTON BOOKS
Lanham • Boulder • New York • London

Published by Lexington Books
An imprint of The Rowman & Littlefield Publishing Group, Inc.
4501 Forbes Boulevard, Suite 200, Lanham, Maryland 20706
www.rowman.com

6 Tinworth Street, London SE11 5AL

Copyright © 2019 by The Rowman & Littlefield Publishing Group, Inc.

All rights reserved. No part of this book may be reproduced in any form or by any electronic or mechanical means, including information storage and retrieval systems, without written permission from the publisher, except by a reviewer who may quote passages in a review.

British Library Cataloguing in Publication Information Available

Library of Congress Cataloging-in-Publication Data is Available

ISBN 9781498567923 (cloth : alk. paper)
ISBN 9781498567947 (pbk: alk. paper)
ISBN 9781498567930 (electronic)

∞™ The paper used in this publication meets the minimum requirements of American National Standard for Information Sciences Permanence of Paper for Printed Library Materials, ANSI/NISO Z39.48-1992.

Contents

Acknowledgments — vii
Introduction — 1

1 Genderblindness and the Wage Gap — 21
2 Genderblindness and Abortion — 53
3 Genderblindness and Rape Culture — 85
4 Genderblindness and Tech Culture — 111

Conclusion — 147
Index — 155
About the Author — 163

Acknowledgments

This book could not have been completed without the support of numerous people in my life. First and most importantly is my amazing friend Sara Rowe. Sara has been with me through the ups and downs not just of writing this book but of life in general. She has always been willing to listen to my latest thoughts on the book and other projects and has supported me through the tough times in life. I consider myself fortunate to have such a wonderful friend in my life. Another friend who deserves similar thanks is Chris Silver. I have known Chris for over a decade now, and our not-nearly-frequent-enough phone calls and trips to anime conventions have been a source of enjoyment and needed relief from the daily grind of life.

Another person who deserves special recognition is Josh Heuman. Josh was one of the co-chairs of my dissertation committee, and through that process and in the years after, Josh has always been willing to lend an ear to my latest research ideas or concerns about the job market, read any research project I sent to him, and write numerous letters of recommendation. I also want to thank Aisha Durham and Kristan Poirot for their support in this area.

Working with the team at Lexington Books has also been a pleasurable experience. I want to specifically highlight the work of Nicolette Amstutz, Senior Acquisitions Editor, for her willingness to work with me to ensure that this project was completed in a timely fashion and that the process of doing so ran smoothly. From originally approaching me about project ideas to the completion of this book, Lexington and Nicolette have made everything from their end straightforward and easy.

Finally, I want to highlight a few of my friends and colleagues at Texas A&M University and academia in general who have helped me in various ways in completing this project. I want to specifically thank Jessica Gantt Shafer for her enthusiastic interest in this project. I also want to thank Leland

Spencer, Brad Serber, Eleanor Amartanth Lockhart, Aimee Upton, Dave Tarvin, Mike Rold, Tommy Adams, Elizabeth Earle, Zoë Hess Carney, Amanda Martinez, Srividya Ramasubramanian, Andrea Terry, Masha Shukovich, Leandra Hernádez, Marissa Doshi, Lucas Logan, Erin Logan, Brittany Collins Hampston, Jennifer Jones Barbour, Brian Altenhofen, Dan De Leon, Ruth Tsuria, Tasha Dubriwny, Jennifer Mercieca, Nancy Street, Joseph Carr, Lital Pascar, Lisa Ellis, Dan Humphrey, Joel Reed, Patrick Burkart, Antonio La Pastina, Patricia Amason, Ryan Rigda, Carrie Murawski, Alex Souza, Victoria Stiegel, Kevin Barge, and Andrea Calland. Without your support in a variety of ways, this project would not have been completed.

Introduction

On November 8, 2016, Hillary Clinton lost her bid for the presidency to Republican candidate Donald Trump. As the first woman to be the nominee of a major party, Clinton's victory in the election would have been historic, but her campaign ended in a crushing defeat. There are many challenges that any woman seeking to become president must overcome, particularly the rhetorical construction of the presidency as masculine, which creates barriers for women seeking the office given the dominance of traditional views of gender in the nation.[1] There have been many articles written since the election analyzing why Clinton lost, but what stands out is that most of them do not even mention gender as a factor. Dan Roberts identifies in his *Guardian* article the economy, lack of trust, a message vacuum, and broken polls as the reasons Clinton lost in 2016.[2] For Molly Ball in *The Atlantic*, lack of outreach to the white working class, Clinton's poor performance with the "Obama coalition," economic message, reliance on experienced campaign staffers, and arrogance explain her loss.[3] In his CNN analysis of why Clinton remains unpopular in 2018, Chris Cillizza offers the fact that President Trump has never let the 2016 campaign end, Clinton has not seemed sorry for losing, she continues to function as the last Republican bogeyman, and we are still too close to the election as explanations.[4] I am not making the argument here that gender is the only explanation for Clinton's loss, but it stands out that in so many articles searching for an explanation, gender is never considered. This tendency to not even consider gender when analyzing the treatment of women in public life in America, I argue, is a sign of genderblindness.

Genderblindness is not the absence of considerations of gender. Instead, genderblindness means a lack of awareness of how gender is absent from public debate and discussion. I argue in this book that genderblindness shapes the current efforts to control women in American society. Unlike previous forms of control that sought to limit women's freedom and access to public space, genderblindness works to control women by reducing their life chances and arguing that men and women should be treated only as individuals because equality has already been achieved. Genderblind rhetoric supports these ideological goals by seeking to remove gender as a means of public persuasive appeals. Women are, thus, unable to ground their arguments in their lived experiences as women because gender is considered invalid as an explanation for treatment in public life. In place of group identities like gender, individual experience and responsibility is favored instead. This focus on the individual disadvantages marginalized groups who do not have the power in the current social structure to make their voices easily heard. Marginalized groups gain power by speaking as a group while dominant members of society maintain power by speaking as individuals. Gender should empower women to take a more active role in public life, so it is disallowed in a rhetoric of genderblindness.

This rhetoric of genderblindness is analyzed in this book in the areas of the workplace, reproductive health, rape culture, and tech culture. Using a critical rhetoric approach, I conduct a critique of domination and a critique of freedom in each of these areas in order to show how women continue to be controlled through public discourse by the dominant groups in American society and how appeals to the increased freedom and equality of women in certain areas are used to maintain the status quo and sustain the marginalization of women. Genderblindness, in this sense, functions as an ideology to keep women in their marginalized place and prevent all citizens from recognizing this continued marginalization. Along with discursively constructing women as marginalized, the rhetoric of genderblindness also has material effects in the lives of women, which are considered through the Foucauldian concepts of biopolitics and disciplinary power.

This introduction proceeds by first discussing genderblindness as an ideology. I give particular attention in this section to the inspiration for my work on genderblindness in previous scholarship on colorblindness. I then discuss the critical rhetoric approach I take to analyzing genderblindness. Finally, I end with a brief summary of the chapters in this book. To begin understanding how genderblindness contributes to the continued marginalization of women, we must first identify its ideological nature.

GENDERBLINDNESS AS IDEOLOGY

Cultural studies theorist Stuart Hall defines ideology as "the mental frameworks—the languages, the concepts, categories, imagery of thought, and the systems of representation—which different classes and social groups deploy in order to make sense of, define, figure out, and render intelligible the way society works."[5] Genderblindness fits this conception of ideology as a mental framework because it helps to clarify and solidify how gender functions in contemporary American society for those who adopt it. Genderblindness is not the only way that gender can be understood, but it is currently favored by the dominant groups because it helps to maintain the status quo. Women's wages can be kept low, access to abortion can be restricted, rape culture can be sustained, and harassment of women online can be encouraged because gender is perceived as no longer relevant in these situations since they are discussed publicly only in very limited ways. Gender is removed from consideration through the framing of these situations as failures of individual effort and responsibility. Dominant groups benefit from maintaining the status quo in these areas of life,[6] so genderblindness as an ideology shapes this discourse so that gender cannot be a rallying point around which their power is challenged.

The current discourses around gender deserve attention in understanding genderblindness as ideology because discourse shapes how people understand an issue. This is not a benign process. Rhetoric theorist Michael McGee argues "that ideology in practice is a political language, preserved in rhetorical documents, with the capacity to dictate decision and control public belief and behavior."[7] This capacity to control public belief and behavior is made possible because of the affective nature of political rhetoric in which "political styles rely on the universal human experience of tension and release, generalize them into mechanisms for the expression and resolution of anxieties, and then use these affective responses to change or stabilize the existing distribution of power."[8] Control by the dominant groups in society is sustained as a result of the fact that the political style in line with the ideology of the dominant groups is the only means citizens have of expressing themselves politically and potentially resisting the dominant groups.[9] If those in power are able to cloak themselves in democratic notions of freedom and equality, the demands by marginalized groups to be free and equal can be framed as asking for special treatment above and beyond the freedom and equality available to all other citizens. Citizens feel that the facts as presented by the dominant groups must be true and find it easier to attack marginalized groups for questioning the system rather than wrestle with their own marginalized place within it.

Genderblindness as an ideology encourages people to not think of the continued marginalization experienced by women as a result of gender discrimination. Sexism itself has changed in the modern context to reflect women's gains in terms of rights. Nijole Benokratis and Joe Feagin have identified three forms of modern sexism: overt, subtle, and covert.[10] The sexism related to genderblindness falls most often under subtle sexism, which is "unequal and harmful treatment of women that is visible but often not noticed because we have internalized sexist behavior as 'normal,' 'natural,' acceptable, or customary."[11] This changing nature of sexism has also shaped how genderblindness is understood by those who enact it. Laurie Cooper Stoll, Terry Glenn Lilley, and Kelly Pinter identify four frames through which genderblindness manifests: abstract liberalism, naturalization, cultural sexism, and minimization of sexism.[12] Genderblindness functions through these frames by arguing that "no demographic group should be singled out for special treatment," differences in outcome for women and men are the result of biological differences, differences are "the result of social processes that distinguish certain types of men and women," and gender inequality either does not exist or is not institutional.[13] The tendency to view rape culture and the gender pay gap as results of individual action are indicative of an abstract liberalist approach: no group should receive special treatment so women should resolve differences in terms of pay inequity and chances of being raped or sexually assaulted on an individual basis. Arguments in the tech industry that women's lack of success is the result of biological differences in women and men that lead to greater affinity for certain positions is clearly an example of the naturalization frame. The work by Cooper Stoll, Lilley, and Pinter is useful for better understanding how genderblind positions are understood by those who hold them.

Genderblindness shapes much of the current discourse around gender in the United States. The discourse used to describe a particular group—in this case, women—is ideological because it "creates the illusion of merely revealing a unified and unproblematic subject."[14] Genderblindness purports to just reflect the current status of women in society while working to keep women under control. Instead of existing outside of discourse, "the people" as a unified group are constituted within and by discourse;[15] this discourse "orients those addressed towards particular future acts."[16] Genderblindness constitutes women as having a reduced role in public life and works to prevent future action to increase that role by convincing women that they will be judged solely as individuals and not as members of a marginalized group. Collective action to address the status of women becomes more difficult because of the genderblind discourse around gender. Any hope in overturning the dominant ideology can be found in the fact that "the people" who have been constituted in this way by the discourse of the dominant ideology will only continue to function as a group so long as the "rhetoric that defined them has force."[17] It is my hope that *Genderblindness in American Society* is able to play some small part in uncovering the dominant rhetoric of genderblindness and helping to undermine its power.

Genderblindness and Colorblindness

Gender, of course, is not the only marginalized social identity that is defined in limited ways by the dominant ideology in American society. My approach to genderblindness is built on the work on colorblindness found in sociology and critical race theory. According to sociologist Eduardo Bonilla-Silva, an ideology of colorblindness, "which acquired cohesiveness and dominance in the late 1960s, explains contemporary racial inequality as the outcome of nonracial dynamics."[18] Colorblindness has historically been defined both as a "prohibition of discrimination against African Americans" and as "restrictions on the state's use of any racial classifications absent a compelling justification," the first based on the assumption that "racism is harmful because it subordinates African Americans through a racialized system of white privilege" while the second is based on the assumption that "racism's harm manifests itself as racial balkanization resulting from race consciousness."[19] The second definition of colorblindness has become the dominant one in the contemporary era. This definition makes the analysis of systemic racism and other forms of discrimination more difficult,[20] and "arguments against color blindness are sometimes dismissed as racist because they foreground difference over similarity."[21] Because of the adoption of colorblindness by the white majority, discussions of race are stifled either through the view that silence is the correct response, particularly by whites,[22] or by the limitations inherent in the "vocabulary of colorblind ideologies that purposefully avoid the language of difference, power, and race consciousness."[23] Colorblindness marginalizes African Americans and other people of color by "dismissing the difference in lived experience of white people and people of color as an irrelevant distinction."[24] The experiences of white people are framed as "natural and neutral" thus allowing "well-intentioned White people [to] generalize their experience to that of people of color."[25]

Colorblindness can be boiled down to "the widespread belief that race no longer matters" in American society.[26] This belief manifests in two ways: (1) race should not be a consideration in any legal, legislative, or social decision,[27] and (2) minority individuals who have success in America prove that a colorblind approach is successful.[28] Michelle Alexander argues that colorblindness is part of the latest system of control that functions to maintain a racial caste system with African Americans at the bottom and that there is a circular pattern of responses to progress that maintains the racial system of control.

> Following the collapse of each system of control, there has been a period of confusion—transition—in which those who are most committed to racial hierarchy search for new means to achieve their goals within the rules of the game as currently defined. It is during this period of uncertainty that the backlash intensifies and a new form of racialized social control begins to take hold. The

adoption of the new system of control is never inevitable, but to date is has never been avoided.[29]

Each new system of control reflects the context in which it is created, with the current mass incarceration of African Americans reflecting a colorblind society by making the policies seem race-neutral and the results solely based on individual action.[30] The individual success of some within a system of control is used to justify the oppression of many others as a result of their own choices. Individualism is highly valued in contemporary society so any system of control must account for it.

Systems of gender social control have also gone through patterns of contestation, transition, and reinforcement. Journalist Susan Faludi referred to this pattern in the early 1990s as a backlash against the rights gained by women. The focus of this backlash was on reframing the rights women had gained through the 1970s as the source of their current mistreatment and unhappiness, but "what has made women unhappy in the last decade is not their 'equality'—which they don't yet have—but the rising pressure to halt, and even reverse, women's quest for that equality."[31] In the transition to a new system of social control, a "preemptive strike" was necessary to ensure that women did not achieve the equality that they had "an increased possibility" to win.[32] As Shulamith Firestone argues in her analysis of the development of the nuclear family, "As civilization advances and the biological bases of sex class crumble, male supremacy must shore itself up with artificial institutions, or exaggerations of previous institutions, e.g., where previously the family had a loose, permeable form, it now tightens and rigidifies into the patriarchal nuclear family."[33]

Genderblindness, in similar ways to analyses of our society's colorblind approach to race, accounts for the ways gender has been rendered inconsequential for legislative and legal outcomes and in the lived experiences of women. Comparing genderblindness and colorblindness is not intended to claim equality in terms of scope or degree of impact. Colorblindness developed out of a legacy of enslavement and terrorism of African Americans while genderblindness has its roots in the restriction of rights and bodily autonomy of women. While the methods and magnitude may differ, the two are connected by efforts of dominant groups in society to maintain control.

Genderblindness as ideology functions along two axes of control: (1) gender is believed to have no impact on legal, legislative, or social decisions, and (2) since women and men are already equal, people are judged solely as individuals. Let's look at each axis separately. First, gender is assumed to no longer have any meaningful effect on legal, legislative, or social decisions. The persistence of the gender pay gap, for example, is frequently attributed to individual choices made by women, such as to take time off to care for an elderly parent or to pursue part-time work in order to have time to devote to childcare, rather than being the result of sexism and the historical devaluation of women's economic goals and contributions. In the workplace, hiring and personnel decisions generally framed as genderblind, such as discussions of flexibility and work–life balance, are still recognized as mostly affecting women.[34] Reproductive rights rollbacks across the country also try to shift the focus from gender to medically essential facility requirements (TRAP laws) and to the rights of the fetus (personhood amendments). These efforts to remove women from considerations of necessary access to reproductive choice attempt to dodge criticism of the undue burden placed on women by claiming that gender is not a consideration at all. From this perspective, arguing for reproductive choice is the *actually* misogynist position for suggesting that women do not want the best care for themselves or their unborn children. Finally, recent efforts to restrict transgender and gender non-conforming people's access to restrooms and other public accommodations, such as the repeal of Houston's HERO law or the signing into law of North Carolina's HB 2 by Governor Pat McCrory, are accomplished by framing the legislation as protecting religious freedom or the safety of children. Framing the legislation in this way allows for a genderblind policing of gender identities and expressions without directly attacking marginalized and vulnerable groups. This policing of gender is a primary goal of genderblindness.

Second, gender is not a factor since men and women are already equal, so as a result, people are judged solely on their individual merit. In practice, this axis of control often manifests in the praising of individual women for the success in the system and for adhering to traditional gender roles. For example, in her analysis of the purity myth, Jessica Valenti found that the morality of women as a whole was judged according to their sexual experience, while individual role models were praised for their adherence to virginity and purity.[35] Women as a group were judged for their failure to meet the standards set by the chosen few. As individuals, women are also expected to anticipate and prevent their own oppression. In the event that led to the passage of the legislation that bears her name, Lily Ledbetter was unable to bring a case against her employer for wage discrimination because the statute of limitations, which began not when she discovered that she earned less than her male peers but when the unequal pay began, had passed. In order to have a successful claim, Ledbetter was expected to have taken individual responsibility for her unequal pay and discovered it sooner. Women are also expected to take sole responsibility for the prevention of rape and sexual assault, through admonitions to not dress in a way that might invite an assault and to not go to certain places alone. These two functions of genderblindness also necessitate greater attention to the material effects of ideology.

The Material Effects of Genderblindness

Rhetoric scholar Dana Cloud finds fault in much of the rhetoric scholarship on ideology for failing to address the material effects of the decisions made and actions taken in line with a particular ideology.

> On the one hand, we find the limited claim that discourse is material because it has material effects and serves material interests in the world. This view, while tending toward idealism, does not equate reality with discourse. On the other hand, a more radical shift is evident, away from structuralist and realist ways of thinking. On this view, discourse not only influences material reality, it *is* that reality. All relations, economic, political, or ideological, are symbolic in nature. This view tends toward relativism.[36]

Ideological critique, instead, is "the only critical stance that suggests discourse may justify oppression and exploitation, but texts do not themselves constitute the oppression."[37] From this perspective, genderblind rhetoric shapes how we talk about the role of women in public life, but this talk does not itself constitute the continued marginalization of women. Instead, the ideology leads people to make certain decisions and take certain actions that contribute to women's continued marginalization in society. The rhetoric of genderblindness is expressive of the ideology but does not constitute the ideology itself.

My understanding of the material effects of ideology is informed by a Foucauldian approach to power at the levels of biopolitics and disciplinary power.[38] Michel Foucault argues that in bio-power's relationship to capitalism, the "investment of the body, its valorization, and the distributive management of its forces were at the time indispensable."[39] The key for our purposes is the "distributive management of its forces" as part of the social control of women under genderblindness, ensuring that women are constrained to certain areas of life and that they encounter problems when trying to enter other areas. Genderblindness prevents women from framing their reactions around their shared experiences as women by framing all actions as the result of individual choice and by encouraging an adherence to traditional values that limit women's roles to certain areas of life. Women's life chances are then reduced as a result of the limited financial, legal, and social support available in their constrained roles. Biopolitics in genderblindness is seen, for example, in efforts to legislatively reduce the life chances of women, such as state legislatures passing TRAP laws that shut down abortion clinics and restrict women's access to legal abortions.

The focus of disciplinary power is on compelling the individual to conform to societal rules and norms.[40] This is accomplished both through strict enforcement of the rules and by encouraging self-surveillance by individuals to ensure that their behavior fits with the established rules. Disciplinary power in genderblindness is found in efforts by women to police their own behavior to make sure that it fits within societal norms, such as accepting a lower salary at work rather than fighting for equal pay in order to be a team player or leaving social media rather than speaking up about harassment.

Disciplinary power and biopolitics intersect in modern society in order to maintain control of the individual. Nikolas Rose argues that the forms of power of "discipline and of bio-power are all relocated within the field of governmentality" which is primarily concerned with "the best way to exercise powers over conduct individually and en masse so as to secure the good of each and of all."[41] The analysis of genderblindness as a system of social control of women focuses on the intersections of individual and mass control in how women are encouraged to view the outcomes they face as the results of their own actions while also facing reduced life chances from a system that maintains gender inequality.

By analyzing the concept at these different levels of power, genderblindness goes beyond male privilege by arguing that society is not only structured to favor men but that societal forces actively function to obscure the continued oppression and discrimination faced by women.[42] Systemic oppression and self-policing behavior are united in limiting the opportunities available to women to fully participate as equals in society. Continuing to ignore the role of genderblindness in perpetuating the oppression of women renders gender justice an unachievable goal.

This focus on individuality reinforces neoliberal ideals which have created a "society of control" that leads to the consideration of individual decisions "in a web of incitements, rewards, current sanctions and forebodings of future sanctions which serve to enjoin citizens to maintain particular types of control over their conduct."[43] Healthcare, for example, becomes "both the responsibility and the obligation of individuals" which "consistently reif[ies] traditional gender roles for women."[44] While a focus on individual responsibility and control of our own lives may appear to be in line with feminist goals of empowering women, "its *logic* is that of neoliberal governmentality."[45]

This focus on individuality also reflects the current postfeminist context.[46] Third wave feminists are products of this context and see themselves as "the beneficiaries of those advances made by the second wave, so their feminist practice relies heavily on celebrating their individual agency in enjoying those rights."[47] This focus on individual freedom in current feminist practice also reflects the feeling that the rights fought for in the second wave are secure so the need to organize against institutional and systemic oppression is minimized,[48] with third wave feminists generally "perceiv[ing] and respond[ing] to sexism only as it occurs in their personal worlds."[49]

The problem with this focus on individual choice and success is that it preserves the status quo. Dominant groups are able to remain dominant because, in a postfeminist context, "the presumption of equality for women in the public sphere has been retained" but this "requires the least ideological adjustment from men and from the culture at large (and, concomitantly, the most adjustment from women themselves)."[50] For Susan Douglas, this reframing of the feminist project as the cause of women's suffering is just "good, old fashioned, grade-A sexism that reinforces good, old-fashioned, grade-A patriarchy."[51] I argue, in contrast, that this is not just the same sexism and misogyny women have faced for centuries but is a new form of social control that seeks to remove the ability for women to even claim misogynistic discrimination because gender does not matter in the decisions made in legal, legislative, or social contexts. Genderblindness is a misogynistic attempt to keep women subordinate to men, but it seeks to accomplish this by removing any power from claims of misogynistic and patriarchal oppression. By removing gender from the legal, legislative, and social realms, oppressive actions against women must be judged as individual actions, not as a product of systemic misogyny. This reframing of legal, legislative, and social decisions as genderblind preserves the status quo by removing any weight from critiques of the current system, a system which still privileges men and their interests.

Members of subordinate groups in a genderblind (or colorblind) system are not supported unless they are able to become success stories. Support is given for policies and individual actions that reaffirm the dominant group while being thought of as genderblind because they are not blatantly misogynist. As Angela McRobbie puts it, "Thus the new female subject is, despite her freedom, called upon to be silent, to withhold critique, to count as a modern sophisticated girl, or indeed this withholding of critique is a condition of her freedom."[52] Women are not only silent in their critique of the system, but some women actively critique and shame those who fail to overcome genderblindness out of a hope that they themselves will then be free from criticism.[53] Thus, women in general are not supported, only those who transcend genderblindness. Clear lines are drawn between those who are able to function as proper subjects of the current regime of gender social control and those who are not.[54] Women's movements and organizing against misogyny will continue to suffer so long as we do not account for genderblind efforts to divide women against each other in order to preserve the dominant position of men. Our genderblind society ultimately removes gender from legal, legislative, and social consideration, celebrates individual choice over recognizing systemic inequality, and demands self-policing of behavior to adhere to societal norms. The workings of power in genderblindness connects the rhetoric of those who adhere to a genderblind ideology to the material effects of their decisions and actions. The discursive and material impacts of genderblindness are analyzed in this book from a critical rhetoric perspective.

A CRITICAL RHETORIC APPROACH TO GENDERBLINDNESS

As defined by Raymie McKerrow, "critical rhetoric examines the dimensions of domination and freedom as these are exercised in a relativized world."[55] The world itself has increasingly been relativized through discourse, but this does not mean that Cloud's concerns about a lack of awareness or interest in the material are misplaced. While examining how discourse works to shape how we understand the world around us, we must never lose sight of the fact that the actions, behaviors, policies, etc. being advocated for in that discourse have real effects on real people. When a woman is raped, denied access to an abortion, or unable to provide for her children because of the lower pay she receives as compared to her male colleagues, real people are affected, and the effects are not solely a matter of perception. Discourse may shape how we think about people in these situations, but those involved are affected outside of the realm of discourse.

McKerrow describes discourse as "the tactical dimension of the operation of power in its manifold relations at all levels of society, within and between its institutions, groups and individuals."[56] It is this tactical dimension that is the focus of the critical rhetoric scholar. Genderblindness as an ideology shapes how people view the world in terms of gender and the decisions and actions that take based on those views. Genderblind rhetoric is how they express their views. Critical rhetoric as a practice focuses on the critique of domination and the critique of freedom. By the critique of domination, McKerrow refers to "the discourse of power which creates and sustains the social practices which control the dominated,"[57] and by the critique of freedom, he refers to how "new social relations which emerge from a reaction to a critique are themselves simply new forms of power and hence subject to renewed skepticism."[58] The critique of domination focuses on how dominant groups maintain their power through control of the dominated while the critique of freedom focuses on the creative aspects of power in which changes to society create new forms of power that must forever be subjected to further critical analysis. The critique of freedom also gives attention to "how forces that constrain are made to appear natural, thereby recognizing the means by which resistance can materialize."[59] Ideology not only seeks to control marginalized groups but also creates new norms through which marginalized groups can be found lacking for failing to measure up. The critique of freedom enables resistance by demonstrating how the norms of a society are marginalizing and oppressive and by revealing, as part of its larger purpose, how these norms can be changed. Genderblindness as an ideology not only seeks to control women by limiting their access to public life but also creates new norms around individual freedom and responsibility that reduce the effectiveness of organizing resistance to the limitations imposed by the dominant groups through gender.

Critical rhetoric is not without its critiques. Maurice Charland criticized McKerrow's "infinite regress of negative critique" in the critique of freedom for turning the role of the critic into merely identifying the existing power relations without being able to make judgments of them.[60] He also criticized McKerrow for failing to address the role of the audience while envisioning critical rhetoric as a mobilizing call to action.[61] Robert Hariman criticized the modernist tendencies in McKerrow's writing, particularly the impersonal nature of his calls for grounding criticism in the experience of the critic.[62] In order to help resolve these criticisms and further develop the project of critical rhetoric, Kent Ono and John Sloop argue for grounding critical rhetoric in a *telos*, which they define as "the moment when a person's pen is put to paper purposively, when ideas become words and when will becomes action."[63] *Telos* serves to direct criticism "while simultaneously recognizing the contingencies of this goal."[64] For Ono and Sloop, "the critic is not only committed to a *telos by necessity*, but that the critic should take hold of the threads of that *telos*—a *telos* that is simultaneously and admittedly contingent—and commit to a purpose."[65]

In order to respond to Ono and Sloop's contributions to critical rhetoric, I want to clearly articulate the *telos* of this book. My purpose in analyzing the rhetoric of genderblindness is to enable people to more effectively use gender as a means of organizing against the marginalization and oppression instituted by the dominant groups in American society. Genderblindness frustrates attempts at this organizing by treating any attempts to ground persuasive appeals in gender as unnecessary because gender is no longer an issue or as demanding special treatment beyond what is available to other citizens. By better understanding the workings of genderblindness and its expressions through rhetoric, more strategic efforts can be made to reassert the important role of gender in public life and our public discourse.

To accomplish this goal, I conduct both a critique of domination and a critique of freedom in this book. Part of taking on a critical rhetoric perspective involves recognizing that the "critique of domination and critique of freedom are effectively one, and are little more than different perspectives about a single discursive struggle."[66] I separate the critique of domination and critique of freedom in the chapters of this book as a means of focusing my attention on the workings of ideology and power through discourse in the specific cases while still recognizing that both forms of analysis are part of the same project. Discourses of domination more obviously seek to control people, but even the creative workings of power in a critique of freedom work to constrain how people see the world around them. Domination is also creative in its attempts to react to any changes in society in order to maintain control. The rhetoric of genderblindness seeks both to control how people think about important issues of gender while also constraining their ability to live freely and equally in society by establishing new norms for how gender issues are currently understood. Specific cases may lean more to one form of power over the other, but both are part of the overall project of genderblindness.

Before proceeding with an overview of how I hope to achieve this goal, it is important to reflect on my role as a critic and how my personal identity helps shape my work. A lack of reflexivity is a problem found in many scholarly discussions of ideology.[67] The absence of reflexivity is only possible by ignoring that "rhetoric is by bodies whose voice and gesture are essential to the production of meaning."[68] Philip Wander and Steven Jenkins argue that the work of a critic is grounded in their personal experience. "Out of his [or her] personal experience, the critic offers a view of social reality. Through his [or her] criticism, the critic invites his [or her] reader to share in this reality."[69] The critic provides evidence to support their claims that can be assessed by the audience, but the claims themselves are based in the critic's own experiences with the world.[70] Ideological criticism "begins from the premise that all criticisms are motivated" and "constitutes an implicit critique of any criticism that does not foreground its ethics or politics."[71] This recognition that all criticism reflects the critic's personal experience and is motivated by the critic's purpose goes beyond just articulating the ethics or politics of the individual critic and leads to an understanding that reality is represented in discourse in different ways according to the political and social positions of the critic with some representations being "more faithful to the interests of ordinary people and their experiences than others."[72] Knowing a critic's personal experience and perspective is not just important for understanding how they approach the topic but also for understanding how their approach shapes their critical analysis.

In order to make my own position on gender clear, I want to share relevant aspects of my personal identity and my perspective on important terms and issues so that you as the reader will be able to understand how my identity and perspective shapes my analysis of genderblindness.

My view on gender and what it means to be a woman is in line with the one articulated by Sara Ahmed in her 2017 book *Living a Feminist Life*.

> Feminism requires supporting women in a struggle to exist in this world. What do I mean by *women* here? I am referring to all those who travel under the sign *women*. No feminism worthy of its name would use the sexist idea "women born women" to create the edges of feminist community, to render trans women into "not women," or "not born women," or into men. No one is born a woman; it is an assignment . . . that can shape us; make us; and break us.[73]

Ahmed's definition of woman invokes Simone de Beauvoir's maxim that "One is not born, but rather becomes, a woman."[74] Contrary to a gender essentialist worldview, de Beauvoir argues that "[n]o biological, psychological, or economic fate determines the figure that the human female presents in society; it is civilization as a whole that produces this creature . . . which is described as feminine."[75] When I speak in this book of women, it is from this position that woman is a socially constructed category from which individuals are expected or required to enact certain behaviors, exhibit certain qualities, and endure certain societal limitations that result in oppression and marginalization. While all who operate under the sign of "woman" face certain limitations, not all women experience oppression and marginalization in the same way. Intersectionality has forced white, Western feminists to reckon with the oppressive and marginalizing effects of their own incomplete understandings of what it means to be a woman.[76] I often speak in this book of a general, undifferentiated idea of woman because I believe the rhetoric being used by the forces of social control do not tend to make distinctions about the different lived experiences of women. However, I also attempt to consider the intersectional realities in terms of race, ethnicity, class, religion, ability, gender identity, and sexual orientation that impact women's lives differently in the areas of the workplace, reproductive health, rape culture, and tech culture. Gender remains the focus of my analysis throughout the book, and this focus is grounded, as Sara Hayden and D. Lynn Hallstein argue, "*not* because we believe it is the central or most important axis of power" but because it reflects the feminist standpoint I occupy as a scholar.[77] The lived experiences of women in the twenty-first century cannot be understood except through an intersectional lens even as the focus of many feminists remains on dismantling forms of oppression and marginalization rooted in gender.

My approach to the topic of genderblindness is shaped by my perspective as a white, middle class, bisexual, transgender woman. Identifying as a feminist and advocating for feminism,[78] for me, is inseparable from my identity as a trans woman. Growing up in a conservative, Christian household and aware of my trans identity from a young age, being trans was a very personal, private thing for me that I rarely expressed out of fear of upsetting my family. As I reached a point in my life where I began to feel comfortable opening up and expressing my trans identity, which culminated in a decision around ten years ago to publicly transition while still in graduate school, I became more aware of my connections to other women and their experiences and began to identify as a feminist. Some women and feminists, though, do not believe it is the place of trans women such as myself to speak for women. Trans scholar Julia Serano responds to this mode of thinking.

> When you're a trans woman, you are made to walk this very fine line, where if you act feminine you are accused of being a parody, but if you act masculine, it is seen as a sign of your true male identity. And if you act sweet and demure, you're accused of reinforcing patriarchal ideals of female passivity, but if you stand up for your own rights and make your voice heard, then you are dis-

> missed as wielding male privilege and entitlement. We trans women are made to teeter upon this tightrope, not because we are transsexuals, but because we are women. This is the same double bind that forces teenage girls to negotiate their way between virgin and whore, that forces female politicians and businesswomen to be aggressive without being seen as a bitch and to be feminine enough so as not to emasculate their alpha-male colleagues, without being so girly as to undermine their own authority.[79]

The struggles and experiences of trans women should not isolate and distance trans women from other women but should bring us closer together. I choose to speak on the issue of genderblindness because as a woman, I do not want to see the continuation of a social structure that maintains the oppression and marginalization of women by preventing them from even raising issues of gender to the level of awareness within the public sphere. All women should feel a similar calling to speak out against the workings of genderblindness. My perspective on gender informs my analysis of the rhetoric of genderblindness as it is expressed in the areas of the workplace, reproductive health, rape culture, and tech culture. I now want to provide an overview of how I conduct this analysis in this book.

OVERVIEW OF CHAPTERS

In *Genderblindness in American Society: The Rhetoric of a System of Social Control of Women*, I rhetorically analyze discourses of the current ideological system of genderblindness. In chapter 1, I begin by discussing the gender wage gap that persists between men and women, with women earning on average around 80 percent of what men earn, and analyzing the rhetoric surrounding the gender wage gap through a critique domination and a critique of freedom that show both how women are controlled by denying the existence of the wage gap and how efforts to encourage women to pursue leadership roles as an expression of individual freedom leads to a reinforcing of the status quo. Women's work continues to be viewed as supplementary based on heteronormative conceptions of the family and life course which undermine efforts to address the disparities. I begin by looking at statements denying the existence of the gender wage gap made by conservative commentators Ben Shapiro and Jordan Peterson. I then analyze self-help books for women in the workplace, including *Lean In* by Sheryl Sandberg, *Earning It* by Joann S. Lublin, *Feminist Fight Club* by Jessica Bennett, and *#Girlboss* by Sophia Amoruso. The books not only perpetuate ideas of individual success but encourage women to find ways to succeed within the constraints of a patriarchal system instead of challenging it. Women need to use their leadership positions to change the existing system rather than telling women ways they can change their behavior to better fit the system.

Chapter 2 begins with an analysis of recent efforts to restrict women's access to abortion through the passage of TRAP laws through a critique of domination. These efforts fit a genderblind system by framing the issue as gender-neutral, concerned only with medical safety and the well-being of the fetus, and completely removing women and their bodies from the debate over reproductive rights. The rhetoric employed by crisis pregnancy centers is analyzed through a critique of freedom for how serves as to discourage women from considering abortion through misleading or inaccurate statements about the procedure. Crisis pregnancy centers have adapted their rhetoric to fit the perceived freedom women have to make choices about their own bodies. The caring tone of the rhetoric seeks to frame abortion as a religious and moral issue while disguising efforts to control women.

In chapter 3, I analyze rape apologia, formal defenses of rapists, for Daniel Holtzclaw and Brock Turner through a critique of domination for how such statements place defending men ahead of supporting women or expecting men to take responsibility for their actions. Rape apologia are genderblind by presenting rape as an individual action and removing the negative aspects of masculinity from consideration. These defenses of rapists work to reduce the life chances of women by tolerating violence by men. Rape culture as a whole is analyzed through a critique of freedom for how it argues that women have the freedom to exist in public spaces but then placing the impetus on women to self-police their behavior in order to avoid being raped or sexually assaulted. I analyze the genderblind rhetoric of rape culture through Katie Roiphe's *The Morning After: Sex, Fear, and Feminism on Campus* for how it seeks to prevent women from grounding their efforts to prevent rape and sexual assault in their shared experiences as women.

Chapter 4 analyzes the rhetorical construction of the tech industry and culture as a male space. I begin with an analysis of James Damore's Google memo through a critique of domination in which he takes a biological determinist view to argue that the lack of success of women in the tech industry is a result of the fact that they have traits that are not suited to the positions that lead to advancement. Damore's argument seeks to control women by reducing their chances at financial success and the benefits that come from it. It is genderblind in attempting to construct the argument as neutral and as reflecting only scientific fact instead of as a worldview that seeks to diminish opportunities for women. This worldview also underlies much of the harassment of women online, which is analyzed through a critique of freedom for seeking to force women to remove themselves from the Internet in order to avoid harassment. Online spaces are generally conceived of as open and welcoming to all, but women receive undue and disproportionate negative attention for being in these spaces. I analyze the specific cases of the women harassed by those associated with GamerGate, particularly Anita Sarkeesian and Zoë Quinn, the actress Leslie Jones's decision to temporarily leave Twitter after being harassed by individuals connected with right-wing provocateur Milo Yiannopoulos, and the decision by actress Kelly Marie Tran to leave Instagram after being harassed by Star Wars fans. The efforts to restrict women's access to tech culture fit a genderblind system by presenting the male dominance of the Internet as its natural state and not a reflection of American society's conceptions of masculinity and femininity.

Finally, I conclude with a review of the arguments made in this book and give specific attention to how the rhetoric used in the specific cases are part of a larger ideological project. I also offer some considerations of how to resist this rhetoric of genderblindness. In particular, I argue that recent efforts, like the Women's March on Washington and the #MeToo movement that work to bring public attention to issues of gender that center women's experiences in those movements and encourage collective action rather than individual solutions, show the greatest promise in eliminating the current system of social control of women. However, other recent events, particularly the campaign and election of Donald Trump to the American presidency, possibly signal a retrenchment of openly sexist and misogynistic attitudes toward women. While there are signs of hope, we need to stay vigilant against a coarsening of opinions.

Genderblindness in American Society seeks to bring attention to the current ideological system of genderblindness. This system of social control of women functions by removing consideration of gender from legal, legislative, and social decisions. It also presents stories of women's individual success in order to encourage a worldview focused on individual freedom and responsibility instead of collective action. Gender is removed from use in public persuasive appeals in a genderblind system which makes it more difficult for women to rally public support and awareness of continuing gender inequality. By bringing attention to the rhetorical functions of genderblindness, I hope this book will serve as a useful tool for resisting and dismantling the current ideological system.

NOTES

1. Kristina Horn Sheeler and Karrin Vasby Anderson, *Woman President: Confronting Postfeminist Political Culture* (College Station: Texas A&M University Press, 2013), 10-12.
2. Dan Roberts, "Why Hillary Clinton Lost the Election: The Economy, Trust and a Weak Message," *The Guardian*, November 9, 2016. https://www.theguardian.com/us-news/2016/nov/09/hillary-clinton-election-president-loss
3. Molly Ball, "Why Hillary Clinton Lost," *The Atlantic*, November 15, 2016. https://www.theatlantic.com/politics/archive/2016/11/why-hillary-clinton-lost/507704/
4. Chris Cillizza, "4 Theories on Why Hillary Clinton Isn't Very Popular Right Now," *CNN*, Last updated January 5, 2018. https://www.cnn.com/2017/12/20/politics/hillary-clinton-bill-clinton-poll-analysis/index.html

5. Stuart Hall, "The Problem of Ideology: Marxism without Guarantees," in *Stuart Hall: Critical Dialogues in Cultural Studies*, ed. David Morley and Kuan-Hsing Chen (New York: Routledge, 1996), 26.

6. Dominant groups benefit by not having to pay their female workers as much as their male colleagues thus saving them money and allowing them to hoard even more wealth, by preventing women from exercising control over their bodies thus allowing them to participate more fully in public life, by the fact that it is generally powerful people who benefit from rape culture by allowing them to avoid consequences for rape and sexual assault, and by preventing women from taking full advantage of the affordance offered by modern technology that might challenge the control of dominant groups in these spaces.

7. Michael Calvin McGee, "The 'Ideograph': A Link between Rhetoric and Ideology," *Quarterly Journal of Speech* 66, no. 1 (1980): 5.

8. James Arnt Aune, "Democratic Style and Ideological Containment," *Rhetoric & Public Affairs* 11, no. 3 (2008): 483.

9. Ibid., 488.

10. Nijole V. Benokraitis and Joe R. Feagin, *Modern Sexism: Blatant, Subtle, and Covert Discrimination* (Prentice-Hall, 1986), 30.

11. Ibid.

12. Laurie Cooper Stoll, Terry Glenn Lilly and Kelly Pinter, "Gender-Blind Sexism and Rape Myth Acceptance," *Violence Against Women* 23, no. 1 (2017): 30-31.

13. Ibid.

14. Maurice Charland, "Constitutive Rhetoric: The Case of the *Peuple Québécois*," *Quarterly Journal of Speech* 73, no. 2 (1987): 139.

15. Ibid.

16. Ibid., 143.

17. Michael C. McGee, "In Search of 'The People': A Rhetorical Alternative," *Quarterly Journal of Speech* 61, no. 3 (1975): 242.

18. Eduardo Bonilla-Silva, *Racism without Racists: Color-Blind Racism and the Persistence of Racial Inequality in the United States*, 3rd ed. (Lanham, MD: Rowman & Littlefield, 2010), 2.

19. Carrie Crenshaw, "Colorblind Rhetoric," *Southern Communication Journal* 63, no. 3 (1998): 248.

20. Margaret L. Hunter and Kimberly D. Nettles, "What about the White Women?: Racial Politics in a Women's Studies Classroom," *Teaching Sociology* 27, no. 4 (1999): 393.

21. Jessica Lyn Simpson, "The Color-Blind Double Bind: Whiteness and the (Im)Possibility of Dialogue," *Communication Theory* 18, no. 1 (2008): 142.

22. Liliana L. Herakova, Dijana Jelača, Razvan Sibii and Leda Cooks, "Voicing Silence and Imagining Citizenship: Dialogues about Race and Whiteness in a 'Postracial' Era," *Communication Studies* 62, no. 4 (2011): 373.

23. Hunter and Nettles, "What about the White Women" 394.

24. Simpson, "The Color-Blind" 142.

25. Ibid., 151.

26. Michelle Alexander, *The New Jim Crow: Mass Incarceration in the Age of Colorblindness*, Revised ed. (New York: The New Press, 2012), 11-12.

27. Ibid., 183.

28. Ibid., 248.

29. Ibid., 21-22.

30. Ibid., 248.

31. Susan Faludi, *Backlash: The Undeclared War against American Women* (New York: Crown Publishers, 1991), xviii.

32. Ibid., xx.

33. Shulamith Firestone, *The Dialectic of Sex* (New York: William Morrow and Company, 1970), 165.

34. Janet Smithson and Elizabeth H. Stokoe, "Discourses of Work-Life Balance: Negotiating 'Genderblind' Terms in Organizations," *Gender, Work and Organization* 12, no. 2 (2005): 164.

35. Jessica Valenti, *The Purity Myth: How America's Obsession with Virginity Is Hurting Young Women* (Berkeley: Seal Press, 2010), 24.

36. Dana L. Cloud, "The Materiality of Discourse as Oxymoron: A Challenge to Critical Rhetoric," *Western Journal of Communication* 58, no. 3 (1994): 142.

37. Ibid., 157.

38. Michel Foucault, *"Society Must Be Defended": Lectures at the Collège de France 1975-1976*, trans. David Macey (New York: Picador, 1997), 245-247; Michel Foucault, *Discipline and Punish: The Birth of the Prison*, trans. Alan Sheridan (New York: Vintage Books, 1995), 182-183.

39. Michel Foucault, *The History of Sexuality Volume I: An Introduction* (New York: Vintage Books, 1990), 141.

40. Focault, "Discipline and Punish" 201.

41. Nikolas Rose, *Powers of Freedom: Reframing Political Thought* (Cambridge: Cambridge University Press, 1999), 23.

42. Self-policing and the control of life chances affect people on many dimensions of identity, including race, ethnicity, socioeconomic class, religion, sexual orientation, and gender identity to name a few. Gender identity deserves particular attention. My use of "woman" should be understood very broadly to include all those who identify as or have been assigned identities as women. As a trans woman myself, I am well aware of the ways gender is rendered a non-issue in the discrimination and marginalization I have experienced, both as a woman and as a trans individual. Gender identity, though, does involve specific forms of discrimination that are beyond the scope of this book's focus on women in general. For more consideration of the impact of disciplinary power and biopolitics on transgender people, see Dean Spade's analysis of the legal system in his book *Normal Life*; Dean Spade, *Normal Life: Administrative Violence, Critical Trans Politics, and the Limits of Law* (Brooklyn: South End Press, 2011), 123-128.

43. Ibid., 246.

44. Tasha N. Dubriwny, *The Vulnerable Empowered Woman: Feminism, Postfeminism, and Women's Health* (New Brunswick, NJ: Rutgers University Press, 2013), 2-3.

45. Kati Kauppinen, "At an Intersection of Postfeminism and Neoliberalism: A Discourse Analytical View of an International Women's Magazine," *Critical Approaches to Discourse across Disciplines* 7, no. 1 (2013): 96.

46. Kristan Poirot, *A Question of Sex: Feminism, Rhetoric, and Differences That Matter* (Amherst, MA: University of Massachusetts Press, 2014), 115.

47. Kristy Maddux, "Winning the Right to Vote in 2004: *Iron Jawed Angels* and the Retrospective Framing of Feminism," *Feminist Media Studies* 9, no. 1 (2009): 81.

48. Astrid Henry, "Solitary Sisterhood: Individualism Meets Collectivity in Feminism's Third Wave," in *Different Wavelengths: Studies of the Contemporary Women's Movement*, ed. Jo Reger (New York: Routledge, 2005), 81.

49. Helene A. Shugart, "Isn't It Ironic?: The Intersection of Third-Wave Feminism and Generation X," *Women's Studies in Communication* 24, no. 2 (2001): 149.

50. Bonnie J. Dow, *Prime-Time Feminism: Television, Media Culture, and the Women's Movement since 1970* (Philadelphia: University of Pennsylvania Press, 1996), 88.

51. Susan J. Douglas, *The Rise of Enlightened Sexism: How Pop Culture Took Us from Girl Power to Girls Gone Wild* (New York: St. Martin's Griffin, 2010), 10.

52. Angela McRobbie, "Post-Feminism and Popular Culture," *Feminist Media Studies* 4, no. 3 (2004): 260.

53. Valenti, "The Purity Myth" 164.

54. McRobbie, "Post-Feminism" 261.

55. Raymie McKerrow, "Critical Rhetoric: Theory and Praxis," *Communication Monographs* 56, no. 2 (1989): 91.

56. Ibid., 98.

57. Ibid., 92.

58. Ibid., 96.

59. Michelle Kelsey Kearl, "The Stolen Property of Whiteness: A Case Study in Critical Intersectional Rhetorics of Race and Disability," *Rhetoric Review* 37, no. 3 (2018): 303.

60. Maurice Charland, "Finding a Horizon and Telos: The Challenge to Critical Rhetoric," *Quarterly Journal of Speech* 77, no. 1 (1991): 71.

61. Ibid., 73.

62. Robert Hariman, "Critical Rhetoric and Postmodern Theory," *Quarterly Journal of Speech* 77, no. 1 (1991): 67-68.

63. Kent A. Ono and John M. Sloop, "Commitment to *Telos*—A Sustained Critical Rhetoric," *Communication Monographs* 59, no. 1 (1992): 48.

64. Ibid., 52.

65. Ibid., 53.

66. Ibid., 52.

67. James Arnt Aune, "The Scholastic Fallacy, Habitus, and Symbolic Violence: Pierre Bourdieu and the Prospects of Ideology Criticism," *Western Journal of Communication* 75, no. 4 (2011): 429.

68. Ibid., 430.

69. Philip Wander and Steven Jenkins, "Rhetoric, Society, and the Critical Response," *Quarterly Journal of Speech* 58 (1972): 450.

70. Ibid., 449.

71. Sharon Crowley, "Reflections on an Argument That Won't Go Away: Or, a Turn of the Ideological Screw," *Quarterly Journal of Speech* 78, no. 4 (1992): 459.

72. Dana L. Cloud and Joshua Gunn, "Introduction: W(h)ither Ideology?," *Western Journal of Communication* 75, no. 4 (2011): 408.

73. Sara Ahmed, *Living a Feminist Life* (Durham, NC: Duke University Press, 2017), 14-15.

74. Simone de Beauvoir, *The Second Sex*, trans. H. M. Parshley (New York: Alfred A. Knopf, 1964), 267.

75. Ibid.

76. Kimberle Crenshaw, "Mapping the Margins: Intersectionality, Identity Politics, and Violence Against Women of Color," *Stanford Law Review* 43, no. 6 (1991): 1242-1245.

77. Sara Hayden and D. Lynn O'Brien Hallstein, "Placing Sex/Gender at the Forefront: Feminisms, Intersectionality, and Communication Studies," in *Standing in the Intersection: Feminist Voices, Feminist Practices in Communication Studies*, ed. Karma R. Chávez, Cindy L. Griffin and Marsha Houston (Albany: State University of New York Press, 2012), 99.

78. bell hooks, *Feminist Theory: From Margin to Center* (New York: Routledge, 2015), 32.

79. Julia Serano, *Excluded: Making Feminist and Queer Movements More Inclusive* (Berkeley: Seal Press, 2013), 39-40.

Chapter One

Genderblindness and the Wage Gap

In November 2017, the Ridley Scott film *All the Money in the World* was reshot in order to replace actor Kevin Spacey, who faced multiple allegations of sexual misconduct, with Christopher Plummer. Actors Michelle Williams and Mark Wahlberg were brought in to reshoot their scenes with Plummer now in the role of J. Paul Getty. In a stark illustration of the gender wage gap, Wahlberg received $1.5 million for his work while Williams only received $1,000.[1]

According to the American Association of University Women, the wage gap between women and men currently stands at 80 percent.[2] Though the overall wage gap has decreased in the past few decades, there are notable differences in terms of race and ethnicity, age, and level of education. In terms of race, the wage gap for white women stands at 79 percent while for black women it is 63 percent, for Hispanic/Latina women it is 54 percent, and for Asian women it is 87 percent.[3] Age shows that there are signs of improvement for younger women. For women 20–24, the wage gap is 96 percent; 25–54, 79–89 percent; and 55–64, 74 percent.[4] Finally, in terms of level of education, the gap in weekly earnings between women and men decreases slightly with higher education levels, from 74 percent to 78 percent.[5] White women earn more than black and Hispanic/Latina women at all levels of education.[6]

Intersections between the gender wage gap and race often lead to less organizational commitment as workers of color are "sensitive to issues of perceived pay equity."[7] The wage gap also intersects with socioeconomic class, with many of the women facing the largest gap holding working-class jobs.[8] Working-class women, for example, face negative impacts on their wellbeing in terms of pay compared to professional women because the difference "literally means having enough money to live."[9] Recent efforts in narrowing the wage gap have been exacerbated by growing class inequality.[10] Despite these intersections between gender and class, the labor movement has not been supportive of all means of reducing the gap. Labor unions, for example, resisted the use of class action lawsuits, such as 1944's *St. John v. General Motors* in which a group of women were awarded damages for pay discrimination, favoring instead administrative solutions to addressing worker pay that would not impact collective bargaining.[11] Ignoring lawsuits in favor of an administrative approach "left wage discrimination largely unregulated."[12]

During the twentieth century, wages shifted from being a product of supply and demand to "management's tool to alter worker behavior," with the package of wages, benefits, and other factors being used to entice and control workers.[13] Segregating women into separate and generally less financially rewarding career paths removed the need for managers to determine which of their female employees would stay rather than leave after becoming mothers.[14] Researchers have identified this segregation of women into lower-paying careers as a primary cause of the wage gap.[15] In an analysis of the Australian labor market, Hiau Joo Kee found that gender was positively associated both with a glass ceiling but also a sticky floor in which women were unable to rise out of low-paying positions.[16]

Paying women less than men on average is often justified by appeals to tradition. Those who deny the reality of the wage gap often draw on a human capital approach that seeks to identify other factors, such as women's individual choices and effort, which lead to the gap, but this approach fails to recognize that discrimination is baked into the variables themselves as they reflect cultural norms and expectations of women and are not gender-neutral.[17] One such attempt at rationalizing away the wage gap is the argument that women are less interested in the competition found in higher-paying positions, but field research has found no evidence that gender determines who pursues these competitive positions.[18]

Economist Joseph E. Stiglitz identifies economic discrimination against women and other groups as among the societal forces that lead to inequality.[19] The wage gap has also been connected to the political position of managers, with women making more working for liberal managers than for conservative ones.[20] A unique situation in which women are valued more than men for positions is when a high-potential woman is seen as adding diversity to the organization.[21] Finally, higher numbers of women in leadership positions has been correlated with increased performance for the companies.[22]

In this chapter, I argue that the rhetoric around the wage gap and women's experiences in the workplace in general works to maintain the existing system and reinforce the wage gap. The material impacts of this rhetoric can be understood as biopolitics by limiting women's life chances by providing justifications for the wage gap and as disciplinary power by advising women to conform to the existing system. I begin with a critique of domination in analyzing how denials of the wage gap seek to present their arguments as self-evident facts and are built on the assumption that equality has been achieved in the workplace and society as a whole. The texts I analyze as examples of denials of the wage gap are an article by conservative commentator Ben Shapiro and an interview with Canadian psychologist Jordan Peterson. Shapiro was an editor at *Breitbart* until 2016. He currently runs the conservative website *The Daily Wire*, which he founded in 2015, and is involved in a number of podcasts and speaking events. Peterson is a clinical psychologist at the University of Toronto who rose to prominence for his video lectures on YouTube in which he advises young men to better themselves through adherence to traditional masculine gender roles and pontificates on the perceived dangers threatening Western civilization. The ideological purpose behind maintaining the wage gap is to keep women in a marginalized, subservient position to men. Women can be controlled by not providing them with the material resources necessary to participate equally in the workplace and in public life in general. Denials of the wage gap serve the ideology of genderblindness by making the wage gap appear to be the natural result of individual actions while framing any attempts to argue for an end to this gender-based wage gap to be a radical effort to upend the natural order.

I then conduct a critique of freedom by analyzing self-help books for women in the workplace that focus on maintaining the system as it is and encouraging women to self-surveil to ensure that their behavior fits the expectations of the system. The texts I analyze are Sophia Amoruso's *#GIRLBOSS*, Jessica Bennett's *Feminist Fight Club: A Survival Manual for a Sexist Workplace*, Lois Frankel's *Nice Girls Don't Get the Corner Office: 101 Unconscious Mistakes Women Make That Sabotage Their Careers*, Joann Lublin's *Earning It: Hard-Won Lessons from Trailblazing Women at the Top of the Business World*, and Sheryl Sandberg's *Lean In: Women, Work, and the Will to Lead*. The ideological purpose in encouraging women to conform to the existing system is that the system as it is will be maintained. The current system diminishes and marginalizes women so any efforts to achieve equality will require remaking the system as a whole. Ensuring that any women who rise to positions of leadership will maintain the existing system is the ideological purpose behind the advice given in these self-help books.

I conclude with a suggestion for addressing the wage gap. To begin analyzing the rhetoric around the wage gap, denials of the wage gap provide insight to the challenges women face in the workplace.

CRITIQUE OF DOMINATION: DENIAL OF THE WAGE GAP

One reason the wage gap persists is the concerted effort made to deny its existence. Such efforts are genderblind because it is more difficult for women to collectively raise consciousness about the realities of the wage gap among other women and seek redress of this systemic discrimination if gender itself cannot be considered a factor in the discrimination. Gender is not the only factor, as wage gap deniers will be quick to tell you, but it is an important factor in unifying various social, political, and organizational practices currently present in American society. In terms of the material impact of denials of the wage gap, these denials can be understood through the lens of biopolitics as reducing the life chances of women. The wage gap as a systemic issue reduces women's earnings over the course of their careers because of a number of factors associated with being women. Denial of the wage gap contributes to the persistence of this systemic issue and reduces the life chances of women because lower earnings lead to lower financial stability, less ability to care for others, and increased chances of being trapped in situations of dependence on others. Denial of the wage gap must be resisted for women to be able to advance toward equality in the workplace.

In order to resist the denial of the wage gap, the rhetorical goals and means of deniers must be identified and understood. These goals and means are more important than debunking specific claims because understanding them can help you to push back against any denials even as the claims being made shift. The primary goal of this rhetoric is to completely deny the existence of the wage gap in terms of gender. The means used by deniers of the wage gap to achieve this goal are (1) presenting their arguments as mere facts that do not support women's equality and (2) assuming that the playing field of the workplace and society at large is already equal so any gap must be the result of women's own individual actions. I analyze the means used by deniers to achieve the goal of a complete denial of the wage gap through two texts: Ben Shapiro's 2016 article "7 Facts You Need to Know to Debunk the #EqualPayDay Lie" from his website *The Daily Wire* and a 2018 interview with Jordan Peterson that aired on Britain's Channel 4.[23] In order to achieve the goal of their argument, deniers must first persuade the audience to accept their claims as fact.

Facts Do Not Support Women's Equality

Ben Shapiro makes the means used by deniers of presenting arguments as mere fact clear in his article, saying, "Women supposedly earn $0.79 cents for every dollar earned by a man—but, of course, this neglects the fact that women choose different jobs, take time off from work for different reasons, work fewer hours, and make different life decisions on average."[24] The argument for the wage gap not existing is presented as a fact supported by the claims Shapiro makes. Choosing different jobs or working fewer hours as causes of the wage gap are claims made in support of an argument, not self-evident facts as Shapiro presents them here. (This is without even getting into the fact that most studies that analyze the wage gap control for other variables as a means of analyzing the gap in terms of equal positions between men and women or examine them in combination with gender in order to understand the nuances of the gap.) Making the argument in this manner is a means of presenting denial of the wage gap as settled fact. By doing so, Shapiro positions himself as not making an argument at all, just presenting facts, which makes countering his argument more difficult because you can get caught up debunking his facts while not addressing his general position. By positioning himself as an arbiter of facts, Shapiro persuades his supporters to continue listening to him even if specific facts he presents are shown to not prove his argument as clearly as he claimed.

Shapiro then highlights a number of claims about women's status in society and the wage gap in his article, from women being the numerical majority in America and making different life choices to men working longer hours and choosing different professions. On women making different life choices, Shapiro says, "My wife is a doctor . . . She took a year off when we had our first child. That means hear [sic] earning was delayed by a year. I took off four days. That's not atypical."[25] Through such anecdotes, Shapiro seeks to portray the normality of women making poor individual decisions that result in the wage gap through his personal experience. Arguing against the facts he presents, such as whether being a numerical majority is the same as having the most power in a society or whether we should change society so that men do not feel pressured to rush back to work four days after their child is born,[26] actually works to Shapiro's advantage because arguing against the facts makes them seem more legitimate. Shapiro can then use that legitimacy and the objective tone he employs through the simple presentation of facts to build his ethos with his supporters; the ethos he has built through his previous work also leads to greater support for this article. By focusing on persuading through ethos, Shapiro ensures that he does not have to fully support his claims, such as by showing how being a numerical majority connects to women's pay, in order to persuade his supporters. The ethos of the speaker is used again as justification for an argument in chapter 3 on rape apologia that is based on defending rapists with appeals to their character. The means employed of presenting claims as facts results in an acceptance of the overall argument even if the evidence does not support his argument or is never provided.

Jordan Peterson uses a similar method of making his argument denying the wage gap during a 2018 interview with Channel 4. Peterson starts by making a broad claim about the issue then presents narrow evidence to support that claim. When he is questioned about his claim or evidence, he denies making the claim by stating that he never said the exact words that were implied through the connection between his claim and evidence. For example, after a statement by the interviewer Cathy Newman about women being dominated in the workplace by men, Peterson responds, "It does seem that way, but multivariate analyses of the pay gap indicate that it doesn't exist"[27] His claim is plainly that the wage gap does not exist. When asked to provide evidence for this claim, Peterson responds, "There's multiple reasons for that. One of them is gender, but that's not the only reason. Like, if you're a social scientist worth your salt, you never do a univariate analysis. Like, you say, well, women in aggregate are paid less than men. Okay, well, we break it down by age. We break it down by occupation. We break it down by interest. We break it down by *personality.*"[28] The only evidence Peterson provides is the fact that multivariate analyses have been conducted. (He emphasizes personality because it has been a primary focus of his psychological practice.) Peterson ignores the fact that these analyses have generally been conducted to add complexity to our understanding of the wage gap, recognizing that gender is still a primary factor but is connected to other variables, like lower-paying career tracks for women and societal expectations for women at work and in the family, and employs the fact that the analyses exist to deny the existence of the wage gap. There is a heated exchange after Newman asks why women should put up with the wage gap, to which Peterson responds, "No, I'm not saying that they should put up with it! I'm saying that the claim that the wage gap between men and women is only due to sex is wrong! And it is wrong! There's no doubt about that! The multivariate analyses have been done."[29] Newman was responding to the implications of Peterson's claim (because the wage gap does not exist, women should accept the realities of the workplace for what they are), and Peterson goes on the attack because he did not make that specific claim. He then goes a step farther, saying, "But I also didn't deny it existed. I denied it existed because of gender. See, because I'm very, very, very careful with my words."[30] This is in direct contradiction to the claim he made at the start of this section of the interview. Newman got caught up in arguing the substance of what Peterson said in the interview without considering why he made his argument that way. Peterson is never required to sufficiently connect his evidence to his claim. The claim then becomes a self-evident fact for his supporters. The denial of the wage gap as a fact persists because of the manner in which Peterson made his argument.

Wage gap deniers like Shapiro and Peterson present their arguments as self-evident fact. The purpose of this method of making an argument is to persuade their supporters that the fact of the wage gap not existing is so obvious that no other evidence is needed to support this claim. This is accomplished through the ethos of the speaker. When Ben Shapiro presents a dry list of facts or Jordan Peterson gets heated when questioned about the implications of his argument, they are perceived as mere deliverers of the truth. You do not have to be persuaded to believe the truth, and positioning themselves in this way as objective truth-tellers allows Shapiro and Peterson to make claims without ever providing sufficient evidence. Resisting denial of the wage gap must begin by considering the ethos of the deniers rather than giving legitimacy to their arguments by trying to debunk their claims. Contesting their claims will not make a difference so long as the speaker is seen as the revealer of objective truth. The value given in critical rhetoric to personal experience as a grounding of analysis should be applied not just to the critic but also to the subject of the analysis. Claims like those made by Shapiro and Peterson should be analyzed as reflective of their personal experience (including their previous work, potential biases, experiences in the workplace, etc.) and not just allowed to stand as objective truth. Truth should be grounded in material reality, but the claims made in advancing an ideological argument should not be treated in the same manner. An assumption that underlies this supposed truth about the wage gap from a genderblind perspective is that the workplace is an equal space so any gap is the result of women's own individual choices and actions.

Assumption of an Equal Playing Field

Along with presenting their arguments as incontrovertible facts, deniers of the wage gap build their arguments on the assumption of equality in the workplace and society. From this viewpoint, each worker's choices and actions should be judged on an individual basis, and systemic issues do not exist. Women have the exact same opportunities, sometimes even better ones, so any gap that exists is the result of their individual decisions. There is no societal expectation that women should place the care of others over their own self-interest resulting in bosses and colleagues assuming that women are not committed to their careers and should not be promoted or paid the same as their male colleagues who do equal work. There is not a history of devaluing women's work, keeping them locked in lower-paying career tracks, and even speeding up the advancement of men in women-dominated fields. Because everything is equal and these other factors do not exist, all arguments about gender discrimination are undercut by the assertion that all individuals must be evaluated on their own merits. Such rhetoric reduces the chances for the existing status quo to be challenged. Women either internalize this viewpoint and question their own lack of advancement or have their concerns dismissed because everything is already equal. Shapiro and Peterson provide examples of this means of denying the wage gap in action.

After presenting what he sees as the facts that prove the wage gap does not exist, Shapiro lays out the argument that the gap is the product of women's choices, saying,

> Equal pay day for women is every day women make the same choices as men. The choices women currently make aren't qualitatively better or worse than men, necessarily, but they do have obvious consequences. Pretending that different decisions do not have disparate consequences is a hallmark of the left, which believes that equal results must be guaranteed regardless of personal choices. But wishes do not shape reality, and quashing Americans' business freedom based on mythology is both counterproductive and immoral.[31]

It is notable in Shapiro's figuring of the issue that it is only women's choices that can have negative consequences for not being the same as men's choices. It is almost as if these choices are made in a system that privileges men! Men's choices are the standard by which all behavior in the workplace is judged, so the wage gap for women is not actually the result of women's individual choices but how those choices are evaluated in relation to the choices made by men, which is the argument that feminists have been making for decades. By demanding that women make the same choices as men, Shapiro reveals the system to not be equal. A completely equal system is the only way Shapiro's argument makes any sense. When complete equality is not assumed, Shapiro's argument falls apart and actually serves to prove that inequality still exists. The success of Shapiro's argument hinges on acceptance of that assumption, so establishing his ethos with his supporters as an objective, unbiased observer who is only relaying facts is key. The two means of denying the wage gap work together to persuade Shapiro's audience that the wage gap is not real.

At one point in Cathy Newman's interview with Jordan Peterson, she asks him if people would be happy if the wage gap was eliminated, and he chuckles and says, "It would depend on how it was eradicated and how the disappearance was measured."[32] She asks if his objection is based on the costs of eradicating it for men, and he responds, "Oh, there's all sorts of things that it could be at the cost of. It could even be at the cost of women's own interests."[33] She asks if he means that women will be less happy if they get equal pay, and he says, "No, because it might interfere with other things that are causing the pay gap that women are choosing to do."[34] She then asks if he means having children, and he responds, "Well, or choosing careers that actually happen to be paid less, which women do a lot of."[35] Peterson is expressing the same viewpoint as Shapiro that equality has already been achieved so if women end up in lower-paying careers, it must be because they choose to make less. The other assumption operating here is that if career fields dominated by women started paying equally, then more men would be attracted to these careers so women would lose out on their chance at getting a job. This argument again reveals the systemic issues at work in producing the wage gap because if the workplace were truly equal, equal numbers of men and women would be attracted to each career based on their own interests and skills. The fact that many lower-paying careers are dominated by women supports the idea that gender does play a role in the wage gap.

Peterson's argument is also reflective of a larger viewpoint he expresses that societal and organizational disparities are a natural part of life. In the interview, Newman asks Peterson if it might be desirable for managers to adopt more feminine traits, and he responds, "They don't predict success. They don't predict success in the workplace. The things that predict success in the workplace are intelligence and conscientiousness. Agreeableness negatively predicts success in the workplace. And so does high negative emotion."[36] After some of his trademark obfuscating about whether he actually meant that feminine traits do not predict success, he argues that he cannot support the idea of feminine leadership styles because there is no evidence for it, saying,

> Well, it's fine if someone wants to start a company and make it more feminine and compassionate, let's say, and caring in its overall orientation towards its workers and towards the marketplace then that's a perfectly reasonable experiment to run. My point is that there is *no* evidence that those traits predict success in the workplace.[37]

The inequalities that exist for women in the workplace must be accepted because no evidence has been produced that shows that other ways of managing organizations will be effective. Toward the end of the interview, Peterson goes even further in his argument that hierarchy is a natural part of life. He argues in the interview and in his other work that certain biological traits that humans share with other animals, particularly lobsters, reveal a predisposition toward hierarchical structure. He then says, "Your biological nature is somewhat like that. It sets the rules of the game, but within those rules, you have a lot of leeway . . . But one thing we can't do is say that hierarchical organization is a consequence of the capitalist patriarchy. It's, like, that's patently absurd! It's *wrong*! It's not a matter of opinion. It's *seriously* wrong."[38] It is revealing that Peterson argues for the naturalness of hierarchy but does not consider that the current structure of human society is not the only form possible. Hierarchy for Peterson means the current status quo. Women's choices do not only lead to the wage gap, but their lower status in the social hierarchy is natural. Arguments for the naturalness of the existing system are also seen in chapter 4 when women's lack of success in the tech industry is attributed to the biological differences between women and men rather than on how the industry was constructed to favor men. That the current system represents true equality for Peterson and others is something with which those who seek to resist this rhetoric must reckon.

Efforts to deny the existence of the wage gap seek to present their argument as fact and are built on the assumption that the workplace is equal so that the outcomes for every worker are the result of their individual actions. The success of these persuasive arguments is dependent on the speaker's ethos, with those supporters who perceive them as objective, unbiased truth-tellers more likely to believe their arguments even if the evidence supporting them is challenged. The arguments against the wage gap also reveal other assumptions about the functioning of society, such as that the current hierarchical structure is natural. Those who seek to resist this rhetoric must give more attention to the means by which the persuasive arguments are made and less on debunking the claims made or evidence provided by the speaker. If you are unable to change the audience's perception of the speaker's ethos, no argument about the accuracy of the evidence provided will be successful.

Denials of the wage gap are genderblind because they prevent gender from being used in persuasive arguments about the need to address the inequalities women face in the workplace. They also function materially as biopolitics because they reduce the life chances of women by providing support and justification for those who contribute to women's inequality. Control over women is made possible in this genderblind system by reducing the material resources available to women. Those who ascribe to this ideology intend for these material effects to lead women to be more dependent on men, serving to reinforce a heteronormative system grounded in traditional conceptions of marriage and the family. Denials of the existence of the wage gap further these ideological goals by making it more difficult for women to actually make changes in the workplace to reduce or remove the gap since it is nothing more than the natural functioning of the individual choices of all involved. Denials of the wage gap are not the only form of the rhetoric of genderblindness takes in the workplace. Advice to conform to the expectations of the existing, unequal system that is found in self-help books for women in the workplace is used to ensure that any women who make the individual effort to improve their status at work by pursuing leadership positions will make decisions that conform to the status quo.

CRITIQUE OF FREEDOM: SELF-HELP BOOKS FOR WOMEN IN THE WORKPLACE

Self-help books are a part of what Dana Cloud labels therapeutic discourse. "The discursive pattern of translating social and political problems into the language of individual responsibility and healing is a rhetoric because of its powerful persuasive force; it constitutes therapy because of its focus on the personal life of the individual as locus of both problem and responsibility for change."[39] This pattern can be seen in self-help books on work-life balance for women that frame gender differences and roles in traditional terms, advise women on the proper emotional responses to their experiences at work and at home, and normalize the idea that women have to choose to maintain the balance on their own.[40]

The reader of self-help books is open to change but may still be defensive about how they see themselves.[41] "The facing, confronting, or confessing of one's personal shortcomings is a central ritual in therapeutic discourse."[42] Self-help readers are "both selective and interpretive" in their interactions with the texts.[43] They make active decisions about which text to read and engage in critical thinking about the advice they are receiving. Reading self-help books is mostly understood through action since that is the only way of determining if the reader has modified themselves according to what they have learned from the books.[44] Success is a prominent feature of the rhetoric of self-help books because we tend to view it "as boundless" when compared to happiness.[45] Happiness also "may be problematic" because it "requires no external validation."[46] The authors of self-help books present themselves as "qualified experts" whom the reader can trust, and they base their authority in their personal experience with the topic.[47]

While the reader may have agency in determining what texts to read and the ability to interpret the advice from their own experience, self-help books still encourage readers to view their problems in individualized terms. Through this focus on individualized solutions to systemic problems, self-help books on women's success in the workplace are genderblind because gender's usefulness in persuasive arguments about addressing the wage gap and other systemic issues women face is undermined when these issues can be dismissed as individual problems. The material impact of this discourse takes the form of disciplinary power by conditioning women to conform to the current status quo in pursuit of personal success.

The wage gap will persist so long as the advice given to women is directed at succeeding within the constraints of the current system rather than remaking the system to be better for all women. The ideological purpose in ensuring that women in leadership positions conform to the current status quo is clear as doing so helps sustain the system as it currently exists. The rhetoric in self-help books helps to achieve this ideological goal by making the reader feel that they are taking individual action and being decisive in how they are going to achieve their goals. This rhetoric also allows the women pursuing leadership positions feel that what they are doing is empowering other women even though conforming to the system only maintains the overall marginalization and oppression of women. The current view that everyone should be judged only on their individual merit without consideration of any other factors convinces women that striving for individual success will benefit all other women while doing so only benefits the individual woman. The genderblind rhetoric of self-help books for women in the workplace is expressed across four themes: awareness of the systemic nature of the wage gap, dealing with representatives of the system, policing your own behavior, and thriving within the system. While the authors advise women to conform to the current status quo in order to achieve personal success, they do at least acknowledge that the problems women face in the workplace are not solely of their own making.

Awareness of the Systemic Nature of the Wage Gap

In line with the research on self-help books, the texts under analysis focus primarily on individual behavior. Their goal is to help the individual woman improve herself so she can succeed and hopefully bring up other women with her. The authors draw on their own experiences as successful women in order to make their case. Sheryl Sandberg is the chief operating officer of Facebook, Sophia Amoruso is the founder of clothing brand Nasty Gal, Joann Lublin is a journalist at the *Wall Street Journal*, Lois Frankel is a psychologist who works as a motivational speaker and executive coach, and Jessica Bennett is the gender editor at *The New York Times*. As with other self-help authors, the authors analyzed in this chapter base their advice in their own experiences as successful women in arguing for individual responsibility and actions leading to success. However, there is at least some recognition in the texts about the systemic nature of the discrimination women face in the workplace. These systemic issues are seen as more futile to address, though, as compared to individual concerns.

Jessica Bennett demonstrates the clearest understanding of the systemic nature of the discrimination women face in the workplace, saying, "today's sexism is insidious, casual, politically correct, even *friendly*. It exists beneath the surface, quietly, in the way we scrutinize a woman's qualifications or simply don't 'like' women who seek power. It is a kind of can't-put-your-finger-on-it, not-particularly-overt, hard-to-quantify, harder-even-to-call-out behavior that maybe isn't necessarily intentional, or conscious."[48] Bennett recognizes the presence of the subtle sexism identified by Benokratis and Feagin in the workplace and the challenges it presents to addressing discrimination against women.[49] If discrimination is friendly, how do you call it out as discrimination? The system also encourages women to shift their targets from the system itself to individual actions, often targeting other women. Bennett pushes back against this tendency to attack other women as the cause of the problem, saying, "The problem isn't *other women*. It's a system that pits us against one another."[50] While Bennett clearly understands the systemic nature of the problems women face in the workplace, her book is still filled with individualized advice for surviving in the current status quo.

This tendency to turn systemic issues into individual action can be seen in how the authors of the other texts respond to systemic problems in their own lives. After beginning to recognize the sexism still present in the workplace as she started her career, Sheryl Sandberg's initial response was to ignore it, saying, "I figured if sexism still existed, I would just prove it wrong. I would do my job and do it well."[51] She later came to recognize the error in that line of thinking, saying, "What I didn't know at the time was that ignoring the issue is a classic survival technique."[52] While she may have come to understand that individual action alone would not solve the problem, individual action was still Sandberg's initial response and continues to be the primary advice she gives women throughout the text. A starker example can be seen in Joann Lublin's reaction to being harassed while interviewing a potential new colleague. "Horrified, I argued against hiring him. My boss disagreed, blaming the applicant's offensive behavior on his laidback lifestyle. But the new hire never fit in well at the *Journal* and lasted less than three years."[53] Lublin turns a systemic issue of why the harasser was even hired into an individual one when he fails to succeed. Women can be confident that harassers will not succeed by this logic. The idea that harassment can be ignored because the harassers will fail in the long run is revisited in chapter 4 when we look at online harassment of women. In relaying their own experiences of dealing with sexism and harassment, the authors privilege individual success and action, which is consistent with the advice they give to other women.

Lublin and Lois Frankel go beyond just encouraging women to take individual action in responding to discrimination in the workplace to actively blaming women for the discrimination they experience. Lublin says of the wage gap, "Various factors account for the gender gap, such as job choices, career interruption, levels of work experience, union membership, hours worked, and available child care. In many cases, women bear a certain responsibility for their pinched pay. They don't get the money they don't ask for."[54] Lublin's argument is consistent with the rationalizations offered by the human capital approach.[55] If a self-help book is going to encourage women to take individual responsibility for their success in the workplace, it must also lay blame for lack of success as a result of discrimination at the feet of women as well. Frankel is even more dismissive of the relevance of systemic issues in the everyday experiences of women in the workplace, saying, "I know all the statistics about gender disparity in pay and benefits. You probably do too. I don't want to downplay the significance of these factors—they're real and they're relevant. But unless you're an equal-pay activist, you have no control over those factors. The real question then becomes, *What are you going to do about it?*"[56] A systemic issue once again becomes an individual action. Seeking to address the systemic issues present in the workplace is better left to the activists so that the individual woman can focus on achieving her own success. There is no issue with maintaining the status quo so long as a few women can achieve personal success within it.

While the texts do demonstrate an awareness of the systemic issues facing women in the workplace, the authors are mostly resigned to leaving these issues unexamined. This is most clearly seen in Sandberg's argument for her individualized approach of leaning in that she contrasts with a focus on systemic issues.

> Others have argued that women can get to the top only when the institutional barriers are gone. This is the ultimate chicken-and-egg situation. The chicken—women will tear down the external barriers once we achieve leadership roles . . . The egg: We need to eliminate the external barriers to get women into those roles in the first place. Both sides are right. So rather than engage in philosophical arguments over which comes first, let's agree to wage battles on both fronts. They are equally important. I am encouraging women to address the chicken, but I fully support those who are focusing on the egg.[57]

This is a common belief across the texts that the best way to change the situation for women in the workplace is to have more women achieve success and rise to the top. While we should applaud the efforts of exceptional women who achieve success, the argument that this is the only way or the best way to end discrimination against women is not persuasive because it fails to dismantle the status quo that perpetuates discrimination against women in the first place. We are attracted to trying to solve the chicken problems of the individual because the egg problems of the system are more difficult to address and do not lead to as many national bestsellers. Again, there is nothing wrong with celebrating the success of exceptional women, but if your only advice for women is to find ways to succeed within the system as it currently exists, you are ultimately in support of that system. We will never be able to end the systems of discrimination and oppression of women and other marginalized groups if we leave the status quo in check. The rhetoric of genderblindness as found in self-help books is grounded in this encouragement to conform to the system. Women are encouraged to pursue success, but finding success within the system will make women less likely to want to change it, not more. The ideological purpose underlying the texts can also be seen in the advice the authors give to women for dealing with representatives of the system.

Dealing with Representatives of the System

The advice the authors of self-help books for women in the workplace offer for dealing with representatives of the system, from bosses who will not pay women equally to clients who sexually harass someone, fits within a genderblind ideology that encourages women to conform to the current status quo rather than trying to change the system. Bad bosses should be learned from so that you know how to be a better manager yourself once you are successful, sexual harassment should be treated in a way that benefits the woman's company rather than as a systemic form of discrimination, and if worse comes to worse, the individual woman should just leave and find a company that will not discriminate against her. These situations represent the most direct interaction with the system, but making substantive changes is never considered because it would not fit the rhetoric of individual responsibility and achievement offered by self-help books. The failures of the authors to truly recognize the systemic issues at work in the experiences of women in the workplace beyond the lip service given to the issue analyzed in the previous section is most clearly illustrated through the advice given to women for how to handle negative encounters with representatives of the system.

Joann Lublin focuses on the strategies successful women have used to succeed in the system, saying, "Several female leaders devised different clever tactics to get accepted by male peers during the early days of their careers, laying a foundation for later success."[58] Linda Hudson, former CEO of BAE Systems,

> feared that an overly emotional reaction or complaint might cut short her advancement. "I wasn't going to let this defeat me," she said about the harassment. "You had to learn to deal with it." For example, she would make comments to the men about their inability to recognize her value to their organization. "That was their problem, not mine," she pointed out.[59]

Hudson's leadership style was defined by her efforts to respond to incidents such as these.[60] As a result of her actions, the "number of women and people of color climbed nearly 10 percent between May 2011 and May 2013."[61] The argument of the authors of these texts is that negative treatment within the workplace can be turned into a positive, teaching valuable lessons in leadership that you can use to advance on your own path to success. Linda Hudson did at least try to make changes from her own position as an executive based on her experience of harassment, but there is still a lack of recognition of the systemic issue that would lead a woman to feel uncomfortable about making a complaint or worried that doing so would negatively affect her career. Women leaders can take the experiences they have had and turn them into positive changes in their workplaces, but so long as the systemic issues around women's discrimination in the workplace persist, then true change will never be possible. Telling women to learn from these experiences is just not enough.

Lois Frankel grounds women's interactions with representatives of the system in gender socialization as children. "Whereas boys are typically taught the art of self-defense, girls are taught to turn the other cheek. As a result, we're more likely to tolerate behavior we should never allow to happen. Unlearning those early childhood messages is a huge step on the path to living an empowered life."[62] This theme of women's socialization holding them back is seen throughout Frankel's book, and she distinguishes between being a girl and being a woman based on whether or not an individual still behaves according to socialization or if they have learned to resist those ingrained behaviors and conform to behaviors that lead to success within the system.[63] Frankel's ideas of success reflecting a prescribed set of limited behaviors would find support from Jordan Peterson and others who deny the realities of the wage gap. This issue of success being defined in narrow ways that benefit men is revisited in chapter 4 in the discussion of the perception of women as not having a place in the tech industry.

Jessica Bennett reflects on the experience of the behavioral expectations in a section advising women on dealing with men interrupting them in meetings. "We speak up, only to hear a man's voice boom over ours. We chime in with an idea, perhaps a tad too uncertainly—and a dude interjects with authority. We may have the smarts, but he has the vocal cords—causing us to clam up, lose our confidence, and credit for our work."[64] As is usual for self-help books, Bennett's advice focuses on individual actions to take in response to being interrupted, from using a talking stick to interrupting the man in order to let another woman continue. This focus on individualized responses once again fails to recognize the systemic nature of what behavior is encouraged in the workplace or how children are socialized into gender. The system does not have to exist or function the way it currently does, and even the advice given to combat the negatives of a system like gender socialization can end up merely reinforcing another system that expects women to conform in ways that are detrimental to their individual success and happiness and to the advancement of all women.

For Sheryl Sandberg, conforming to the current system is just part of a larger goal of getting more women into positions of leadership. "I understand the paradox of advising women to change the world by adhering to biased rules and expectations. I know it is not a perfect answer but a means to a desirable end. It is also true, as any good negotiator knows, that having a better understanding of the other side leads to a superior outcome."[65] The problem with this means-to-an-end line of argument is that the women who succeed by conforming to the system will be less likely to want to make substantive changes to the system once they have achieved power. They become products of the system and will defend the overall value of the system. Because of this, they end up pursuing only minor changes that help reduce the barriers to entry for marginalized groups but do not threaten the positions of any of those already in power. The hope is that these minor changes will be enough to reduce the sheer amount of discrimination experienced by women and other marginalized groups. However, a system that is discriminatory at its core needs to be completely remade rather than just tinkered with.

In contrast to the general advice provided in the texts to seek minor changes when interacting with representatives of the system, Lois Frankel portrays making any changes as an ultimately futile effort. First, she argues that most of the discrimination women report in the workplace is not actually discrimination at all.

> The common thread through 90 percent of these cases was not discrimination, but poor management. And like it nor not, poor management is not illegal. Despite the fact there are also laws to protect those who file claims of discrimination from retaliation, I never saw a claim that helped *anyone's* career. It didn't always hurt, but it never helped.[66]

Discrimination is not discrimination; it is just having a boss that is bad at their job. Frankel's purpose is to discourage women from reporting discrimination out of concern that her rhetoric of individualized responsibility and resisting socialization will lead women to more actively reporting the discrimination they experience. Doing so would upset the system, which would contradict Frankel's advice on how to conform.

Second, Frankel is very explicit about the negative effects on women from even discussing the discrimination they have experienced.

> Even if you don't go so far as to file a formal internal or external charge of sex discrimination, there is a stigma attached to women who "make noise" publicly about it—people suddenly become uncomfortable with you. They begin to act differently around you and treat you more carefully. In most cases this is counter to what women want—to be treated fairly. These are a few reasons why I strongly urge women to explore every other alternative available to them before playing the gender card.[67]

Framing discussions of discrimination as "playing the gender card" is unnecessarily reductive and dismissive of the experiences of women. It presents these discussions as illegitimate and only seeking to win, by using gender as a trump card, at the expense of the company that had not really done anything wrong. There is also the impression of sneakiness, as if the individual woman had the card up her sleeve the entire time and was just waiting for the chance to use it. Finally, Frankel goes over the options available to any woman who cannot handle the situation in the workplace, ultimately arguing, not surprisingly, for an individual response. "If gender is a legitimate impediment to your success in your current workplace, you have only three options: Put up with it (which I don't recommend—it will only further diminish your self-esteem), pursue formal internal channels for addressing it (which may or may not yield the desired results), or leave (which is the only option over which you truly have control)."[68] Making any sort of change is actively discouraged while the only option presented is to leave and hope that things will go better at the next company. The result of this rhetoric is that the system is preserved, and women are more likely to doubt whether their own experiences of discrimination rise to a high enough level to even give voice to them.

Joann Lublin provides one final piece of advice for women in how to deal with representatives of the system through the case of Charlotte Beers, former CEO of Ogilvy & Mather Worldwide. "Beers was ill-equipped for being sexually harassed by a senior executive at a major client of Tatham-Laird & Kudner, a small and struggling ad agency that named her its first female chief executive in 1982, when she was in her forties."[69] She accepted a dinner invitation from an executive at a client of the agency, and after dinner, the executive invited her up to his private apartment while he picked up some documents. On the elevator, she realized he was drunk.[70] While stumbling around in the dark apartment searching for a light switch, Beers stumbled onto the bed at which point the executive forced himself on her.[71] Afterward, the question was raised about whether or not to drop the account, which Beers found ridiculous after all of the effort the agency had put into securing it. Her goal, instead, was to find a solution that addressed the situation while still preserving the agency's relationship with the client. Beers's solution was to offer a male executive to take over the account.[72] Even the systemic issue of sexual harassment is turned into an individual one where women must outthink their harasser and try to find a way to benefit the company from the situation. Conformity to the system is a survival mechanism as presented in these texts, and experiences like Beers's are the scars that prove women have earned their success in the workplace. Instead of trying to create a new system in which no one would receive such scars, the advice given to women focuses instead on how to survive the scars you do receive so that you can achieve your goals of success. The texts seem to ask, "Is success even valid if you have not received these scars?" Having advised women that conformity to the system is the only way to achieve success, the texts then turn to encouraging women to police their own behavior in order to remain compliant.

Policing Your Own Behavior

It is with the advice on how women should police their own behavior that the self-help books for women in the workplace move from promoting conformity to the system to self-surveillance in order to ensure conformity. While before the texts were preaching the value of the system as a means of organizing the workplace and women's experiences in it, now the texts advise women to alter their behavior if it does not already fit within the expectations of the system. This is the primary domain of self-help rhetoric in general in its encouraging of people to view any problem in their lives as something they can address solely through individual responsibility and action. Any problem a woman might face in the workplace can be solved by fitting her behavior within the constraints of the system. This is where the project of shaping women to be nothing more than cogs in the existing system takes place. The conformity that is demanded of individuals in order to be successful means that anyone, woman or man, who succeeds within the system will continue to uphold it. This is particularly dangerous for women in the workplace because they are being molded to support a system that is built on discrimination against women at its very core. Even if women achieve success within the system, if their values are completely in line with the existing system, their rise to the top will not bring about change because it will only end up reproducing the system as it is. It is through the individualizing rhetoric of self-help books and the advice for women to police their own behavior to make sure it conforms to what is already successful within the system that women leaders end up reproducing a system that is discriminatory toward women.

Sophia Amoruso offers the most conventional, "power of positive thinking"-style advice for achieving success in the workplace in any of the texts. "If you believe that what you're doing will have positive results, it will—even if it's not immediately obvious."[73] While her advice may appear more generic, it is still built on the premise that you are doing something wrong and need to change your behavior. "You get back what you put out, so you might as well think positively, focus on visualizing what you want instead of getting distracted by what you don't want, and send the universe your good intentions so that it can send them right back."[74] Amoruso goes beyond just thinking positively to advocating for changes to behavior in her definition of a successful woman, or #GIRLBOSS in her parlance.

> A #GIRLBOSS is someone who's in charge of her own life. She gets what she wants because she works for it. As a #GIRLBOSS, you take control and accept responsibility. You're a fighter—you know when to throw punches and when to roll with them. Sometimes you break the rules, sometimes you follow them, but always on your own terms. You know where you're going, but can't do it without having some fun along the way. You value honesty over perfection. You ask questions. You take your life seriously, but you don't take yourself too seriously. You're going to take over the world, and change it in the process. You're a badass.[75]

Amoruso's advice may sound like something you would see on an inspirational poster, but she lays out specific behavioral changes, such as accepting responsibility, fighting for what you want, knowing when to follow the rules, working hard, and so on, that are necessary for success. Her text is also interesting because unlike the other authors who assume that women are making numerous mistakes and need correction, Amoruso frames her message around the assumption that anyone reading her book is already a #GIRLBOSS and so would already be doing the majority of the things she is advocating. Behavior change results from wanting to live up to the expectations of someone who already sees you as successful.

The majority of the advice in the texts centers on individual feminine behaviors that are portrayed as incompatible with success in the workplace. Lois Frankel makes this incompatibility explicit, saying, "By emphasizing your femininity, you diminish your credibility."[76] The authors have long lists of behaviors they see as problematic. Joann Lublin says of many women's lack of executive presence, "Strong competence and ability matter the most. But smaller and less obvious things, such as the way a woman speaks, can dramatically affect how she is regarded in the workplace. Women often lack executive presence because they have a weak handshake, gesture a lot, slouch, or speak tentatively with too many qualifiers."[77] Sheryl Sandberg critiques women for not speaking up, saying,

> If we want a world with greater equality, we need to acknowledge that women are less likely to keep their hands up. We need institutions and individuals to notice and correct for this behavior by encouraging, promoting, and championing more women. And women have to learn to keep their hands up, because when they lower them, even managers with the best intentions might not notice.[78]

In her book, Sandberg recognizes the systemic forces that limit women's opportunities for success but chooses to focus on women's individual behaviors instead.[79] She is also very fond of the idea of the self-fulfilling prophecy and makes repeated references to it as an explanation for how women's behaviors limit their own success.[80] As an example, she says of women's reluctance to go after new roles for which they do not feel they meet all of the qualifications, "This can become a self-fulfilling prophecy, since so many abilities are acquired on the job."[81] This position ignores the fact that most women are hired or promoted based on performance while men are more likely to be hired or promoted based on their potential.[82] Men are more likely to have the opportunity to develop their abilities on the job while women who try to change their behavior to meet this systemic norm may still find themselves unsuccessful.

Lois Frankel spends the most time identifying specific individual behaviors that must be corrected. Her advice ranges from how you should wear your hair to delivering bad news. "The most common mistake I see women make is to wear their hair too long."[83] "Public primping emphasizes your femininity and detracts from your credibility. Real women avoid PDG (public displays of grooming)."[84] "This is the most common mistake I hear women make: asking a question as a safe way of expressing an idea without being perceived as too direct or pushy."[85] She says of a woman wearing her glasses on a chain, "At the risk of sounding ageist, I need to say once again that, unlike men, it's the rare woman who finds her credibility increasing with age. Although I don't think it's something to hide or lie about, I do think it's not necessary to emphasize it."[86] On women's presentation styles, she says, "When you combine taking up too little space with using too few gestures, the overwhelming impression conveyed is that of being demure, careful, unwilling to take risks, timid, or frightened with little to contribute."[87] She even critiques women for spending time in lower-level positions, saying, "Spending time in a 'female ghetto' makes you more likely to be branded as unworthy of a senior assignment. Do I think this is right? Of course not . . . Remaining too long in such a role or department will eventually limit your marketability."[88] These are just a small portion of the numerous behaviors Frankel advises women to correct in order to fit the expectations of the workplace. The main problem with Frankel and the other authors' advice on changing specific behaviors is that they do not consider systemic causes for behaviors, just individual problems. Asking questions rather than stating opinions, not taking up too much space during a meeting, or taking gender-segregated positions are also the result of how women are treated in the workplace because it is structured to privilege men, not just because of problems with their individual socialization. Focusing on how women can change their behaviors to fit the expectations of the system reinforces the privileging of men in the workplace since it is the standards set according to their behavior that women are expected to meet. Rather than chastising women for their feminine behaviors or leadership styles, we need to be creating a new system in which these behaviors are no longer devalued.

One of the most problematic forms of advice on policing your own behavior is the arguments that systemic issues like sexual harassment and the wage gap should be responded to in line with the expectations of the system or that women's individual behaviors create the system itself. Joann Lublin advises women who are dealing with sexual harassment to be strategic, saying, "Pick your battles and don't overreact."[89] She quotes Carol Bartz, former CEO of Yahoo and Autodesk, on the advice she gave her daughter when she was dealing with sexual harassment in the workplace as a new employee: "'You haven't earned the right to make a big deal of this,' Bartz told [her daughter]. 'Just stay out of his way.'"[90] The advice here is to conform, to not cause problems by expecting men to not harass women. The best interests of the company are placed ahead of the experiences of the individual woman. Beyond just the advice to put your head down and avoid the harasser as the proper response, the idea that the right to challenge systemic discrimination is tied to your position within the company is pretty disgusting.

After acknowledging that the wage gap is real, Jessica Bennett lays the blame for it on women's inability to negotiate effectively, saying, "People—especially women—often don't ask for what they want, which is one reason why the wage gap (and many other things) still exists."[91] In trying to advise women to conform to the system by negotiating better, Bennett goes a step further to argue that women's individual behaviors create the wage gap itself. The Catch-22 here for women is that conforming to the system will not fix the wage gap but not acting in accordance with the expectations of the system also seemingly creates the wage gap itself. Women are literally damned if they do, damned if they do not.

Along with these specific behaviors, the authors identify women's lack of confidence and unwillingness to take risks as barriers to their success. Sheryl Sandberg identifies fear as the main thing holding women back. "Fear is at the root of many of the barriers that women face. Fear of not being liked. Fear of making the wrong choice. Fear of drawing negative attention. Fear of overreaching. Fear of being judged. Fear of failure. And the holy trinity of fear: fear of being a bad mother/wife/daughter."[92] Fear is an individualized failing as Sandberg uses it, not an emotion that implies connection to others or a legitimate contextual response to the oppressive environment a woman finds herself in. The fear that holds women back is just another challenge to be conquered, so women are advised in these texts to just choose to be confident rather than giving in to fear. As Lublin says of the women leaders she interviewed, some "contend that strong self-confidence should trump any imposter fears about taking a top-level job . . . After all, 'if you don't have confidence in yourself, you shouldn't be aspiring to get ahead,' said Pat Russo, a former chief of Lucent Technologies and Alcatel-Lucent."[93] Self-confidence becomes another requirement for women who want to succeed.

Paired with confidence is a willingness to take risks. Risks can potentially damage a woman's career, such as in a glass cliff situation where a recently promoted woman is set up to take the fall for the company's failures, but Joann Lublin found that "the chance of failure didn't deter most women I interviewed from taking a mission impossible and becoming more resilient as a result of their inevitable setbacks."[94] Lublin offers Gracia Martore, CEO of TEGNA, as an example of a risk-taker who critiques her female colleagues for not matching her fearless attitude, saying, "They cite 'all the reasons why they can't do the job,' she noted. 'Men, even though they have the same inability to do the job, will sit there and say, "I can do that. That's no sweat.""'[95] Sheryl Sandberg, in a familiar pattern, offers gender socialization as the reason many women are afraid to take risks, saying, "Career progression often depends upon taking risks and advocating for oneself—traits that girls are discouraged from exhibiting. This may explain why girls' academic gains have not yet translated into significantly higher numbers of women in top jobs."[96] Sandberg does at least acknowledge that expectations for women and men in the workplace are different in regards to taking risks, saying, "Professional ambition is expected of men but is optional—or worse, sometimes even a negative—for women . . . Aggressive and hard-charging women violate unwritten rules about acceptable social conduct."[97]

Even though she acknowledges these differences in expectations, Sandberg still wants to push women to take more risks, especially when it comes to staying in a career or leaving to raise a family. This is the major theme of her book: women need to lean in to their jobs rather than always preparing to leave. Leaving may seem like a single, big decision, but Sandberg argues that it is actually the result of many smaller decisions.

> But when it comes to integrating career and family, planning too far in advance can close doors rather than open them. I have seen this happen over and over. Women rarely make one big decision to leave the workforce. Instead, they make a lot of small decisions along the way, making accommodations and sacrifices that they believe will be required to have a family. Of all the ways women hold themselves back, perhaps the most pervasive is that they leave before they leave.[98]

Women are too cautious, according to Sandberg, and do not give their careers their all until they have to leave, essentially letting the situation make the decision for them because their careers are not at the level where they would want to stay. Sandberg wants women to take the risk of giving their careers their all so that the decision they have to make about having a family will be a real one. "Anyone lucky enough to have options should keep them open. Don't enter the workforce already looking for the exit. Don't put on the brakes. Accelerate. Keep a foot on the gas pedal until a decision must be made. That's the only way to ensure that when that day comes, there will be a real decision to make."[99]

Risk is often partnered with confidence in these texts because you have to have true confidence in yourself to take the necessary risks to succeed. The ideal work norm expects all employees to exhibit complete devotion to the company, and women have been changing their behavior, such as through hookups and other non-committed romantic relationships, to demonstrate how they meet this workplace expectation.[100] The advice on taking risks feeds into this expectation by making women feel that they are at fault and will never succeed if they have to step away from work. Instead of empowering women, this advice leads women to feel guilty about having to conform to societal expectations. Rather than seeing successful women as role models, many women may not even try to succeed after receiving the message about what is required of them.

The advice on policing your own behavior is the clearest example of genderblindness to be found in the texts under analysis. In their reflection of a genderblind ideology, these self-help books ignore the realities of women's experiences with discrimination and oppression in the workplace and society at large to spread a message that individual success can be achieved so long as you alter your behavior to conform to the expectations of the workplace. Women's manner of dress and speaking style are not the product of centuries of societal pressure on how women are supposed to present themselves in public but just individual decisions to express their femininity excessively. Women are not more cautions in making decisions and taking risks because their entire lives and livelihoods have historically depended on making sure everyone is happy and taken care of but just a product of an individual fear of trying something new. Women are not choosing to leave the work force to raise a family or take care of sick and elderly family members because society has expected women to be caretakers since the beginning of time but just because they are looking for the exit as soon as they start their careers and so make leaving the only viable option. These realities of women's lives are ignored for the most part in favor of framing women's experiences in the workplace as the result of their own individual actions so that their problems can be solved by the individualized advice offered by the authors. This advice is offered as a foolproof plan that will succeed for every woman so long as she is ever-vigilant to make sure she does not slip in her conformity to the system. It is truly genderblind because the only way that foolproof promise could possibly be true is in a world where the constraints placed on women in terms of gender were no longer present. Only in that world would women be free to be judged solely on their individual actions. This foolproof promise also ignores the intersectional identities, particularly race and class, that shape women's experiences in the workplace. No acknowledgment is made of the differing experiences women who hold other marginalized identities have in the workplace. By offering this promise to a universal woman, the authors fully reveal their lack of awareness of the various systemic issues that impact women's everyday lives and their lack of interest in truly changing the system. In order to make their promise of foolproof success seem viable, the final theme in the self-help rhetoric for women in the workplace is offering examples of how to thrive within the system.

Thriving within the System

As successful women themselves, the authors of the texts analyzed in this chapter have found ways to succeed within the current system. Their ethos as authors is grounded in that success because if they could not achieve it themselves, no one would listen to their advice on how to be successful. Because of their success, they obviously believe that success within the system as it is currently constructed is not only achievable but something that every woman should strive for. Having advised women to police their own behavior so that it conforms to the expectations of the system, the authors now turn to showing how such conformity can lead to thriving within the system. This final theme of self-help books for women in the workplace solidifies the idea that the primary limitation of this rhetoric is that it prevents actual change to the system because those who thrive within the system will be reluctant to change it. Success does not preclude critiquing the system and fighting for change, but the messages about thriving within the system are presented as the reward for conformity rather than as new platforms of power that can be used to enact necessary changes.

Joann Lublin ties success in the workplace to fighting for gender pay equity, saying, "Several executive women I met pocketed sizable rewards only after they pushed for more equitable financial treatment. Deft pay negotiations for themselves and female colleagues often made them stronger leaders."[101] What is notable here is that Lublin is not saying that women succeeded because of the changes to the system but from the skills learned from fighting for change. These skills tend to fit the expectations of the system even if what is being fought for is ostensibly a change in the system. Thriving in the system for Sophia Amoruso also entails a willingness to fight, saying, "I, along with countless other #GIRLBOSSes who are profiled in this book, girls who are reading this book, and the girls who are yet to become a #GIRLBOSS will do it not by winning—but by fighting."[102] The process of fighting itself is rewarding even if they goals fought for are never achieved.

Sheryl Sandberg highlights the fact that women are achieving more success now than ever before, saying, "Today in the United States and the developed world, women are better off than ever. We stand on the shoulders of the women who came before us, women who had to fight for the rights that we now take for granted."[103] Amoruso makes a direct connection between the fight for women's equality and success, saying, "I believe the best way to honor the past and future of women's rights is by getting shit done."[104] While a certain debt may be owed to the women who have come before, the authors quickly refocus success on the individual behaviors highlighted before. Lublin identifies the key traits shared by the successful women she interviewed, saying, "They displayed tremendous confidence, calculated risk taking, and a stubborn refusal to admit defeat when career obstacles loomed."[105] Sheryl Sandberg argues for restarting a stalled revolution in women's rights through a focus on changes to individual behavior, saying, "We can reignite the revolution by internalizing the revolution. The shift to a more equal world will happen person by person. We move closer to the larger goal of true equality with each woman who leans in."[106] Finally, Sophia Amoruso states that she is fine with the current system that privileges men so long as she achieves personal success, saying, "You don't get taken seriously by asking someone else to take you seriously. You've got to show up and own it. If this is a man's world, who cares? I'm still really glad to be a girl in it."[107] Thriving within the system is the product of individual responsibility and action. The clear message from the authors is that success is all that matters. Since success is defined in individual terms, individual behavior is privileged over changes to the system. The policing of behavior is rewarded through personal success. The ultimate argument of self-help books for women in the workplace is that if women will just conform to the system, they will achieve personal success too. And if they are not successful, then they must be doing something wrong.

The focus of the texts under analysis has been on changing individual behavior in order to conform to the expectations of the system. These texts do provide useful advice for women looking for ways to find success within the system. If you are woman who is looking for advice on how to be promoted at your company and advance your career, the texts have numerous tips and tricks you can try to change your behavior and signal to others in the company that you are serious about advancing. If you are a woman who has felt unfairly passed over for promotions and is looking for practical advice for things you can change that are within your control, these texts have suggestions for you, from changes you can make to your hairstyle or clothing to changes in behavior in meetings and negotiations that will make you a more readily identifiable candidate for leadership. In this sense, self-help books for women in the workplace fulfill their stated goal of helping more women succeed. The problem is that these books are not marketed toward women in these specific situations but as guides for all women to achieve success without taking into account the various systemic constraints and limitations preventing all women from rising to the same level. Greater awareness of the specific audience for self-help books like these could have reduced the criticism of these texts.

This lack of awareness is part of how the texts function in service to a genderblind ideology by defining what proper behavior is within the system and advising women to self-surveil their own behavior to make sure that it conforms to those expectations. This advice is genderblind because it reduces the usefulness of gender as a persuasive appeal in addressing women's discrimination in the workplace because any arguments for making changes to the system to address this discrimination can be defeated through references to women just needing to change their individual behavior, using these texts as proof. Framing the issues women face in the workplace as individual problems with individual solutions prevents necessary changes from being made that would benefit all women. In the conclusion, I suggest some steps that can be taken to change this framing of the issue.

CONCLUSION

The wage gap is real and cannot be solved by changes to women's individual behavior. The rhetoric around the wage gap and women's experiences in the workplace in general, though, works to maintain the existing system and reinforce the wage gap. Denials of the wage gap seek to present their arguments as self-evident facts and are built on the assumption that equality has been achieved in the workplace and society as a whole. The material impact of this discourse is the reduction of women's life chances by providing justification for the gender inequality that exists in the workplace. Self-help books for women in the workplace advise women to conform to the existing system. While there is some acknowledgment of the systemic discrimination women face, the focus is on working to maintain the system as it is and encouraging women to self-surveil to ensure that their behavior fits the expectations of the system. Women who find success according to the expectations of the system end up just reproducing the system that shaped them into leaders. The ideological purpose in genderblindness of maintaining the system as it currently exists is fulfilled in the rhetoric around the wage gap.

What can we do to address the wage gap? We need to demand that women leaders do more than just succeed. Most of the advice given to women on what to do after achieving success is just about using that success to help other women succeed. Joann Lublin says of the successful women she interviewed, "A number of business leaders I spoke with 'pay it forward' by trying to guide and propel the careers of their junior female executives."[108] Jessica Bennett advises women who succeed, "And when you've trailblazed your way to the top, remember your FFC [Feminist Fight Club] duty: to bring other women with you."[109] In reference to moving parking spaces for pregnant women at Google closer to the door when she was pregnant, Sheryl Sandberg says, "The other pregnant women must have suffered in silence, not wanting to ask for special treatment. Or maybe they lacked the confidence or seniority to demand that the problem be fixed. Having one pregnant woman at the top—even one who looked like a whale—made the difference."[110] The benefits of having more women as leaders may seem obvious, but we need women in those positions who will seek to make substantive changes to the system they now have power within. Instead of teaching women how to survive in a system designed to privilege men, women leaders need to be at the forefront of creating a more equal and just system. Instead of telling women how to wear their hair or how to use gestures while giving a presentation, women leaders should be reforming the hiring and promotion processes so that things like personal appearance and speaking style are not factors in decisions. Instead of telling women how to negotiate better, women leaders should be reforming HR practices so that all workers in the same job with the same time at the company earn the same pay. Instead of telling women to ignore harassment or use it to benefit the company, women leaders should be taking decisive action against anyone who harasses or discriminates against anyone else. As Audre Lorde says, "For the master's tools will never dismantle the master's house."[111] We need women leaders to truly be leaders and not think that their success is all that is necessary.

The self-help books analyzed in this chapter are correct that we need more women leaders. However, we need to stop advising women to only strive for success within the existing system. We need women leaders who are aiming to create the new, more equal system that is yet to come rather than women leaders who are content with the system as it currently exists.

NOTES

1. Andrea Mandell, "Exclusive: Wahlberg Got $1.5M for 'All the Money' Reshoot, Williams Paid Less Than $1,000," *USA Today*, January 10, 2018, https://www.usatoday.com/story/life/people/2018/01/09/exclusive-wahlberg-paid-1-5-m-all-money-reshoot-williams-got-less-than-1-000/1018351001/.

2. American Association of University Women, *The Simple Truth about the Gender Pay Gap* (AAUW, 2017), 6.

3. Ibid., 11.

4. Ibid.

5. Ibid., 14.

6. Ibid., 15.

7. E. Holly Buttner and Kevin B. Lowe, "The Relationship between Perceived Pay Equity, Productivity, and Organizational Commitment for US Professionals of Color," *Equality, Diversity and Inclusion: An International Journal* 36, no. 1 (2017): 83.

8. Joan Acker, *Doing Comparable Worth: Gender, Class, and Pay Equity* (Philadelphia: Temple University Press, 1991), 13.

9. Judith K. Pringle, Sharyn Davies, Lynne Giddings and Judy McGregor, "Gender Pay Equity and Wellbeing: An Intersectional Study of Engineering and Caring Occupations," *New Zealand Journal of Employment Relations* 42, no. 3 (2017): 40.

10. Ruth Milkman, *On Gender, Labor, and Inequality* (Urbana, IL: University of Illinois Press, 2016), 293-295.

11. David Freeman Engstrom, "'Not Merely There to Help the Men': Equal Pay Laws, Collective Rights, and the Making of the Modern Class Action," *Stanford Law Review* 70, no. 1 (2018): 75.

12. Ibid., 85.

13. Claudia Goldin, *Understanding the Gender Gap: An Economic History of American Women* (New York: Oxford University Press, 1990), 90.

14. Ibid., 116.

15. Mohamad G. Alkadry and Leslie E. Tower, "Slowly but Can We Say 'Surely'? Pay Equity & Segregation a Decade Later in West Virginia State Government," *Public Administration Quarterly* 37, no. 2 (2013): 230; Maria Karamessini and Elias Ioakimoglou, "Wage Determination and the Gender Pay Gap: A Feminist Political Economy Analysis and Decomposition," *Feminist Economics* 13, no. 1 (2007): 56.

16. Hiau Joo Kee, "Glass Ceiling or Sticky Floor? Exploring the Australian Gender Pay Gap," *The Economic Record* 82, no. 259 (2006): 424.

17. Hilary M. Lips, "The Gender Pay Gap: Challenging the Rationalizations, Perceived Equity, Discrimination, and the Limits of Human Capital Models," *Sex Roles* 68, no. 3-4 (2013): 178.

18. Alan Manning and Farzad Saidi, "Understanding the Gender Pay Gap: What's Competition Got to Do with It?," *Industrial and Labor Relations Review* 63, no. 4 (2010): 694.

19. Joseph E. Stiglitz, *The Price of Inequality: How Today's Divided Society Endangers Our Future* (New York: W. W. Norton & Company, 2013), 85.

20. Forrest Briscoe and Aparna Joshi, "Bringing the Boss's Politics In: Supervisor Political Ideology and the Gender Gap in Earnings," *Academy of Management Journal* 60, no. 4 (2017): 1433.

21. Lisa M. Leslie, Colleen Flaherty Manchester and Patricia C. Dahm, "Why and When Does the Gender Gap Reverse? Diversity Goals and the Pay Premium for High Potential Women," *Academy of Management Journal* 60, no. 2 (2017): 426.

22. Marcus Noland, Tyler Moran, and Barbara Kotschwar, "Is Gender Diversity Profitable? Evidence from a Global Survey," *Peterson Institute for International Economics*, Working Paper 16-3 (2016): 3.

23. Ben Shapiro, "7 Facts You Need to Know to Debunk the #EqualPayDay Lie," *The Daily Wire*, April 12, 2016, https://www.dailywire.com/news/4858/7-facts-you-need-know-debunk-equalpayday-lie-ben-shapiro; "Jordan Peterson Debate on the Gender Pay Gap, Campus Protests and Postmodernism," *Channel 4 News*, January 16, 2018, https://www.youtube.com/watch?v=aMcjxSThD54.

24. Shapiro, "7 Facts."

25. Ibid.

26. For more on numerical majorities and power, see Shaun, "So, About the Amazing Atheist Video . . .," November 13, 2017, https://www.youtube.com/watch?v=6Lce4eZFZ2E&t=812s.

27. "Jordan Peterson Debate."

28. Ibid.

29. Ibid.

30. Ibid.

31. Shapiro, "7 Facts."

32. "Jordan Peterson Debate."

33. Ibid.

34. Ibid.

35. Ibid.

36. Ibid.

37. Ibid.

38. Ibid.

39. Dara L. Cloud, *Control and Consolation in American Culture and Politics: Rhetorics of Therapy* (Thousand Oaks, CA: Sage, 1998), 1.

40. Katherine J. Denker, "Are You Managing It All? Just Read This: Working Mothers Search for Work-Life Balance through Therapeutic Discourse and Self-Help Texts," in *Gender in a Transitional Era: Changes and Challenges*, eds. Amanda R. Martinez and Lucy J. Miller (Lanham, MD: Lexington Books, 2015), 11-16.

41. Kelly Coyle and Debra Grodin, "Self-Help Books and the Construction of Reading: Readers and Reading in Textual Representation," *Text and Performance Quarterly* 13, no. 1 (1993): 66-67.

42. Ibid., 67.

43. Debra Grodin, "The Interpreting Audience: The Therapeutics of Self-Help Book Reading," *Critical Studies in Mass Communication* 8, no. 4 (1991): 410.

44. Scott Cherry, "The Ontlogy of a Self-Help Book: A Paradox of Its Own Existence," *Social Semiotics* 18, no. 3 (2008): 344-345.

45. John Ramage, *Twentieth-Century Success Rhetoric: How to Construct a Suitable Self* (Carbondale, IL: Southern Illinois University Press, 2005), 33.

46. Ibid., 34.

47. Rebecca Hazleden, "'You Have to Learn These Lessons Sometime': Persuasion and Therapeutic Power Relations in Bestselling Relationship Manual," *Continuum: Journal of Media & Cultural Studies* 24, no. 2 (2010): 294-295. See also Louise Woodstock, "All about Me, I Mean, You: The Trouble with Narrative Authority in Self-Help Literature," *The Communication Review* 9, no. 4 (2006): 328.

48. Jessica Bennett, *Feminist Fight Club: A Survival Manual for a Sexist Workplace* (New York: Harper Wave, 2016), xxv-xxvi.

49. Nijole V. Benokraitis and Joe R. Feagin, *Modern Sexism: Blatant, Subtle, and Covert Discrimination* (Edgewood Cliffs, NJ: Prentice-Hall, 1986), 30.

50. Ibid., 85.

51. Sheryl Sandberg, *Lean In: Women, Work, and the Will to Lead* (New York: Alfred A. Knopf, 2013), 142-143.

52. Ibid.

53. Joann S. Lublin, *Earning It: Hard-Won Lessons from Trailblazing Women at the Top of the Business World* (New York: Harper Business, 2016), 68.
54. Ibid., 81-82.
55. Lips, "The Gender Pay Gap" 178.
56. Lois P. Frankel, *Nice Girls Don't Get the Corner Office: 101 Unconscious Mistakes Women Make that Sabotage Their Careers* (New York: Warner Business Books, 2004), 72.
57. Sandberg, "Lean In" 8-9.
58. Lublin, "Earning It" 54.
59. Ibid., 69.
60. Ibid.
61. Ibid.
62. Frankel, "Nice Girls" 215.
63. Ibid., 132.
64. Bennett, "Feminist Fight Club" 6.
65. Sandberg, "Lean In" 48.
66. Frankel, "Nice Girls" 246.
67. Ibid., 247.
68. Ibid., 248.
69. Lublin, "Earning It" 75.
70. Ibid.
71. Ibid., 75-76.
72. Ibid., 76.
73. Sophia Amoruso, *#GIRLBOSS* (New York: Portfolio/Penguin, 2014), 29.
74. Ibid., 117-118.
75. Ibid., 11.
76. Frankel, "Nice Girls" 78.
77. Lublin, "Earning It" 208.
78. Sandberg, "Lean In" 36.
79. Ibid., 8.
80. Ibid., 22, 33, 62, 114, 171.
81. Ibid., 62.
82. Rosamund Unwin, "Are You Falling into the Promotion Gap?," *The Sunday Times* (London), Mar. 18, 2018, 32-33.
83. Frankel, "Nice Girls" 198.
84. Ibid., 204.
85. Ibid., 148.
86. Ibid., 208.
87. Ibid., 188.
88. Ibid., 140.
89. Lublin, "Earning It" 78.
90. Ibid.
91. Bennett, "Feminist Fight Club" 81.
92. Sandberg, "Lean In" 24.
93. Lublin, "Earning It" 119.
94. Ibid., 103.
95. Ibid., 107.
96. Sandberg, "Lean In" 15.
97. Ibid., 17.
98. Ibid., 93.
99. Ibid., 103.
100. Kendra Knight and Benjamin Wiedmaier, "Emerging Adults' Casual Sexual Involvements and the Ideal Worker Norm," in *Gender in a Transitional Era: Changes and Challenges*, eds. Amanda R. Martinez and Lucy J. Miller (Lanham, MD: Lexington Books, 2015), 151-165. It is ironic here that the excessive pressure places on young people to adhere to workplace norms is actually undermining traditional ideas of relationships and the family. The gender-blind ideology in the workplace generally works in sync with ideas of the traditional family

with its continuing to pay women less for equal work and its limiting of many women to more traditionally feminine positions. Should the pressures to maintain the traditional family become even stronger, I believe the pressures on women to demonstrate commitment to the company as ideal workers will lose out, and women will begin to be forced out of their jobs and back into the home.

  101. Lublin, "Earning It" 81.
  102. Amoruso, "#GIRLBOSS" 15-16.
  103. Sandberg, "Lean In" 4.
  104. Amoruso, "#GIRLBOSS" 14.
  105. Lublin, "Earning It" 258.
  106. Sandberg, "Lean In" 11.
  107. Amoruso, "#GIRLBOSS" 16.
  108. Lublin, "Earning It" 187.
  109. Bennett, "Feminist Fight Club" 112.
  110. Sandberg, "Lean In" 4.
  111. Audre Lourde, *Sister Outsider: Essays and Speeches* (Trumansburg, NY: The Crossing Press, 1984), 112.

Chapter Two

Genderblindness and Abortion

On June 27, 2018, Justice Anthony Kennedy announced his retirement from the Supreme Court effective July 31.[1] Kennedy served on the Court for thirty-one years after being appointed in 1987 by President Ronald Reagan. Kennedy's role as a swing vote in many important cases has led many who are pro-choice to be concerned about the future of abortion access in America.[2] President Donald Trump wasted no time in announcing his nomination on July 9, 2018, of Brett Kavanaugh, one of many potential nominees who has signaled a willingness to overturn 1973's landmark decision in *Roe v. Wade* that made abortion legal throughout the United States.[3] As the debate over abortion is sure to ratchet up in the coming months and years, it is important to analyze the rhetoric surrounding the issue.

Abortion is generally understood as a women's health issue, but gender is not the primary predictor of support for abortion rights. In terms of support for abortion, women are not statistically more likely to support abortion than men, but religiosity was found to have a significant indirect effect as "women are more religious than men, and religiosity is negatively associated with support for legal abortion."[4] This intersection of gender and religion will be particularly important in my analysis of the rhetoric of crisis pregnancy centers.

Opposition to abortion is generally framed as love of and caring for children, and state laws are presented as necessary for achieving this mission. However, states with strict abortion regulations are also less interested in the health and well-being of children.[5] This supposed care for children does not seem to apply once the child has been born.

Anti-abortion activists frequently argue that abortion causes mental and emotional stress for the women who have abortions, but denial of abortion initially leads to higher stress levels than having an abortion, though stress levels return to similar levels within a few weeks.[6] Social disapproval was also identified as a primary reason women experienced negative feelings after having an abortion.[7] Abortion is a complex issue that impacts women's lives in fundamental ways, but the anti-abortion rhetoric of Targeted Regulation of Abortion Providers (TRAP) laws and crisis pregnancy centers increases the stress women feel when making decisions around abortion by restricting their options or making their choices seem less valid. The discourse surrounding this issue has been developing for decades.

The discourse around abortion has gone through different stages of development over the last century. In the early twentieth century, Margaret Sanger and other family-planning activists had to construct other means of delivering their message as access to the official public sphere for such discourse was restricted by the state, the medical community, and the church.[8] In this period, doctors positioned themselves as authorities by claiming that young women had lost touch with the messages they received from their bodies that encouraged maternity.[9] Storytelling became a means through which women were able to share their experiences with childbirth and abortion while adhering to the expected norms of femininity.[10]

This use of narrative continued into the 1960s and 1970s. Women's health advocates at this time made use of three narratives: ones that "place[d] women's experiences in a historical context to understand them more clearly as evidence of a larger, systemic problem," "'horror stories' women tell of the ways they were treated by physicians and other health care providers created a compelling case for changes in women's health care," and they "used their own experiences to test what they read in books, or were told by their physicians, and created new knowledge about women's health."[11] While these narratives were intended to communicate the difficulties women faced in accessing abortion, they also led to further stigmatizing of women who had abortions and created the expectation that it was women's duty to take the necessary actions to prevent abortion.[12]

In the late 1960s, pro-choice rhetoric was inspired by the civil rights movement to shift from narratives of personal experiences to a focus on abortion restrictions as discrimination against women.[13] The pro-life movement responded by drawing more direct connections between the fetus and "life" in the early 1970s.[14] Around the same time, "choice" replaced "discrimination" as the primary ideograph for the pro-choice movement.[15] After the Supreme Court's decision in *Roe v. Wade* in 1973, the discourse "was characterized by two competing tendencies: (1) attempts to normalize abortion by working it into the daily understandings of Americans and (2) an escalation of the opposition to such normalization, focusing on a constitutional amendment."[16] By the early 1980s, the anti-abortion movement had moved away from an effort to persuade others through rhetoric to an ideology restricted to only true believers as supported by a discursive strategy of "over-weighing" in which "rhetors attempt to show that the values and interests on their side carry more weight than those of the opposition."[17] The closing off of this discourse has made persuading opponents of abortion more difficult as any such efforts would be seen as inferior to the anti-abortion position.

In the current political discourse surrounding abortion and other reproductive health issues as seen through the discourse surrounding health care reform, "the political subjects who emerge through these discourses fall into two categories: those citizens who deserve to have the individual freedom that is so greatly emphasized and those biocitizens whose power needs to be curbed to preserve the nation's best interests."[18] Women are positioned within this discourse as subjects who need to be controlled rather than as citizens with the rights and freedoms to make decisions over their own bodies. The state must ultimately intervene in service to women's best interests since they are not able to make the correct decisions themselves.

Anti-abortion discourse continues to seek to shut down discussion as activists encourage their supporters to view the other side as radical and to "engage in apocalyptic confrontation" with any efforts to expand abortion access.[19] This discourse has also moved from a focus on the fetus to personhood, which entails a shift "from a moral to a legal proposition."[20] The anti-abortion movement historically has framed itself as the moral position because as the maintainer of order, its discourse implies a return to sexual innocence as contrasted with the unruly sexual promiscuity of the pro-choice position.[21] The shift from framing the anti-abortion position as a moral position to a legal position raises questions about what should happen to women should anti-abortion activists succeed in making abortion illegal. Such questions about how much jail time women should receive if abortion was made illegal bring the focus back to women.[22] While such questions may re-center women at the micro-level, I show in this chapter how the macro-level discourse around abortion tends to frame the discussion around the state's ability to restrict access and anti-abortion activists' support for families rather than on women's health or bodies.

The abortion debate continues to be highly contentious. Pro-choice and anti-abortion activists both tend to vilify their opponents as a strategy in their public discourse.[23] The news media plays an important role in public perception of the contentious nature of the debate by presenting activism around abortion as illegitimate through providing viewers with "two major subject positions in the war: activists on both sides of the issue versus the imagined community of people like you and me."[24] Presenting both sides of the abortion debate as equivalent does viewers a disservice by flattening the contours of the discourse.

In the current discourse surrounding abortion, there has also been an increase in the recognition that not all women experience abortion the same way. Abortion access, for example, intersects with class because the Hyde Amendment and other restrictions on abortion have particularly negative effects on low-income women.[25] The providers and services most directly impacted by these restrictions are more likely to be accessed by low-income women; higher-income women have greater ability to travel long distances in order to access abortion services and greater capacity to access services from private physicians who are not as likely to be affected by the restrictions. Women of color are often positioned in anti-abortion rhetoric "as a danger to the nation in their capacity to perpetuate 'anti-American' values and, as potential reproducers and carriers of innocent fetal life, as essential to nation building."[26] While women of color are often framed as a problem in constructing a national identity, they are also constructed as sympathetic to anti-abortion discourse that focuses on abortion as destructive to communities of color. Conservatives have made efforts to appeal to people of color by presenting themselves as defenders of children, which has often been a more effective discursive strategy than liberals' efforts to address the material needs of women and children.[27] Pro-choice liberals also often fail to appeal to women of color through their framing of abortion. Framing abortion access and reproductive health as a matter of choice does not reflect the lived experiences of all women. For Latinx women in particular, "<choice> is unable to convey Latin@ reproductive health intricacies and barriers to well-being, including and especially abortion rights broadly construed."[28] As part of recognizing how abortion affects women differently, pro-choice activists must also recognize how abortion is still frequently presented as something to be ashamed of rather than celebrated.

In our attempts to account for the heterogeneity of women's lives and concerns, we acknowledge that not all women experience abortion in the same way, that it can be liberatory and painful, devastating and empowering, all at the same time. Some women find it entirely liberating while others describe being traumatized by the experience. In our attempts to recognize the complexity of women's experiences, we find ourselves responding to and perpetuating the false claims of anti-abortion activists who have constructed the medically unrecognized "post-abortion stress syndrome," a condition that does not exist.[29] In order to fully recognize the diverse experiences women have, we must also recognize that our rhetoric around abortion still privileges certain experiences over others.

Pro-choice efforts have not solely failed women of color as transnational feminist groups have played an important role in making information about abortion more accessible to women in Latin American countries.[30] Intersectional activism around abortion can be facilitated by following three strategies: seeking strength from the community rather than attacking opponents, employing public narratives and dialogues on the issue, and making connections with allies from diverse groups in the community who have not always been involved with the issue.[31] Activism that recognizes the diverse experiences of women will be extremely important in order to counter the current genderblind discourse around abortion.

The discourse surrounding abortion works to restrict women's access and make them feel that abortion was never a valid choice in the first place. Women are absent from much of this discourse, which leads to it being reflective of a genderblind ideology. Increased regulation of abortion has a material effect on women's lives as biopolitics by limiting women's access to reproductive services which can have negative impacts in terms of health, finances, and social status. These laws are genderblind because they shift the debate on abortion from women's rights, health, and bodily autonomy to more abstract issues like safety and states' rights. The rhetoric in support of laws restricting women's access to abortion is in line with a genderblind ideology through its focus on treating the restrictions on abortion as being in the best interest of women. Women are removed from the discussion as their needs become an abstract justification for controlling their bodies. The rhetoric in support of abortion restrictions rarely grounds its arguments in the lived experiences of actual women and instead appeals to an abstract, generalized conception of what women need in order to avoid having to wrestle with the needs of actual women.

Genderblindness in the area of reproductive health is also found in crisis pregnancy centers. Crisis pregnancy centers are often at the front line of the anti-abortion movement as they try to convince women in their most vulnerable moments to not have an abortion. Genderblindness as an ideology is furthered through these efforts by centering efforts not around the needs of women but on the potential located in the fetus. Crisis pregnancy centers have a material effect through disciplinary power of removing women's individual control of their own bodies by making them conform to the idea that abortion is an immoral choice that exists outside of the norms of society. The rhetoric of the centers preys on the implied freedom of choice that has existed since the decision in *Roe v. Wade* to convince women that deciding against an abortion is the only valid choice. Instead of trying to directly control women as in restrictive anti-abortion laws, crisis pregnancy centers take choice to be the new status quo and seek to convince women that having limited choices is actually a sign of having true freedom of choice.

In this chapter, I proceed by first conducting a critique of domination of the discourse surrounding the regulation of abortion through the oral arguments in the Supreme Court case *Whole Woman's Health v. Hellerstedt*. Then, I conduct a critique of freedom of the rhetoric of crisis pregnancy centers for how the organizations limit the reproductive health options available to women. Finally, I end with suggestions for how to re-center women in the debate over reproductive health. This re-centering is necessary because women are largely absent from the discourse around abortion regulations that seeks to reduce the life chances of women.

CRITIQUE OF DOMINATION: TRAP LAWS

Targeted Regulation of Abortion Providers (TRAP) laws are a legislative effort to make abortion more difficult to access by placing unnecessary regulations on abortion providers, from requiring that doctors have admitting privileges at a local hospital to requiring clinics to make changes to the physical space of the clinic, such as the size of the hallway or procedure room. These new requirements are often difficult or expensive to meet, leading to the closure of abortion clinics.[32] Even if a provider was able to meet the requirements, the state could just change them and force the provider to shut down. "TRAP laws purport to regulate for women's health, not potential life, but this reason is clearly pretextual. The laws single out abortion for different and more stringent treatment than comparable or even more dangerous procedures."[33] These laws "make access more difficult and impose greater burdens on many women who seek an elective abortion."[34] While these laws do make abortion more difficult for women to access, they fail in their stated goal of decreasing the demand for abortion.[35] Abortion providers are forced to try to make often costly changes in response to the laws while providing services to an equal number of women. After TRAP laws have been enacted, abortion providers have worked to minimize the impact on their patients so that the financial burden is not transferred to them.[36] These efforts have led to providers taking on greater cost and time burdens.[37]

If TRAP laws have not achieved their goal of decreasing abortion demand and have only led to greater burdens being placed on abortion providers, why do states continue to pursue them? One reason states continue to pursue strict abortion regulations is because the "opposition is concentrated in a few demographic groups which hold their beliefs intensely."[38] Also, partisan political attention to abortion increases as abortion becomes more salient to the public.[39] Finally, while conceding that the ultimate choice on terminating a pregnancy lies with the individual woman, the Supreme Court has given the states a lot of leeway "to try to persuade pregnant women how to understand the act of abortion."[40] As TRAP laws have proven to be unpopular with the public, personhood amendments have been tried instead.[41]

Even though TRAP laws haven proven to be unpopular, states continue to pursue them. The case under analysis in this chapter involves Texas House Bill 2 (HB 2) that was enacted in 2013.[42] Two major provisions of the law required abortion providers to obtain admitting privileges with a local hospital and for the clinics to meet the facilities requirements for an ambulatory surgical center (ASC). After the law was enacted, "the number of facilities providing abortions dropped in half, from about 40 to about 20."[43] A group of abortion providers brought suit against the state contesting the admitting privileges and ASC provisions. While the Supreme Court ruled in favor of the plaintiffs 5-3, the case is still of interest for what it reveals about the rhetoric used by proponents of TRAP laws. The main statements analyzed in this section are those made during oral arguments by Scott Keller, the solicitor general of Texas.

Proponents of TRAP laws make specific arguments in defense of the laws that are centered not on improving women's health but on the state's ability to take action in passing TRAP laws. In the case of TRAP laws, the state is argued to be able to do anything in the name of increasing safety. When it is pointed out that other medical procedures are statistically more dangerous than abortion, proponents state that the state is merely responding to public opinion and will pursue regulating other procedures when there is enough public outcry to warrant such regulation. Safety now becomes dependent on the public, putting the state at a remove from actively promoting safety. The attempt to defend the original position has only undermined it. If the state was truly concerned with increasing safety, it should be a proactive agent searching for instances where the public is unsafe rather than waiting for the public to demand action. For the safety argument to truly hold weight, proponents would need to stand firm in their conviction that it is the state's duty to protect the safety of its citizens. The fact that they quickly retreat to the shelter of public opinion when questioned about the safety of abortion reveals the targeting of abortion to be purely ideological rather than the duty of the state.

Women are entirely absent from consideration in this argument. They are present only as the subject of the procedure. Proponents make no claims about any special duty to defend women's safety. The patriarchal overtones of protecting women are absent in the current discourse surrounding abortion based on the belief that a more neutral/objective tone will make regulating abortion more palatable and harder to argue against. This is reflective of an ideology of genderblindness that seeks to use perceptions of total freedom and equality as means of controlling women. The argument made by proponents of TRAP laws is not that they are ideologically driven to control women's lives and bodies but that they have made a strategic decision to remove that element from the current discourse. Genderblindness is presented as more palatable in contrast to more patriarchal efforts to control women in the past. Analysis of the rhetoric around TRAP laws reveals these efforts to still be ideologically driven even if the ideology has shifted to reflect the contemporary era. The only time women enter into the discussion of regulating abortion at all is in terms of access, with proponents claiming that ensuring that abortion is technically accessible is all they are required to do by law even if it is not practically accessible for a large number of women. From this position, all regulations are acceptable so long as access to abortion is not removed entirely. This move is an attempt to deflect criticism that TRAP laws are intended to restrict access to abortion. So long as access is still technically available, the state has fulfilled its duty to women.

This section proceeds with an analysis of these three aspects of the argument in support of TRAP laws. First, I analyze the arguments about the state's right to pursue any measure in the name of increasing safety. I then analyze the qualification that the state only pursues regulation in response to public opinion. The argument that any level of access to abortion fulfills the state's requirements under the law is analyzed for how women are invoked as a subject but not directly addressed. Finally, I end this section by analyzing the arguments made to overturn the regulations.

The State's Right to Pursue Any Measure to Increase Safety

In his opening statement, Scott Keller says Texas "acted to improve abortion safety."[44] He concludes by arguing that the law will not negatively impact access to abortion for the majority of Texas women, saying, "Abortion is legal and accessible in Texas. All the Texas metropolitan areas that have abortion clinics today will have open clinics if the Court affirms, and that includes the six most populous areas of Texas."[45] Keller's opening statement summarizes the general argument that the state is motivated to improve safety and that the state has fulfilled its duties under the law since abortion remains accessible.

During the Justices' questioning, Keller focuses more on the state's ability to regulate abortion in the name of safety rather than on how the law actually increases safety. In response to a question by Justice Kennedy about Texas favoring surgical abortions, which goes against the trend nationwide toward medically induced abortions, Keller says, "It would certainly be permissible to regulate both surgical and—and drug-induced abortions, and in drug-induced abortions, since there are greater complications."[46] In his response, Keller avoids addressing both whether the state actually favors surgical abortion and the necessity of doing so, focusing instead on the state's ability to regulate. The only justification he provides is his frequently referenced "complications."

One of Keller's major claims as representative of the state is that abortion as a whole and medically induced abortions specifically have a high risk of complications that require additional surgery. The regulations are warranted because of this risk. At a later point in the oral argument, Keller is questioned directly by Justices Ginsburg, Sotomayor, and Breyer about these complications, and Keller fails to adequately defend the argument. When asked about the percentage of women who die from complications from abortion, Keller estimates the rate to be "lower than 1 percent," to which Justice Sotomayor responds, "there are people who die from complications from aspirin. May be unusual, but there's a certain percentage that do that. Yet, we don't require that people take aspirins in ASC centers or in hospitals."[47] Justice Sotomayor then asks Keller about the relationship between the perceived minimal benefit of decreasing the less than 1 percent of women who die as a result of complications and the additional burden placed on a significantly greater number of women in accessing abortion, and Keller responds that this relationship is only important "[i]n examining not effect, but the purpose. The constitutional analysis would be did the Texas legislature have an invalid purpose?"[48] Keller's contention is that the regulations do not have to have the actual effect of protecting women so long as that was their purpose. The state, in essence, can do anything it wants so long as its purpose is increasing safety.

Keller returns to this line of argument when pushed by Justice Breyer on the actual effect of the regulations even if their purpose was justifiable, saying,

> Justice Breyer, about self-induced abortion, the evidence in the record on that were two points of testimony, both from McAllen where Petitioners prevailed, as-applied challenges could be brought in areas for instance, if there could be shown a substantial obstacle based on travel distance, the four clinics that closed in West Texas between El Paso and San Antonio, all those closed before the admitting-privileges requirement took effect. They were all Planned Parenthood facilities.[49]

Keller completely avoids the actual question and instead falls back on the claim that many of the clinics that closed in Texas did so before the regulations went into effect. He twists the effects on women to the effects on the clinics. Rather than argue for actual benefits to women, Keller instead retreats to the genderblind discourse of TRAP laws to claim that the effects of the regulations cannot be understood because the clinics shut down before they went into effect. Despite his frequent appeals to protecting women from complications, Keller and proponents of TRAP laws are revealed to be more interested in the power of the state to impose regulations rather than on providing material benefits to women.

The State Responds Only to Public Opinion

After making the argument that the state is able to enact any regulations it chooses in the name of protecting safety, Keller begins to backtrack on this argument when questioned by Justice Kagan about why Texas chose to pursue stricter regulations at this specific time. He responds, "Justice Kagan, this bill was passed in the wake of the Kermit Gosnell scandal that prompted Texas and many other States to reexamine their abortion regulations."[50] Kermit Gosnell was a Pennsylvania doctor who ran an abortion clinic in West Philadelphia since 1979 and who was found to have neglected patients and run his clinic in unsanitary conditions.[51] Gosnell was found guilty of three counts of murder and one of involuntary manslaughter in 2013 for his actions at the clinic.

The Gosnell case is cited by proponents of TRAP laws as the inciting incident that led to an increase in state interest in regulating abortion. The case is presented as so horrific that any state is justified in taking whatever necessary actions in order to prevent a similar case from occurring in their state. Justices Kagan and Ginsburg, however, push back against Keller's invocation of Gosnell by asking if Texas had existing regulations to prevent such a case from happening. Keller responds, "Texas did have existing regulations, but increasing the standard of care is valid."[52] Justice Sotomayor continues the line of questioning, saying,

> Well, no, no, no. A real problem, meaning, Gosnell, the governor of Pennsylvania, said was a regulatory failure. And only in that, not—this clinic had not been inspected for 15 years. He—the doctor was fabricating his reports. That could happen almost in any setting. Anyone who intends to break the law is going to break the law, whatever the regulatory rules are.[53]

Her statement to Keller raises the issue that if a case like Gosnell is used to justify new abortion regulations, it begs the question if similar cases are happening in Texas and other states who justified their regulations in preventing another Gosnell. If the state's existing regulations were strong enough to prevent Gosnell, then no new regulations would be necessary. The state cannot claim to both have strong regulations and need new ones to prevent a Gosnell-like case. Keller then backtracks again, saying, "The constitutional standard for whether a State can make abortion safer can't be that it can only prevent the Gosnell situation, and there are complications."[54] After using Gosnell to justify the new regulations, Keller argues that Gosnell cannot be the only standard for passing regulations. Safety and the specter of complications are invoked again as warrants for the new regulations. Keller then lays the argument bare, saying, "But legislatures react to topics that are of public concern . . . When the legislature sees that there's a problem, and maybe that there wouldn't rise to the same level of a Gosnell problem, but the legislature can still act to make abortion safer, which is precisely what Texas did here."[55] After repeated questioning of the use of the Gosnell case, the state's position is now that it acts only in response to public opinion. Where the state had initially positioned itself as an active agent working to protect women, it is now a passive entity that takes action only in response to public outcry. The effort to regulate abortion is revealed to be nothing more than a bald effort to curry favor with the public by giving it what it wants. It is also genderblind in that instead of centering women's health, proponents of TRAP laws are basing their policy in public opinion. It is possible to envision an abortion policy that truly centers the needs of women, but such a policy would not be subject to the whims of the public.

In his dissent to the majority opinion, Justice Alito takes Keller's argument one step further, saying,

> I do not dispute the fact that H. B. 2 caused the closure of some clinics. Indeed, it seems clear that H. B. 2 was intended to force unsafe facilities to shut down. The law was one of many enacted by States in the wake of the Kermit Gosnell scandal, in which a physician who ran an abortion clinic in Philadelphia was convicted for the first-degree murder of three infants who were born alive and for the manslaughter of a patient . . . And if there were any similarly unsafe facilities in Texas, H. B. 2 was clearly intended to put them out of business.[56]

By Alito's reasoning, any clinic that closed as a result of the new regulations was obviously unsafe since the law was intended to shut down Gosnell-like clinics. We have now moved from the potential for preventing another Gosnell to the certainty of having done so. The actions of the state are justified because they have already shut down dangerous clinics like Gosnell's. Also, the state is once again not motivated by a desire to protect women's safety but by public awareness and outcry related to a specific case. The state is rather limited to act in this reasoning despite its claim of the right to do so.

The idea that proponents of TRAP laws are only operating in response to public opinion is also on its face ludicrous since most of the politicians pursuing such legislation are openly anti-abortion. Events like the Gosnell case provide rhetorical cover for pursuing abortion regulations because any regulations can be justified as a response to current events. Rather than own up to their ideological positions, proponents of TRAP laws seek to deflect responsibility onto the public. The public's rightful horror at the Gosnell case provides justification for actions proponents were intending to do anyway. By using the public in this way, though, proponents end up undermining their other argument that they are acting on the behalf of women. You cannot be both an active agent and a passive responder. Claiming to be both reveals the arguments to be nothing more than justifications for ideologically motivated actions. The ideological motivations of TRAP laws are also seen in the lack of attention given to actually helping women safely exercise their rights.

Providing Minimum Access to Women

An important issue of access to abortion is the capacity of clinics to meet the demand. Keller is questioned by Chief Justice Roberts about what evidence he could provide to support the claim that the remaining clinics would have the capacity to meet the demand. Keller responds, "But the Houston Planned

Parenthood ASC they estimated could perform 9,000 abortions annually. 9,000. That's 175 a week is what their chart says."[57] He then estimates that with the nine other facilities "it does not stretch credulity to believe that those remaining facilities would suffice to meet the demand for abortions."[58] It is important to note that he does not make any claims about the actual demand for abortions in Texas but that the perceived capacity of the clinics must surely be enough. There is an undertone to his response that implies that the current figures are already too high. The capacity is already more than enough because it is higher than the zero that abortion opponents seek. This neglect of the actual demand in favor of the implication that the current abortion rate is already too high demonstrates how the seemingly neutral discourse of TRAP laws works to reduce women's access to abortion.

One of the major provisions of *Planned Parenthood v. Casey* is that state laws cannot create an undue burden on women's access to abortion, so Justice Ginsburg begins the questioning of Keller by asking him how many Texas women will be more than 100 miles from an abortion provider. Keller responds, "Justice Ginsburg, JA 242 provides that 25 percent of Texas women of reproductive age are not within 100 miles of an ASC. But that would not include McAllen that got as-applied relief, and it would not include El Paso, where the Santa Teresa, New Mexico facility is."[59]

Justices Ginsburg and Sotomayor zero in on the claim that women in El Paso are not included in the number of women who are further than 100 miles from an abortion provider since they have access to a clinic in New Mexico. The state's argument is that the regulations are necessary to protect women's safety, but they have now claimed that the new regulation does not create an undue burden on the women of El Paso because they are able to access abortions in a state that does not have the same regulations, implying from Texas's point of view that abortions in New Mexico are less safe. If the goal of the regulations was to protect women's safety, sending them to a state without the same regulations would fail to achieve this goal. Keller responds to this line of inquiry by focusing on access, saying, "The policy set by Texas is that the standard of care for abortion clinics should rise to the level of ASCs for clinics, and admitting privileges for doctors. Texas obviously can't tell New Mexico how to regulate, but the substantial obstacle inquiry examines whether there is the ability to make the ultimate decision or elect the procedure."[60] Keller's argument on behalf of the state of Texas is that the state is required only to ensure that enough women have access to abortion so that the regulation of abortion providers does not rise to the level of creating an undue burden. It does not actually matter, according to Keller, if all women have access to the same quality of care so long as they have access. Those looking to restrict access to abortion have shown that they do not actually care about women's health and safety through arguments such as these. Any argument will be employed if the goal of restricting access to abortion is achieved, even arguments that undermine the major claim of protecting women. If the state truly cared about protecting women, it would accept the reality of a higher percentage of women not having access to abortion in pursuit of this higher goal. Instead, the state knows that access must be available to a certain percentage of women in order to not create an undue burden and pass legal muster, so the stated goals are abandoned in order to preserve the regulation. Controlling women and their bodies is shown to be the true goal of restricting abortion access.

Moving from access to abortion to women's health, Justice Sotomayor questions Keller about the relationship between health benefits and restricting access to abortion, saying, "according to you, the slightest health improvement is enough to impose on hundreds of thousands of women even assuming I accept your argument, which I don't, necessarily, because it's being challenged but the slightest benefit is enough to burden the lives of a million women. That's your point?"[61] Keller responds by returning to what the state is required to do under the law, saying, "what *Casey* said is the substantial obstacle test examines access to abortion. Now, if a law had no health benefits, presumably it would be irrational. But even their expert—and this is at JA 256 and 258—acknowledged that some doctors do believe that there are benefits for the ASC and admitting-privileges requirement."[62] Ginsburg then tries to question Keller about the specific benefits, particularly the requirement that women have access to an ASC when obtaining a medically induced abortion. In a back and forth in which Ginsburg attempts to get Keller to state the specific benefit to this requirement, Keller only repeats the claim that medical abortions have higher levels of complications that would require surgery. When asked by Ginsburg if the law would require women to return to the ASC or just to the nearest hospital, Keller responds, "Although when the significant majority of women are living within fifty miles of the clinic, in most situations they are going to be in the facility. And it is beneficial to have continuity of care, to check for clinical competence, to prevent miscommunication and patient abandonment to have the admitting-privileges requirement."[63] The message here is that the law is fine because the majority of women will be close enough to the facilities that they would make use of them anyway.

The greater purpose of this argument is to make abortion seem dangerous and justify the state's regulation of it. If complications are common as claimed by Keller, the state's regulations seem reasonable. However, even if you accept the state's claim about abortion's inherent dangers, Keller avoids answering the specific question posed by Justices Sotomayor and Ginsburg about why abortion medications need to be administered in an ASC and why an ASC would be the best place to treat someone should complications arise. Keller's avoidance is a result of the fact that the feigned interest by the state in women's health serves the purpose of making abortion more difficult to obtain. The state wants women to have to travel long distances of up to fifty miles to obtain even a medically induced abortion because the distance will often serve to prevent women from obtaining an abortion. Women's health and safety are merely excuses for making abortions more difficult to obtain. There is no medical reason women should have to go to an ASC to obtain a medically induced abortion or be treated for any complications that might arise. Requiring women to travel there is intended to make it harder for them to get there, either because of financial or travel limitations. If something is too far away to get to easily, many people will not pursue the options available to them. Keller struggles to explain the medical reason for the regulation because the regulation is not motivated by medical reasons. The medical reasons are sought after the fact to justify the regulation rather than being the inspiration for it.

In the end, the Court ruled 5-3 to overturn the regulations as unconstitutional. Justice Breyer, in this majority opinion, frequently refers to the lack of health-related reasons for the regulations. He specifically centers women's needs toward the end of his opinion, saying,

> More fundamentally, in the face of no threat to women's health, Texas seeks to force women to travel long distances to get abortions in crammed-to-capacity superfacilities. Patients seeking these services are less likely to get the kind of individualized attention, serious conversation, and emotional support that doctors at less taxed facilities may have offered. Healthcare facilities and medical professionals are not fungible commodities. Surgical centers attempting to accommodate sudden, vastly increased demand . . . may find that quality of care declines. Another commonsense inference that the District Court made is that these effects would be harmful to, not supportive of, women's health.[64]

The state claims to be regulating in the name of protecting women's health but ends up making things worse for women. The rhetoric of the state is genderblind because it takes a position of working toward the neutral value of safety while actually harming women. Abortion policy that centered women's needs would place not causing harm to women as its central concern. In her concurring opinion, Justice Ginsburg lays out the future prospects for TRAP laws, saying, "Targeted Regulation of Abortion Providers laws like H. B. 2 that 'do little or nothing for health, but rather strew impediments to abortion' . . . cannot survive judicial inspection."[65] Future Courts may be more sympathetic to the genderblind rhetoric of the proponents of TRAP laws, but we can continue to resist them so long as we call attention to the emptiness of their claims to protect women and continue to center women in our own policies on abortion.

TRAP laws work to control women through access to abortion which limits their freedom to exercise their reproductive rights. The material effects of these laws are felt disproportionality by women who do not have the financial resources to access abortion because of the constraints imposed by these laws. The rhetoric in support of these laws helps to further the ideological goal of controlling women by framing that control in neutral terms of safety. Protecting women is the stated goal of TRAP laws, but the genderblind rhetoric focuses more on the state's ability to impose the regulations than on actually helping women. Protecting women is merely a façade for the true goal of maintaining state control of their bodies. TRAP laws are not the only avenue taken to restricting abortion access as crisis pregnancy centers working to persuade women not to seek an abortion in the first place.

CRITIQUE OF FREEDOM: CRISIS PREGNANCY CENTERS

Crisis pregnancy centers are generally religious non-profit organizations that seek to intervene with pregnant women and persuade them not to seek an abortion. One of the primary concerns with these organizations is that they are not always entirely honest in their efforts to prevent an abortion. Amy Bryant and Erika Levi found in their research on crisis pregnancy centers in North Carolina that 53 percent of those contacted by the researchers provided false or misleading information, and 86 percent of the websites visited contained similarly misleading information.[66] Nationally, 80 percent of the websites for crisis pregnancy centers contained false or misleading information.[67]

Activists who work for these organizations view themselves as "contributing a needed practical, woman-centered approach to pro-life movement strategy."[68] They feel that their "feminized, relational approaches carried out woman-to-woman represent the best strategies for preventing abortion and converting clients."[69] In contrast to this perception of their work, I argue that the rhetoric of crisis pregnancy centers reveals an absence of women except in the roles of wife and mother that are consistent with a traditional view of the family. Rather than being woman-centered, the rhetoric of these organizations privileges the needs of maintaining a traditional, heteronormative family structure above all else.

In line with the religious nature of the organizations, activists tend to define their success not in terms of how many abortions they prevented or women they helped. Instead, activists "believe their task is to act in accordance with their faith and God will determine the outcomes."[70] This helps to inure activists from setbacks in achieving their ultimate goal of seeing abortion made illegal again. According to the leaders of crisis pregnancy centers, setbacks can actually be helpful "by raising the visibility of the abortion issue and increasing pro-life citizens' urgency about changing its status quo."[71] While ending abortion access may be the ultimate goal of these organizations, I argue that their rhetoric reveals a need for continued access to abortion in order for their arguments to be persuasive. Achieving their goal might actually be the worst thing for these organizations.

Recent events have also necessitated a deeper analysis of the rhetoric of crisis pregnancy centers. On June 26, 2018, the Supreme Court ruled 5-4 in *National Institute of Family and Life Advocates v. Becerra* that requiring crisis pregnancy centers to disclose information about abortion violates their First Amendment rights.[72] The case concerned a California law that required crisis pregnancy centers to disclose that abortion services would be provided by the state. Pro-choice activists have long wondered how doctors can be compelled by the state to read anti-abortion statements to women and force them to view ultrasounds before having an abortion while the rhetoric of crisis pregnancy centers is protected as free speech.[73] Courts have ruled that the speech of doctors can be regulated as commercial, professional speech, but crisis pregnancy centers as non-commercial, non-professional entities are given free speech protections.[74] This difference in regulation demands greater attention to the rhetoric of crisis pregnancy centers.

Through their rhetoric, crisis pregnancy centers seek to advance the cause of restricting access to abortion by making abortion seem inconsistent with women's proper place in society. In contrast to the rhetoric in support of TRAP laws that directly advocates for changes in the laws regulating abortion, the rhetoric of crisis pregnancy centers accepts women's freedom to make choices regarding their pregnancies as the current status quo and seeks to convince women that having a baby within the confines of traditional marriage is the only acceptable choice. Crisis pregnancy center leaders, workers, and supporters are still outspoken in their opposition to abortion and their hopes to make abortion illegal again, but instead of advocating solely for an end to abortion access, they have adapted to the freedom of choice that women supposedly have gained through reproductive rights and use that freedom as a means of limiting women's choices. Having a baby and opposing abortion are presented as nothing more than choices that must be respected in the supposedly pro-choice status quo. Accepting this as the foundation for their arguments, crisis pregnancy centers then seek to limit women's choices. A primary means of accomplishing this goal for crisis pregnancy centers is espousing support for traditional, heteronormative family structures as guided by a Christian belief system. Women who come to these organizations seeking help and support are not only told that considering an abortion is immoral and wrong but that they are immoral and wrong if they become pregnant outside of the confines of heterosexual marriage. The organizations see it as their greater purpose to guide women down the proper path in life. This guidance is again framed as a choice made by the individual woman. Opposition to crisis pregnancy centers can then be rendered as actually anti-choice for interfering in the decisions made by individual women.

The rhetoric of crisis pregnancy centers reveals how the decision is not made as freely as it is presented by the centers themselves.

As a result of this construction of the traditional family as the only valid option for women, women are absent from the rhetoric of crisis pregnancy centers except in their roles as wives and mothers. Abortion is not a decision made by a woman in control of her own body but a failure to follow God's true plan for her life. Removing women from an active role in making decisions about their own reproductive health leads to a genderblind rhetoric which reduces pregnancy decisions to nothing more than the perpetuation of the traditional family. Crisis pregnancy centers play an important role in disciplining women to see this as their only option.

In this section, I analyze the rhetoric found on the websites of the following national crisis pregnancy center organizations: Bethany Christian Services, Birthright, Care Net, Heartbeat International, 1st Way Life Center, Option Line, and The Nurturing Network. To create this list, I analyzed all active national crisis pregnancy center networks as of June 2018 as identified by Christian Medical & Dental Associations.[75] The organizations make four arguments for their services: a focus on families and support, positioning themselves as acting on God's behalf, the use of testimony and artistic expression, and direct statements on abortion. These arguments work together to convince women of their limited options when it comes to an unwanted pregnancy. The first of these arguments is that crisis pregnancy centers are chiefly devoted to supporting families.

Focus on Families and Support

A primary tactic employed by crisis pregnancy centers is to frame their efforts as providing support for families. Doing so presents having a child as a choice that must be supported. Bethany Christian Services makes supporting this choice incontrovertible, saying, "When women choose life, it is essential that we support that choice."[76] As will be shown in later sections, this is the only choice that these organizations actually respect.

Providing support is often framed by crisis pregnancy centers as offering a helping hand when someone is in the midst of trouble. The feelings associated with struggling are exacerbated by the emotional appeals employed by the organizations. 1st Way Life Center makes a direct appeal to women who are seeking support. "If you are feeling alone, frightened or just plain angry, call us. Let us help you through this. You need to know also that there is a God who loves you more than you can imagine and He is always waiting to care for you and shower this love upon you. No matter what your circumstances or lifestyle may be, He will be waiting for you."[77] Option Line also uses fear tactics in appealing to women to use its services.

> Scared. Pressured. Trapped. If a baby is not in your plans right now, it's possible you're feeling at least one of these emotions—and abortion might seem like the best way out. Your feelings are valid; this is a big decision. There are at least three options available to you. Each option will have immediate and long-term impacts on your life.[78]

Once a woman feels isolated through the use of this rhetoric, she will be more receptive to the message from the organization. Crisis pregnancy centers create their own need for support that they then seek to provide.

Not all crisis pregnancy centers use fear and other emotional appeals to prey on women in times of trouble. Birthright presents itself as taking a "non-moralistic, non-judgmental approach toward helping women through their pregnancy dilemmas."[79] Birthright describes its mission in this way: "The essence of Birthright is love. Birthright is unique and committed to offering free, non-judgmental help to women facing unplanned pregnancies. Birthright offers love, hope and support to each woman, to help her make a realistic plan for her future and the future of her unborn child."[80] Bethany Christian Services presents itself as "a global nonprofit organization that brings families together and keeps families together. Strengthening families for the well-being of children is our top priority."[81] While these organizations take a neutral stance in their public organizational messaging, their position on abortion is communicated in other ways as explored in a later section.

This focus on support for families also intersects with more direct messaging on abortion opposition. Care Net explicitly frames supporting families as part of an effort to end abortion access, saying, "Care Net works to end abortion, not primarily through political action but by building a culture where woman and men receive all the support they need to welcome their children and create their own success stories."[82] Support is merely a means to an end rather than being motivated by a special concern for families.

The support provided by crisis pregnancy centers is obviously conditioned on the acceptance of particular views on abortion and family structure. Their support is always framed within the context of the family, and the frequent references to men and women make the traditional, heteronormative contours of the family clear for these organizations. This focus on the family means that women as individuals are absent from their rhetoric. Women only exist as part of a heterosexual couple, and the role of the organization is to encourage the maintenance of the family. Crisis pregnancy centers are not here to support women in the actual circumstances they find themselves in but only as part of a larger project that moves these women into either maintaining or achieving the traditional family structure. They will use any tactic, even making women feel isolated and alone, in order to achieve their goals. These tactics can be rationalized since they are understood as being in the service of a higher calling and as fitting within the current framework of choice.

Position Themselves as Acting on God's Behalf

Crisis pregnancy centers do not only present themselves as working to support families. They also view themselves as acting directly on God's behalf. Many of these organizations are explicitly Christian and view their services as part of a Christian mission to provide for those in need and ensure that people will "be fruitful and multiply."[83] Heartbeat International frames its services as part of fulfilling God's plan: "Heartbeat International does promote God's Plan for our sexuality: marriage between one man and one woman, sexual intimacy, children, unconditional/unselfish love, and relationship with God must go together."[84] The services provided by crisis pregnancy centers are often framed in this way as serving a larger purpose. They do not see themselves as only preventing abortion but also as taking an active role in promoting a heteronormative viewpoint on what it means to be a family. Positioning themselves in this way allows crisis pregnancy centers to claim an interest in the child and family beyond just ensuring that the child is born that is often missing from the larger anti-abortion movement. Invoking God's plan also allows the organizations to promote traditional views on the family and sexuality while abdicating responsibility for those views; "we are not saying that all families have to be heterosexual couples who did not have sex before marriage, we are just following what God says." Doing so allows them to promote restrictive views while claiming to care about the well-being of all children and families.

Care Net frames its alternatives to abortion as fulfilling God's plan, saying,

> When doing so, we don't lose sight of God's design, which is for a child to be raised by a mom and a dad that are married. Recognizing that life decisions need life support, Care Net helps our clients build Godly families, get connected to a local church, and ultimately, follow Christ as Lord and Savior.[85]

Along with working to prevent abortion, Care Net makes sure to mix in some explicit compulsive heteronormativity into its messaging. Bethany Christian Services positions its support of families as following the will of God, saying, "God loves children and so do we. Every child deserves a loving family—that's where children thrive best—but so many children don't have this blessing."[86] They go on to claim an even more direct role in fulfilling God's will, saying, "We strive every day to be the hands and feet of Jesus—working toward a world where every child, everywhere, has a loving family."[87] Evangelical Christian theology views the Church as the body of Christ which is able to take action on Jesus's behalf on Earth. It is notable that Bethany claims to be the most active parts (hands and feet) of the body, thus positioning itself as essential to fulfilling Jesus's plans. They are not just passive participants but are actively directing Christ's actions. Testimony of clients is offered by the organizations as specific examples of their direct action at work.

Use of Testimony and Artistic Expression

Crisis pregnancy centers frequently use testimony from clients and artistic expressions like poetry to communicate an indirect message opposing abortion. Presenting the message in this way allows the organizations to downplay criticism of their positions on abortion by claiming that they are only communicating the experiences of their clients. In this way, the message to women that they should not pursue an abortion is made clear, but it is not coming directly from the organization itself.

I want to be clear here that while these are called testimonies, they are not the same as reviews of the services provided by the organizations. Instead, they are testimonies in the Christian sense, meaning stories of personal conviction and revelation. In this case, they are stories of the personal conviction to not pursue an abortion and that abortion itself is wrong. Testimony is frequently used in the Evangelical Christian tradition to persuade people to seek personal salvation through Jesus. I do not take issue with personal religious experience, but I do find the use of testimony as public persuasion by crisis pregnancy centers troubling.

1st Way Life Center shares the testimony of a woman who sought their services after having an abortion. She specifically describes feeling pressured to have an abortion by the baby's father and his family.

> At the age of 17 when I found out that I was pregnant, I knew in my heart that the right thing to do, would be to carry the baby to full term. There was so much pressure on me from the baby's father to have an abortion. And from his family. I kept telling them that I didn't want to have an abortion. But my cries for support were pointless. My voice was hoarse and no one heard me.
> So one day, just like that, I caved into the pressure. I told my boyfriend that I had decided that I would do it, I would do what he was asking me to do. I heard a sigh of relief on the other end of the phone. [88]

Having an abortion is presented as a sign of weakness in giving in to the pressure when she knew what the "right thing to do" was. This feeling is amplified in the description of her reaction to having an abortion.

> Laying in my bed, I started to feel the drugs that had put me under begin to wear off more and more which meant I was coming back to reality. I wanted to

die. I was praying that the feeling of death would go away. Actually, I was praying to find the strength to stay here, among the living. I felt that I wanted to be with my baby. My baby that I took a huge part in murdering. But I didn't realize. I didn't realize how final my decision was. I wanted it back. I wanted it back in my womb. I didn't want to be a murderer. Not only a murderer. I murdered my own child. I wouldn't wish the feelings that I felt so intensely on my worst enemy.[89]

References to death, murder, and "my worst enemy" are obviously intended to scare women away from having an abortion. And while this experience may be legitimate as a personal experience with abortion, it is being mobilized here as part of a campaign to restrict abortion access entirely. Rather than serving as a personal conviction to not have an abortion in the future, this woman's story is now part of a larger effort to restrict access for all women. These stories are used in this way because of their effectiveness. It is important to understand why they are effective and the motivations behind their use in order to effectively resist restrictions being placed on abortion access.

Birthright positions itself in its public messaging as not taking any political or moral stance on abortion and promises that it "treats each woman as an individual who deserves love and respect, as well as personal attention to her unique situation." However, its newsletters communicate a different message. In their November 2016 newsletter, they present the testimony of an unnamed mother who had previously used their services.

When she first found out she was pregnant, she told her mother who took her for an abortion. Lying on the table, she glanced at the ultrasound screen and saw her baby for the first time. She saw that it was much more than the blob of cells they had told her it was. She jumped up off the table, out the door and to the nearest pay phone to call Birthright. This is when things started to change.[90]

This mother's story follows a common pattern for anti-abortion testimony: the personal struggle with what to do, outside pressure to have an abortion, personal conviction that abortion is wrong (including a dramatic leap from the table at the abortion clinic!), and finding support from a crisis pregnancy center. The message presented in the newsletter through this testimony and other essays does not fit with the neutral, "we're here to support all women in a non-judgmental way" tone that is found on the rest of the website.

A poem in the April 2017 newsletter makes the organization's stance on abortion abundantly clear.

> I will not raise my precious child
> to kill your precious child ...
> or to learn how to kill the one you cherish

- A Mother's Pledge to and Covenant with Every Other Mother[91]

Birthright's non-judgmental organizational messaging may be particularly effective for women who are struggling with the decision to have an abortion but who are also suspicious of the overt Christianity of other crisis pregnancy centers. These newsletters must be sought out by the user as they are not easily accessible on the website. It is entirely possible that a woman could have a complete experience with Birthright through the birth of her baby without ever knowing the organization's actual stance on abortion. In this way, Birthright is able to condition women to believe that having a baby is their only option who might be reluctant to listen to an organization that is openly opposed to abortion.

Bethany Christian Services presents testimony from a donor named Doris whose daughter Tara struggled with the decision of whether or not to have an abortion after becoming pregnant at seventeen.

> Tara was raised in a Christian home. Faith-based values were a strong part of her childhood, but when she discovered she was pregnant a guidance counselor at school encouraged her to have an abortion. Tara was confused about what to do. Conflicting messages were all around her. Her mother wanted her to keep the baby, but her father wanted her to have the abortion. "It was hard, being so young, to make the right choice. At that age, you want to take the easy way out," Tara said. "But I did ask God what to do. It was a really big thing to find pennies in the hallway at school, and one day I said to God, 'Lord, if you want me to keep the baby, you need to send some pennies my way.' Well, you have no idea how many pennies I found that day. I knew that I was supposed to keep the baby, but I still struggled to commit to it."[92]

Tara's story is similar to the testimony found on other crisis pregnancy center websites. She struggled with her decision, even having people in her life encourage her to have an abortion, before making the decision to have the baby. Such stories can be comforting to women who are concerned that their own struggles with decisions about whether or not to have a baby might be viewed as somehow wrong or sinful. While organizations like Bethany do not fully support the idea that the decision should be a struggle, the use of these testimonies recognizes the realities that many women face and send the message that struggling is okay so long as you make the right decision at the end. Women are persuaded through these testimonies that having a baby is the only acceptable outcome.

Tara's story goes even further, though, than just her struggle with the decision about having an abortion.

> The night before her abortion, Tara couldn't sleep. Still unsure what to do, she agreed to speak with a family friend who was a Christian counselor. The woman helped Tara make up her mind to keep her baby. Miraculously, when

Tara called the clinic the next morning to cancel her appointment, they claimed to have no record of it. It was a final, albeit unnecessary, sign from God.[93]

Where before Tara's story was simply the recognition that women may struggle with their decision and that is okay so long as they come to the conclusion that they should have the baby, now her testimony is being used as a sign that having a baby is the miraculous will of God. For a woman struggling with the decision to have an abortion, claiming that doing so will go against God's will makes the decision almost impossible. The use of these testimonies on crisis pregnancy center websites goes beyond personal revelation in a moment of crisis to actively manipulating women to believe that their decision to terminate a pregnancy will have consequences for their immortal souls. These organizations take what should be an extremely personal decision that every woman is free to make for themselves and add in a layer of religious guilt. Tara's experience is legitimate for herself but to use it in this way to persuade other women, not of the value of the services provided by Bethany but of a position on abortion itself, goes to the core of how crisis pregnancy centers do not present women with true choices as their rhetoric claims. These testimonies condition women to believe that the choice about what to do with their own bodies is not actually a choice at all. The direct statements by crisis pregnancy centers of their anti-abortion position makes the lack of choice even clearer.

Direct Statements on Abortion

Crisis pregnancy centers do not only attempt to convince women that having a baby is their only option through indirect means such as supporting families and personal testimony. Many organizations are very direct about their opposition to abortion. Care Net, for example, has a "Donate Now" button on their website that says, "Nearly one million children are expected to lose their lives in abortions this year . . . unless we act!"[94] Heartbeat International centers opposing abortion in its vision as an organization: "Heartbeat's Life-Saving Vision . . . is to make abortion unwanted today and unthinkable for future generations."[95] While such direct messaging on abortion will obviously appeal to those who are already anti-abortion, these organizations are still seeking to persuade other people to accept their position.

The Nurturing Network frames their opposition to abortion clearly within a perceived status quo of choice.

> Freedom of "choice" without real options is meaningless.
> Of the two basic choices . . . abortion and birth . . . only the first has been made easily and widely available to single pregnant women.

> The absence of real choice is of particular concern because it is known that the single most significant influence on both the speed and degree of recovery from any life crisis is a person's ability to regain control over one's life.
> The woman wanting to exercise her choice for the birth alternative often does not have the financial, medical or emotional resources necessary to carry out this decision.[96]

The phrase that stands out in their statement is "the birth alternative." They have chosen to frame abortion as more common than giving birth so that giving birth can be understood as an option that women, specifically single women, are not given the freedom to pursue. This stands in contrast to the rhetoric of the rest of the anti-abortion movement that frames birth as God's natural plan for your life while abortion is the evil aberration. The motivation behind this rhetorical framing is to paint abortion as the option given to women in lieu of financial, social, and emotional support. It is ironic, then, that this lack of support after having children is most common in states that have the most restrictive abortion laws.[97] If The Nurturing Network truly wants to achieve its goal of making the "birth alternative" available to more women, they should be pursuing greater legal access to abortion rather than trying to restrict that access.

While first declaring that "There is no right or wrong way to feel after your abortion," Option Line then makes it clear that you should expect negative feelings after having an abortion. "If you have had an abortion (or know someone who has), maybe you have noticed changes emotionally or physically, and you wonder what has brought on the change. Some women and men who have been involved in an abortion decision have feelings of sadness, loneliness, anger, or a lack of interest in work, school, or even sex."[98] 1st Way Life Center also raises concerns about the emotional impact on women who have an abortion.

> One way to decide what is right is to look at the results in the lives of other women. When choosing parenting, most women struggle with being a mom, but nearly all say it is worth it. With adoption, there is normally a [sic] some regret, but there is also, normally, an acceptance of having done the best you could. With abortion, the most common feeling is regret. As a matter of fact, one survey found that 93 percent of women regret their abortion. "The majority of women wish that they had not chosen abortion. Of all the choices you have, abortion is the choice regretted most by women who have gone through it."[99]

While research has shown that this idea of regret is not true,[100] it is still frequently employed as a persuasive appeal by crisis pregnancy centers because it preys on the struggles women have when they seek advice and support from such organizations. When you are struggling with a decision, one of the main things you are looking for is reassurance that you will not regret the decision you make. If crisis pregnancy centers can plant the seed of doubt in a woman's mind that she might regret having an abortion, they have increased the likelihood that she will not have one. The problem with this tactic is that misleading women does not allow them the freedom to make their own choices but manipulates them into making the choice favored by the organization. The use of such misleading information shows a lack of confidence in crisis pregnancy centers and the larger anti-abortion movement that their position can stand on its own merits.

Heartbeat uses the metaphor of David vs. Goliath to frame itself as the underdog in a battle to end abortion.

> It seems like every day there is a new attack on pregnancy help organizations. Attacks come from NARAL pro-choice America, mainstream media's "unbiased" coverage, and state and federal legislator's malicious new laws.
> Our pregnancy help organizations are engaged in a David vs. Goliath battle (1 Samuel 17) against powerful pro-abortion forces.
> What is at risk? Innocent lives.[101]

Underdog framing is popular in the anti-abortion movement because it elicits sympathy from the audience. If you present yourself as constantly under attack from more powerful forces, some people will feel compelled to support you, either by volunteering or through financial donations. That support will not go unrewarded, though, as Heartbeat and other organizations also claim inevitable victory: "Just like David defeated Goliath with just five smooth stones and God on his side, we will overcome the abortion giant with your help!"[102]

Care Net is very clear in their mission statement about their opposition to abortion: "Acknowledging that every human life begins at conception and is worthy of protection, Care Net offers compassion, hope, and help to anyone considering abortion by presenting them with realistic alternatives and Christ-centered support through our life-affirming network of pregnancy centers, churches, organizations, and individuals."[103] In seeking to persuade others to accept its position, Care Net uses the format of an FAQ section. In response to a hypothetical question about why a pro-choice person should support the organization, Care Net says,

> It is equally sensible and logical for both pro-life and pro-choice people to support the work of Care Net and pregnancy centers. The core of the pro-choice argument is that women should have the ability to exercise their free choice about what they do with their own pregnancies. So, once a choice has been made by a pregnant woman, a pro-choice person should be equally supportive of whichever choice she made for herself. That of course implies that if a woman *chooses* to keep her baby, then pro-choice people are just as obligated to support her in her decision as pro-life people are.[104]

Care Net subverts the meaning of pro-choice to make having a baby and opposing abortion just choices that people make. The intent is to appeal to a sense of respect in that pro-choice people should respect all choices, which is ironic given that Care Net clearly does not respect the choice to have an abortion.

In response to a hypothetical question about the political nature of abortion, Care Net says, "It is more accurate to say that abortion has become politicized to the advantage of those who want to maintain the status quo of relatively unfettered access to abortion in the United States. It is a tactic to silence any debate or discussion on abortion."[105] This framing of abortion as politicized is part of an effort by anti-abortion activists to shift the grounds upon which the abortion debate takes place since cultural values like personal freedom and liberty work against their position in the political arena. Care Net goes on to say that debating abortion in political terms is the equivalent of silencing them: "So, if you have been silenced by someone who has told you that abortion is a political issue or if you have silenced someone using this argument, then consider these other aspects of abortion that warrant a continued dialogue about this critical topic—a dialogue that considers the medical and moral aspects of abortion."[106] This encouraging of people to consider the medical and moral aspects of abortion ignores the fact, of course, that these aspects are also political since they are ideologically motivated efforts to prevent women from choosing abortion. Presenting their lack of success in the political arena as silencing ensures that any setbacks to advance their political agenda can be framed as no one wanting to hear their side rather than as society shifting away from their position.

Crisis pregnancy centers are engaged in the debate over abortion in the political arena even if they like to present their actions as more grounded in the everyday experience of caring for women in contrast to the more political wings of the anti-abortion movement. The absence of women from the rhetoric of crisis pregnancy centers except as mothers and as part of a heterosexual couple, however, reveals that those involved in these organizations know that the freedom to choose is actually what is best for women. Crisis pregnancy centers speak of supporting the family because the family is perceived both as a social organization that always already implies parents and children and as a more neutral institution that exists outside of an individual woman's choice. They speak of supporting families in fulfilling God's plan, but they do not want to speak to women directly. The only time they speak directly to women is to make them feel isolated and afraid so that they can then push them toward their traditional views of life.

Crisis pregnancy centers actively oppose abortion and seek to restrict women's access, but they know that they could not survive without abortion to oppose. Their entire messaging centers on providing an alternative to abortion, so if abortion was made illegal, how would they convince women of the necessity of their services? Making abortion illegal also will not push women seeking the procedure to organizations like crisis pregnancy centers but will only push them underground where these organizations will not be able to reach them. The rhetoric of crisis pregnancy centers reveals that they need abortion to be legal. This is most clearly seen in how they frame the abortion debate as a battle in which they are the underdogs who are frequently losing. While they may be triumphant immediately after abortion is made illegal, the reality that they do not know how to communicate with women except in opposition to abortion will soon set in. The messages about helping women when they are alone and isolated or fulfilling God's plan for your life ring hollow when there are no longer any other options. The rhetoric of crisis pregnancy centers is only effective when it is being used to train women away from another choice. Browbeating women into having a child after an unwanted pregnancy loses its rhetorical force when there is no other legal alternative available.

Women are absent from the rhetoric of crisis pregnancy centers except in certain roles because the organizations do not know how to actually talk to women as women. They have spent so long fighting against abortion that they do not know how to communicate except within that framework. Their only message to women is to make them feel bad for even considering an abortion, and that message is no longer available once abortion is made illegal. Achieving their long sought-after goal will ironically make the rhetoric of crisis pregnancy centers less effective.

CONCLUSION

The retirement of Justice Kennedy and the appointment of Brett Kavanaugh to the Supreme Court in October 2018 raises legitimate concerns for the future of abortion access and sets the stage for a contentious fight over the right to abortion. The rhetoric by supporters of TRAP laws and crisis pregnancy centers reveals how the anti-abortion movement will attempt to persuade the American people to support their position. Women are entirely absent from this discourse as increased regulations are used to make abortion less accessible and then crisis pregnancy centers work in defense of the traditional family to convince women that abortion was never a legitimate option in the first place. Anti-abortion rhetoric fits the ideological goals of genderblindness by making the control of women seem to be in their best interest and of their own choice. The material effects of genderblind beliefs about abortion are that women have less control over their own bodies, less freedom to be active participants in public life, and an increased belief that they are not able to legitimately determine the shape of their own lives.

Countering the arguments made in support of genderblind beliefs on abortion is essential to winning the fight over abortion rights.

I end with two suggestions. First, all women and all individuals capable of and desiring to bear children should assert their right to bodily autonomy in regards to reproductive health. (I specifically limit this right to the realm of reproductive health so that it cannot be used to exclude trans and gender nonconforming people from certain public spaces in the name of bodily autonomy.) This right should trump the right of the state to take whatever actions it wants in the name of protecting women. Instead, the state should only be responsive to women's claims that their right has been violated. If the state wants to protect women, it should listen to the actual needs and concerns of women as it concerns their reproductive health instead of manufacturing concerns as a pretense for controlling their bodies.

Second, along with this right to bodily autonomy in the realm of reproductive health should come a right to accurate information to make an informed decision. Instead of forcing doctors to read unnecessary statements after a woman has already made her decision, the focus should be on preventing misinformation and false statements being used to interfere with a woman's decision. Women are fully capable of making their own decisions about what to do with their bodies and only need protection from those who would maliciously seek to mislead them. These are just a couple of places based on an understanding of genderblind beliefs on abortion to start the conversation over how to continue to fight for women's reproductive rights.

NOTES

1. Michael D. Shear, "Supreme Court Justice Anthony Kennedy Will Retire," *The New York Times*, June 27, 2018. https://www.nytimes.com/2018/06/27/us/politics/anthony-kennedy-retire-supreme-court.html

2. Mary Ziegler, "What Does the Future of Abortion Rights Look Like?," *The Atlantic*, July 2, 2018. https://www.theatlantic.com/politics/archive/2018/07/kennedy-abortion-supreme-court/564191/

3. Mark Joseph Stern, "How Brett Kavanaugh Will Gut *Roe v. Wade*," *Slate*, July 9, 2018. https://slate.com/news-and-politics/2018/07/how-brett-kavanaugh-will-gut-roe-v-wade.html

4. Steven E. Barkan, "Gender and Abortion Attitudes: Religiosity as a Suppressor Variable," *Public Opinion Quarterly* 78, no. 4 (2014): 944.

5. Marshall Medoff, "Pro-Choice Versus Pro-Life: The Relationships between State Abortion Policy and Child Well-Being in the United States," *Health Care for Women International* 37, no. 2 (2016): 168.

6. Laura F. Harris, Sarah C. M. Roberts, M. Antonia Biggs, Corinne H. Rocca, Diana Greene Foster, "Perceived Stress and Emotional Support among Women Who Are Denied or Receive Abortions in the United States: A Prospective Cohort Study," *BMC Women's Health* 14, no. 76 (2014): 10.

7. Katrina Kimport, "(Mis)Understanding Abortion Regret," *Symbolic Interaction* 35, no. 2 (2012): 110-111.

8. Jennifer Emerling Bone, "When Publics Collide: Margaret Sanger's Argument for Birth Control and the Rhetorical Breakdown of Barriers," *Women's Studies in Communication* 33, no. 1 (2010): 20-22.

9. Nathan Stormer, "In Living Memory: Abortion as Cultural Amnesia," *Quarterly Journal of Speech* 88, no. 3 (2002): 266.
10. Bone, "When Publics Collide" 30.
11. Matthew J. Sobnosky, "Experience, Testimony, and the Women's Health Movement," *Women's Studies in Communication* 36, no. 3 (2013): 228, 232, 235.
12. Paige Settles and Jessica Ferguson, "The Acceptable Abortion: Thematic Consistencies of Prominent Narratives within the U.S. Abortion Debate," *Kentucky Journal of Communication* 34, no. 2 (2015): 34.
13. Celeste Condit Railsback, "The Contemporary American Abortion Controversy: Stages in the Argument," *Quarterly Journal of Speech* 70, no. 4 (1984): 414.
14. Ibid., 415.
15. Ibid., 416.
16. Ibid.
17. Celeste Michelle Condit, *Decoding Abortion Rhetoric: Communicating Social Change* (Urbana, Illinois: University of Illinois Press, 1990), 159.
18. Lora Arduser and Amy Koerber, "Splitting Women, Producing Biocitizens, and Vilifying Obamacare in the 2012 Presidential Campaign," *Women's Studies in Communication* 37, no. 2 (2014): 124.
19. Cat Duffy, "States' Rights vs. Women's Rights: The Use of the Populist Argumentative Frame in Anti-Abortion Rhetoric," *International Journal of Communication* 9 (2015): 3496.
20. Catherine L. Langford, "On Making <Person >s: Ideographs of Legal <Person >hood," *Argumentation and Advocacy* 52, no. 2 (2015): 128.
21. Randall A. Lake, "Order and Disorder in Anti-Abortion Rhetoric: A Logological View," *Quarterly Journal of Speech* 70, no. 4 (1984): 438.
22. Joseph C. Packer, "How Much Jail Time? Returning Women to the Abortion Debate," *Argumentation and Advocacy* 50, no. 2 (2013): 95.
23. Marsha L. Vanderford, "Vilification and Social Movements: A Case Study of Pro-Life and Pro-Choice Rhetoric," *Quarterly Journal of Speech* 75, no. 2 (1989): 179.
24. Ginna Husting, "Neutralizing Protest: The Construction of War, Chaos, and National Identity through US Television News on Abortion-Related Protest, 1991," *Communication and Critical/Cultural Studies* 3, no. 2 (2006): 163.
25. Brooke McGee, "Pregnancy as Punishment for Low-Income Sexual Assault Victims: An Analysis of South Dakota's Denial of Medicaid-Funded Abortion for Rape and Incest Victims and Why the Hyde Amendment Must be Repealed," *Civil Rights Law Journal* 27, no. 1 (2016): 102.
26. Jennifer M. Denbow, "Abortion as Genocide: Race, Agency, and Nation in Prenatal Nondiscrimination Bans," *Signs* 41, no. 3 (2016): 605.
27. Gillian Frank, "The Colour of the Unborn: Anti-Abortion and Anti-Bussing Politics in Michigan, United States, 1967-1973," *Gender & History* 26, no. 2 (2014): 353.
28. Kathleen M. de Onís, "Lost in Translation: Challenging (White, Monolingual Feminism's) "Choice" with *Justicia Reproductiva*," *Women's Studies in Communication* 38, no. 1 (2015): 5.
29. Carly Thomsen, "From Refusing Stigmatization toward Celebrating New Directions for Reproductive Justice Activism," *Feminist Studies* 39, no. 1 (2013): 151.
30. Julia McReynolds-Pérez, "No Doctors Required: Lay Activist Expertise and Pharmaceutical Abortion in Argentina," *Signs* 42, no. 2 (2017): 351.
31. Patricia Zavella, "Intersectional Praxis in the Movement for Reproductive Justice: The Respect ABQ Women Campaign," *Signs* 42, no. 2 (2017): 510.
32. In the case of admitting privileges, an abortion provider may not admit enough patients to the hospital to meet the requirements for admitting privileges. Also, many hospitals are run by religious organizations that may be opposed to abortion.
33. Caitlin E. Borgmann, "Borrowing from Dormant Commerce Clause Doctrine in Analyzing Abortion Clinic Regulations," *Health Matrix* 26, no. 1 (2016): 49.
34. Linda J. Beckman, "Abortion in the United States: The Continuing Controversy," *Feminism & Psychology* 27, no. 1 (2016): 105.

35. Marshall H. Medoff, "State Abortion Policy and Unintended Birth Rates in the United States," *Social Indicators Research* 129, no. 2 (2016): 597.

36. Rebecca J. Mercier, Mara Buchbinder, Amy Bryant and Laura Britton, "The Experiences and Adaptations of Abortion Providers Practicing under a New TRAP Law: A Qualitative Study," *Contraception* 91, no. 6 (2015): 512.

37. Rebecca J. Mercier, Mara Buchbinder and Amy Bryant, "TRAP Laws and the Invisible Labor of US Abortion Providers," *Critical Public Health* 26, no. 1 (2016): 82.

38. Gerald N. Rosenberg, "The Surprising Resilience of State Opposition to Abortion: The Supreme Court, Federalism, and the Role of Intense Minorities in the U.S. Political System," *Saint Louis University Public Law Review* 34, no. 2 (2015): 247.

39. Marshall H. Medoff, "State Abortion Politics and TRAP Abortion Laws," *Journal of Women, Politics & Policy* 33, no. 3 (2012): 255.

40. Edward Schiappa, "Analyzing Argumentative Discourse from a Rhetorical Perspective: Defining 'Person' and 'Human Life' in Constitutional Disputes over Abortion," *Argumentation* 14, no. 3 (2000): 330.

41. Steven R. Morrison, "Personhood Amendments after *Whole Woman's Health V. Hellerstedt*," *Case Western Reserve Law Review* 67, no. 2 (2016): 467.

42. Whole Woman's Health v. Hellerstedt, 579 U. S. ___, 1 (2016).

43. Ibid., 2.

44. Transcript of Oral Argument at 36, Whole Woman's Health v. Hellerstedt, 579 U.S. ___ (2016) (No. 15-274).

45. Ibid.

46. Ibid, 43.

47. Ibid., 55.

48. Ibid.

49. Ibid., 57.

50. Ibid., 63-64.

51. Sarah Kliff, "The Gosnell Case: Here's What You Need to Know," *The Washington Post*, April 10, 2013. https://www.washingtonpost.com/news/wonk/wp/2013/04/15/the-gosnell-case-heres-what-you-need-to-know/?utm_term=.415c451dffbe.

52. Transcript of Oral Argument, 66.

53. Ibid.

54. Ibid., 67.

55. Ibid., 68.

56. Whole Woman's Health (Alito, S., dissenting), 26.

57. Transcript of Oral Argument, 45.

58. Ibid., 46.

59. Ibid., 37.

60. Ibid., 37-38.

61. Ibid., 40.

62. Ibid., 40-41.

63. Ibid., 43.

64. Whole Woman's Health, 35-36.

65. Ibid. (Ginsburg, R., concurring), 2.

66. Amy G. Bryant and Erika E. Levi, "Abortion Misinformation from Crisis Pregnancy Centers in North Carolina," *Contraception* 86, no. 6 (2012): 753.

67. Amy G. Bryant, Subasri Narasimhan, Katelyn Bryant-Comstock and Erika E. Levi, "Crisis Pregnancy Center Websites: Information, Misinformation and Disinformation," *Contraception* 90, no. 6 (2014): 603.

68. Laura S. Hussey, "Crisis Pregnancy Centers, Poverty, and the Expanding Frontiers of American Abortion Politics," *Politics & Policy* 41, no. 6 (2013): 1004.

69. Kimberly Kelly, "In the Name of the Mother: Renegotiating Conservative Women's Authority in the Crisis Pregnancy Center Movement," *Signs* 38, no. 1 (2012): 217.

70. Kimberly Kelly, "Evangelical Underdogs: Intrinsic Success, Organizational Solidarity, and Marginalized Identities as Religious Movement Resources," *Journal of Contemporary Ethnography* 43, no. 4 (2014): 432.

71. Laura S. Hussey, "Political Action versus Personal Action: Understanding Social Movements' Pursuit of Change through Nongovernmental Channels," *American Politics Research* 42, no. 3 (2014): 426-427.
72. Adam Liptak, "Supreme Court Backs Anti-Abortion Pregnancy Centers in Free Speech Case," *The New York Times*, June 26, 2018. https://www.nytimes.com/2018/06/26/us/politics/supreme-court-crisis-pregnancy-center-abortion.html
73. For more, see Aziza Ahmed, "Informed Decision Making and Abortion: Crisis Pregnancy Centers, Informed Consent, and the First Amendment," *Journal of Law, Medicine & Ethics* 43, no. 1 (2015): 54.
74. B. Jessie Hill, "*Casey* Meets the Crisis Pregnancy Centers," *Journal of Law, Medicine & Ethics* 43, no. 1 (2015): 59.
75. Christian Medical & Dental Associations, "Crisis Pregnancy Centers," Last accessed July 26, 2018. https://www.cmda.org/resources/publication/crisis-pregnancy-centers
76. Bethany Christian Services, "Impacting Lives in Iowa," Last accessed July 26, 2018. https://www.bethany.org/campaigns/impacting-lives-in-iowa
77. 1st Way Life Center, "Message from Founder," Last accessed July 26, 2018. http://www.1stwaylifecenter.com/message-from-founder/
78. Option Line, "Options," Last accessed July 26, 2018. http://optionline.org/options
79. Birthright International, "Discover Birthright," Last accessed July 26, 2018. http://birthright.org/en/discover-birthright
80. Birthright International, "Our Philosophy," Last accessed July 26, 2018. http://birthright.org/en/our-philosophy
81. Bethany Christian Services, "About Us," Last accessed July 26, 2018. https://www.bethany.org/about-us
82. Care Net, "History," Last accessed July 26, 2018. https://www.care-net.org/history
83. Genesis 1:28 (KJV).
84. Heartbeat International, "Our Commitment," Last accessed July 26, 2018. https://www.heartbeatinternational.org/about/our-commitment
85. Care Net, "Mission & Vision," Last accessed July 26, 2018. https://www.care-net.org/mission-and-vision
86. Bethany Christian Services, "About Us."
87. Bethany Christian Services, "Our Success," Last accessed July 26, 2018. https://www.bethany.org/about-us/our-success
88. 1st Way Life Center, "Testimonials," Last accessed July 26, 2018. http://www.1stwaylifecenter.com/testimonials/
89. Ibid.
90. Birthright International, "Birthright Newsletter – November 2016," Last accessed July 26, 2018. http://birthright.org/en/blog/item/newsletter-november-2016
91. Birthright International, "Birthright Newsletter – April 2017," Last accessed July 26, 2018. http://birthright.org/en/blog/item/birthright-newsletter-march-2017
92. Bethany Christian Services, "Consider Parenting," Last accessed March 12, 2019. https://www.bethany.org/pregnancy-support/options/consider-parenting
93. Ibid.
94. Care Net, "Homepage," Last accessed July 26, 2018. https://www.care-net.org/
95. Heartbeat International, "Our Passion," Last accessed July 26, 2018. https://www.heartbeatinternational.org/about/our-passion
96. The Nurturing Network, "TNN's Founder Reflects Upon the Meaning of Practical Compassion," Last accessed July 26, 2018. http://nurturingnetwork.org/history/strategic_approach
97. Medoff, "Pro-Choice Versus Pro-Life" 168.
98. Option Line, "After Abortion Support," Last accessed July 26, 2018. https://optionline.org/after-abortion-support/
99. 1st Way Life Center, "Abortion Information," Last accessed July 26, 2018. http://www.1stwaylifecenter.com/abortion-information/
100. Harris et al., "Perceived Stress" 10; Kimport, "(Mis)Understanding" 110-111.
101. Heartbeat International, "Representation and Defense," Last accessed July 26, 2018. https://www.heartbeatinternational.org/our-work/representation-defense

102. Ibid.
103. Care Net, "Mission & Vision."
104. Care Net, "FAQ," Last accessed July 26, 2018. https://www.care-net.org/FAQ
105. Ibid.
106. Ibid.

Chapter Three

Genderblindness and Rape Culture

On April 26, 2018, comedian Bill Cosby was found guilty of three counts of indecent assault for the 2004 drugging and sexual assault of Andrea Courtland.[1] The conviction came a year after a previous trial ended in a mistrial. Cosby's celebrity brought a lot of attention to the trial, and many celebrated his conviction since convictions are so rare in cases of rape and sexual assault. Cosby was not without his defenders, though, as his wife Camille released a statement claiming that the media had played a role in publicly convicting her husband.

> Now enters an American citizen, Bill Cosby. The overall media, with their frenzied, relentless demonization of him and unquestioning acceptance of accusers' allegations without any attendant proof, have superseded the Fifth and Fourteenth Amendments, which guarantee due process and equal protection, and thereby eliminated the possibility of a fair trial and unbiased jury. Bill Cosby was labelled as guilty because the media and accusers said so...period. And the media ensured the dissemination of that propaganda by establishing barricades preventing the dissemination of the truth in violation of the protections of the First Amendment. Are the media now the people's judges and juries?[2]

Along with blaming the media for preventing her husband from having a fair trial, Camille Cosby also made connections to the injustice black men have experienced in the past when accused (usually falsely) of rape and sexual assault by specifically referencing the cases of Emmett Till and Darryl Hunt before claiming similar treatment of her husband, saying, "In the case of Bill Cosby, unproven accusations evolved into lynch mobs, who publicly and privately coerced cancellations of Bill Cosby's scheduled performances."[3] While the lynching of black men based on false accusations is an important part of American history that this country continues to fail to reckon with, Camille Cosby's statement also fits into the American tradition of defending those who have been convicted of rape and sexual assault as the true victims. The defense of rapists fits into a larger rape culture that refuses to investigate accusations of rape seriously, fails to convict or imposes light sentences on those brought to trial, blames women for the violence visited upon them, and expects women to change their behavior in order to prevent rape.

Rape is "not about sex; it's about power."[4] This is the primary way rape has been understood by Western feminists at least since Susan Brownmiller's analysis of rape as a method of maintaining control over women through violence, fear, and terror.[5] Rape is a "constitutive element of women's experience,"[6] shaping the "bodily comportment" of women in a way "that holds women responsible for their own physical, sexual victimization."[7] In order to address Christine Helliwell's call to not universalize this understanding,[8] I want to clearly state that my discussion of rape and rape culture focuses solely on how they are understood within an American context.

Rape culture makes possible the individualization of rape, in accordance with American society's increased focus on the individual, and the continued underestimation of its impact on women.[9] Rape culture "denotes a culture where we are inundated, in different ways, by the idea that male aggression and violence toward women is acceptable and often inevitable."[10] It is a society that "condones physical and emotional terrorism against women *as the norm*."[11] Rape culture encourages a view of rape as insignificant and individualized, forces women to deal with the physical and emotional fallout of rape on their own, and encourages society to blame the victim for their own rape; "its most devilish trick is to make the average, non-criminal person identify with the person accused, instead of the person reporting a crime."[12]

Peggy Miller and Nancy Biele argue that the violence of rape "comes from bias, hatred, and inequality" and that this violence can be overcome by men viewing women as equals.[13] Genderblindness problematizes this call for equality and maintains rape culture by presenting the illusion that men and women are already equals while maintaining a societal system that privileges men. One way that men are privileged by rape culture is by the entire onus of preventing rape being placed on women. Ann Burnett and colleagues introduce the term "shadowboxing" to refer to the ways women prepare for situations in which rape might be possible.[14] "The most common shadowboxing strategy for women was going to parties with trusted friends."[15] While encouraging women to do what they can to take care of themselves may have its value, these shadowboxing strategies "may further mute actual and potential date rape victims by highlighting an individual responsibility for self-protection."[16] The specter of individual choice and responsibility appears to prevent any attempts to address systemic violence against women while preserving the privilege of men. If women are solely responsible for protecting themselves from rape, then men are removed from playing any role in preventing rape. If women are also muted from reporting rape out of fear of repercussions or a feeling that it is their own fault for not doing enough to prevent rape, the underestimating of the prevalence of rape and sexual assault continues unabated.

How can we understand efforts like Camille Cosby's to defend the actions of rapists? What leads to this search for external, mitigating explanations for such violent behavior? What allows for the perpetuation of a rape culture that places the blame on women for rape? The defense of rapists I term *rape apologia* and argue that such rhetoric increases the likelihood that women will be raped by leading men to believe their actions are defensible. Rape apologia also functions as genderblindness by seeking to remove gender from public discussions of rape and turn it into an issue of men's lack of control of their own actions and relationships with authorities. Rape culture persists because it performs the useful function of persuading women that they are at fault for their own victimization. Contemporary rape culture is genderblind for seeking to prevent women from grounding their efforts to prevent rape and sexual assault in their shared experiences as women.

In this chapter, I first conduct a critique of domination of rape apologia through the cases of Brock Turner and Daniel Holtzclaw. Brock Turner and his father Dan A. Turner made statements to the court in Brock's defense that laid the blame for his actions on alcohol and the stress of being a college athlete. Daniel Holtzclaw was defended by journalist Jeff Arnold in an article titled "Who Is Daniel Holtzclaw?" In the article, Arnold raises a number of possible explanations for Holtzclaw's actions from performance-enhancing drug use to disappointment at not playing professional football. Such defenses of the actions of rapists seek to control women by making it clear that women should expect their rapist to be supported over them should they be raped. Genderblindness as an ideology supports rape apologia on the belief that men are unfairly targeted by women with accusations of rape and sexual assault, so the defense of rapists is necessary to keep things in balance. Rape apologia seeks to remove women's voices from public discussion of rape by drowning them out with defenses of rapists. These defenses are seen as men necessarily exercising their individual responsibility to defend themselves, an individual responsibility women are constructed as having not exercised in making decisions that led to them being raped. The material effects of these beliefs about rape and sexual assault are that rapists either do not face charges or receive lighter sentences if convicted, and women are less likely to come forward with accusations or to press charges if they are raped.

I then conduct a critique of freedom of rape culture through the case of Katie Roiphe's *The Morning After: Sex, Fear, and Feminism on Campus*. Roiphe's book is based on the belief that a new status quo has been created in which women are believed, supported, and celebrated after being raped or sexually assorted. This support has, according to Roiphe, led some women to falsely claim to be victims in order to receive the notoriety and sense of community that comes with public support of victims. Roiphe also accuses women of working to change the definition of rape, particularly through her claims that date rape is not real, in order to claim the status of victims. Roiphe's arguments work to maintain a rape culture in which women are not believed or supported by are instead attacked for not taking the proper actions to protect themselves from being raped. Women bare sole individual responsibility for preventing rape as men's actions are never considered. The ideological goals of genderblindness are achieved through rape culture in rendering rape an individualized act in which differences in status and power in terms of gender play no role. The material effects of this belief are that women are not able to fully participate in public life as equals out of fear of having to always protect themselves from possible rape.

Finally, I provide suggestions for how we can begin to dismantle the current genderblind system of control in the context of rape apologia and rape culture. We must particularly move away from grounding our attempts at addressing issues of rape and sexual assault at the level of individual responsibility by only women. Rape apologia reveals how power works to protect men as a group from facing any blame for the persistence of cultural attitudes of dismissiveness toward rape and sexual assault.

CRITIQUE OF DOMINATION: RAPE APOLOGIA

"Typically, the primary goal of apologia is the restoration or reconstruction of a positive reputation."[17] Apologists are "motivated to deny, to mitigate, or to purify the resultant image."[18] For apologists, denial strategies tend to work better than those designed to bolster the image of the accused.[19] Another important function of contemporary apologia is providing explanations for the actions of which the individual is accused or convicted.[20] A final function of apologia is differentiating aspects of the character of the accused from the context of their status. Differentiation separates "some fact, sentiment, object, or relationship from some larger context within which the audience presently view that attribute."[21]

Rape apologia, as a specific instance of apologia in defense of a rapist, supports genderblindness' focus on individual behavior and reveals the lengths people will go to in order to deny how American society conceives of rape in ways that benefit men. Rape apologia reflects the focus on individual behavior in genderblindness as a form of gender social control in their defense of the perpetrators' character and their search for alternative explanations for the events that occurred. There is a need to understand who the perpetrator is as an individual since in a genderblind system of control, the individual is most important. Individual stories are especially important for dominant group members as a way of trying to deflect blame for the transgressions from the group as a whole. First, the rapist is presented as not the type of person who would have raped and sexually assaulted women (or committed any other kind of crime) thus raising doubt that they committed the crimes they were convicted of at all. Second, even if they did rape and sexually assault women, there were extenuating circumstances that remove culpability from them. Michelle Holling, Dreama Moon, and Alexandra Jackson Nevis found in their analysis of apologia in response to racist statements and actions that the figures involved "reproduce the harm already done in their apologetic rhetoric,"[22] so it should come as no surprise that attempts to defend rapists would support a genderblind system of control that seeks to maintain the privileges of men.

This need to try to understand the motivations of convicted rapists is intended to remove blame from the dominant group. Individual men may commit acts of rape and sexual assault, but these crimes are obviously not related to their gender or the prevailing rape culture that tells men that they have the power to pursue sex and dominate women whenever they want to. Even though individual men may fail, there is no need to examine the culture of toxic masculinity in America in more depth since, in a genderblind society, gender has no role in public life.

In this section, I begin by relaying details of the specific cases I analyze, those of Brock Turner and Daniel Holtzclaw. I then discuss the intersectional component of rape apologia as gender intersects with race and class through the various persona evoked in the statements. I then analyze the rape apologia for Turner and Holtzclaw for how they and their defenders support a system of genderblind control of women that limits their ability to seek redress in cases of rape. The cases of Turner and Holtzclaw serve as useful examples of the genderblind defense of rapists.

Details of the Cases of Brock Turner and Daniel Holtzclaw

Brock Turner, a former student athlete at Stanford University, was arrested on January 17, 2015, for sexually assaulting a young woman. When he was found digitally penetrating the unconscious woman behind a dumpster, Turner tried to run away before being tackled by one of the foreign exchange students who noticed him. After he was sentenced to just six months in jail for the crime,[23] a court statement made by Turner was released online in which he blamed his behavior solely on alcohol consumption and pledged to devote his efforts to ending campus drinking culture. A statement by his father, Dan A. Turner, was also released in which the elder Turner argued against a lengthy prison sentence for his son by saying it would be "a steep price to pay for 20 minutes of action out of his 20 plus years of life."[24]

Daniel Holtzclaw, a former police officer from Oklahoma City, was found guilty on December 9, 2015, of eighteen out of thirty-six counts of sexual assault against thirteen women that took place from December 2013 to June 2014. "Mr. Holtzclaw targeted women he stopped while on patrol, singling out poor, black victims with criminal backgrounds whose stories would not be believed."[25] His victims spoke of a sense of powerlessness during a news conference after he was convicted.

> Sharday Hill said at the news conference on Friday that Mr. Holtzclaw had assaulted her while she was handcuffed. "I didn't know what to do," she said. "I felt I was in survival mode, so I had to do what he wanted me to do." Ms. Hill earlier told the authorities: "I thought stuff like that only just really happened on movies. I couldn't believe what was going on was really going on."[26]

Jannie Ligons, whose complaint after being sexually assaulted following a traffic stop led to the investigation of Holtzclaw, said, "I was so afraid, and I was out there so helpless." On deciding to file the complaint, she said, "he just picked the wrong lady to stop that night."[27] In January 2016, Holtzclaw was sentenced to 263 years in prison for his crimes.[28]

On February 17, 2016, sports website SB Nation published a 12,000 word story by journalist Jeff Arnold titled "Who Is Daniel Holtzclaw?" The story served as an apologia for Holtzclaw, providing interviews with family and friends to attest to how out of character the rapes were and offering possible steroid use, brain damage, or disappointment resulting from a failed attempt to play in the National Football League (NFL) as explanations for his crimes. After an outcry from readers, the story was taken down five hours after being published.[29] The defenses of Turner and Holtzclaw not only reveal the lengths people will go to in order to make rape and sexual assault women's fault, they also reveal in the audiences that are addressed and not addressed the intersectional qualities of rape apologia.

Persona, Intersectionality, and Rape Apologia

While gender is the focus of this chapter, rape apologia also intersect with race and class through the different personae employed in the rhetoric in defense of rapists. The first persona is the implied author of the statement, and the second persona is the implied audience.[30] The first persona, not surprisingly, in rape apologia is the rapist or their defender, but the second persona is not the victims of their crimes but the authorities and society at large that the rapist has inconvenienced or offended. The victims function as the third persona in rape apologia. The third persona is who is implied but not directly addressed in the rhetoric and involves "being negated" in relation to the second persona; "being negated in history, a being whose presence, though relevant to what is said, is negated through silence."[31] The victims are implied but not directly addressed in rape apologia because of the intersections of gender, race, and class in the identities of the rapists, their defenders, and their victims.

Rape apologia and rape culture more broadly are built on a foundation of white, male fragility, a concept that has its roots in Robin DiAngelo's more general white fragility.[32] Men, as rendered by rape culture, are unable to handle the consequences of their actions and must be shielded from them. Genderblindness works against the typical assumption that women are weak for allowing themselves to be violated and failing or refusing to report the crime. Instead, men are now the ones who are weak, either unable to control their need to dominate women or with too much to lose in terms of potential or material wealth to accept the consequences of their actions. Rape apologia clearly exhibit this feature of genderblindness in rape culture. Dan Turner describes his son Brock as a changed man, saying, "he barely consumes any food and eats only to exist. These verdicts have broken and shattered him and our family in so many ways. His life will never be the one that he dreamed about and worked so hard to achieve."[33] If combined with a sense of shame or regret for what he had done, the changes Turner had gone through would be evidence of the effects of accepting his responsibility, but when combined with efforts to deflect blame for his actions, the changes serve as evidence of Turner's fragility. The crime had so devastated him that any further punishment was unwarranted, an argument Judge Aaron Persky was only too happy to oblige with his short, six-month sentence for Turner. Jeff Arnold also presents Daniel Holtzclaw as fragile, unable to successfully deal with his inability to make it to the NFL and the stresses of his new job as a police officer to avoid sexually assaulting multiple women. By ignoring the role of masculinity's focus in American culture on independent individualism, no acceptance of failure, and reticence to express emotions, men will continue to be rendered as too fragile to responsibly contribute to efforts to prevent rape and sexual assault since men in general will continue to be shielded from the consequences of their actions. Protecting men's fragility reduces the life chances for women who continue to be the majority of victims of rape and sexual assault.[34] Women's victimhood is not a product of their own weakness, as reflected in an ideology of genderblindness, but a result of American culture's inability to reckon with the fragility of men.

Men's fragility also reflects genderblindness when contrasted with the prevalence of victim-blaming in American media coverage and society as a whole. For example, *New York Times* reporter James McKinley Jr., in a story on the gang rape of an eleven-year-old girl in Cleveland, Texas, "focused on how the men's lives would be changed forever, how the town was being ripped apart, how those poor boys might never be able to return to school . . . Little word space was spent on the girl, the child. It was an eleven-year-old girl's life that was ripped apart, not a town."[35] In her coverage of the conviction of two young men of rape in the Steubenville, Ohio, case, CNN reporter Poppy Harlow focused on how "[t]hese two young men who had such promising futures — star football players, very good students — literally watched as they believed their life fell apart."[36] Even cases were rape allegations are proven to be false, such as the Duke Lacrosse case or *Rolling Stone*'s article on a rape at the University of Virginia, reflect the speed with which a gender-blind system of control seeks to blame the victim, serve as examples to support the claim that false rape allegations are rampant, and silence women from coming forward with legitimate cases. Along with protecting men's fragility, silencing women is also part of American culture's acceptance of male violence.

From a young age, children learn to associate violence with being masculine in American society.[37] Syed Haider, in his analysis of the Pulse nightclub massacre, argues that the constitutive nature of violence for masculinity prevents attempts to address its harms because "a disillusionment with violence-*qua*-violence would mean a disenchantment with masculinity itself," transforming into something toxic instead.[38] Along with physical violence, Pierre Bourdieu identifies male domination as the primary form of symbolic violence in which dominated groups come to view the world and themselves from the perspective of dominant groups.[39] Rape apologia functions as symbolic violence by preventing society from seeing the role gender plays in perpetuating rape culture through the acceptance of a genderblind ideology. The violent act of rape cannot be fully understood unless we accept the role played by American society's conception of masculinity, but genderblindness prevents that full reckoning by denying any role to gender at all in rape or rape culture. Strikingly, in his court statement, Brock Turner removes gender from his assertion that he will not commit similar acts if shown leniency, instead saying that he "would never have any problem with law enforcement. Before this happened, I never had any trouble with law enforcement and I plan on maintaining that."[40] Law enforcement is the wronged party in this statement, not the victim or women in general, because as the symbols of power in American society, they are the ones negatively affected by Turner's actions. As a man, Turner sees disrupting the existing power structure as his greatest error, and he must now commit to complying in the future in order to be shown leniency. Gender is removed entirely as rape becomes violence toward the system rather than violence toward women.

Turner's violence is also tolerated within the system becomes of its connection to his white, male fragility. Devon Carbado argues that in these cases, the intersectionality of gender and race tend to be overlooked outside of certain typical understandings.[41] The benefits Turner received from his whiteness and his perceived class status as a student at a prestigious university should not be overlooked as non-white, lower-class men may not receive the same benefits of fragility. The intersectional nature of male violence can also be seen in Holtclaw's case. The thirteen women he was convicted of raping are all black and mostly lower socioeconomically. Holtzclaw himself used the differences in race and class between himself and his victims to paint them as lying for financial gain during an interview with *20/20* in May 2016, saying, "Detectives approached these women and said, 'We have a tip that you've been sexually assaulted by an Oklahoma City Police Officer' . . . That's basically giving them a lottery ticket to say, 'Yes.'"[42] He went on to say that "all they have to do is go throughout the court case, cooperate, go on the stand, and then now they're gonna be, you know, billionaires for something, you know, that I didn't do."[43] Black women are generally presented by media as more susceptible to violence because of their naiveté or hypersexuality.[44] Holtzclaw draws from that cultural perception of black women in order to undermine support for his victims.

The genderblindness that removes gender from our conceptions of masculine domination and violence should not be disconnected from other forms of oppression and marginalization. The intersections of gender, race, class, and other identities work together to limit women's life chances. The victims of Turner's and Holtzclaw's actions are silenced because the intersectional differences in their gender, race, and class from the perpetrators means that society already cares less about them, so why should rapists and their defenders be concerned with addressing them? The truly wronged parties, according to rape apologia, are the authorities who had to waste time arresting and detaining the rapists and society at large for being disappointed in them for not living up to their potential. They address their apologies to these groups because they are the ones whose forgiveness matters. The victims are not even are an afterthought given their low status on the social hierarchy. While gender is the focus in this chapter, other forms of oppression that lead to the silencing of victims are also worthy of similar attention. The focus now turns to Turner, Holtzclaw, and their defenders.

Rape Apologia for Turner and Holtzclaw

> Dressed in a black suit, aqua blue shirt and striped tie, Holtzclaw sobbed audibly, overwhelmed by the day's sudden gravity. His body, folded in two, see-sawed back and forth, almost in an attempt to find solace within himself and the confined space he occupied along with his lawyers behind a wooden table. As he rocked, his future in the balance and his past in question, Holtzclaw stared mostly at the floor, but glanced up every few seconds and nodded his head from side to side in apparent disbelief while a 36-count litany of sins that included sodomy and rape, was read aloud by Judge Timothy Henderson.[45]

With these opening lines, it is clear that the focus of Jeff Arnold's *SB Nation* story is on defending the reputation and character of a convicted rapist. The story functions as rape apologia for Holtzclaw, presenting his individual narrative as worthwhile not as a way to understand how someone could have abused his power in committing such heinous acts but to explain his actions away. Rape apologia refers to formal defenses of a rapist in order to distinguish such statements from the general defense or downplaying of rape and the blaming of rape victims that are a part of rape culture. Rape apologia is particularly troubling in the context of rape culture's encouragement of blaming the victim. As Kate Harding notes about rape culture,[46] readers of Arnold's story are being asked to identify with a convicted criminal while society frequently blames victims of similar crimes. In this section, I analyze how Arnold's story and the court statements by the Turners serve as examples of rape apologia.

One purpose of apologia is to improve the perpetrator's reputation, and in rape apologia, this often involves painting the rapist as the true victim. Arnold notes that to his lawyer, "Holtzclaw was the victim."[47] Framing Holtzclaw as the victim, whether of circumstances, thwarted desires, or a political climate out to punish police officers, provides license for restoring his reputation. Brock Turner paints himself as a victim of alcohol. After a preamble in which he talks about how much his life has changed, Turner then seems to take responsibility for his actions, saying, "I am the sole proprietor of what happened on the night that these people's lives were changed forever."[48] He quickly finds an external cause for his actions, saying, "I wish I had the ability to go back in time and never pick up a drink that night."[49] In just a few lines, Turner has betrayed his positioning of himself as the "sole proprietor" of what happened and now places all of the blame at the feet of alcohol. Dan Turner also seeks to deny Brock's full responsibility for his actions by seeking an external cause, saying, "it's clear that Brock was desperately trying to fit in at Stanford and fell into the culture of alcohol consumption and partying."[50]

As a way of restoring Holtzclaw's image, Arnold presents frequent denials of the facts presented in and the outcome of the case against him. When one of his former college football teammates, Cortland Selman, considered Holtzclaw's case, he always "reached the same conclusion: *There was just no way*. There was nothing he could point to in his time with Holtzclaw that squared with that of the man in [*sic*] trial, or the testimony from the 13 women victims during Holtzclaw's trial."[51] Rather than being presented as the inability to accept the truth about someone you know, Arnold's interviews with Selman and Holtzclaw's other friends and family are intended to deny the charges against him and support the claim that he is the innocent victim. As with the use of ethos in denying the wage gap discussed in chapter 1, the audience here is being asked to believe in the character of the accused rapist. By identifying an external cause in alcohol for Turner and offering statements from friends and family that the rapes did not fit Holtzclaw's character, the rape apologia for the two men seek to fulfill the purpose of restoring their character as upstanding members of society.

Another primary purpose of apologia is offering explanations for the perpetrator's actions, and the tactic used by defenders in rape apologia is generally to throw any explanation at the wall to see if something will stick. Providing alternative explanations for Holtzclaw's crimes is one of the primary purposes of Arnold's story. Among the many explanations offered by Arnold are the political climate surrounding police brutality, the effects of using performance-enhancing drugs, brain damage resulting from playing football, feeling out of place and under suspicion from residents in the lower socio-economic and racially diverse neighborhood he patrolled in Oklahoma City, and pent-up frustration at failing to achieve his dream of playing professional football in the NFL. It is this last explanation that Arnold really zeroes in on. Growing up in the small town of Enid, Oklahoma, football provided Holtzclaw, according to Arnold, a way "to escape the town's rural setting" which has "never been uncommon among players at Enid High."[52] Playing professional football is presented as a believably achievable dream, which Holtzclaw pursued with determination. "He wanted to make the game his life, to claw his way from college football and into the NFL."[53] When others doubted his ability to succeed, calling him "too small and too slow for the NFL," Holtzclaw responded by saying he "would make up for it with dedication and willpower. He would do whatever it would take."[54] His character is also tied to his desire to play professional football, with a former teammate saying that "Holtzclaw studiously avoided off-the-field issues not only for moral reasons, but because of his intense desire to play in the NFL."[55] Holtzclaw frequently felt unappreciated and "acknowledged that being known as a player who, for the most part, flew under or off scout's radar screens constantly pissed him off."[56] Arnold concludes that football had given Holtzclaw a sense of power and the feeling that anything could be achieved if he worked hard enough for it. Having all of that taken away came as a stinging blow.

> If anything caused Holtzclaw to become unhinged, that may, in part, be what did. For the first time in his life, he had failed and the goal he had long sought was no longer available. For the first time, his strength and will had not been enough. Without an NFL dream to aspire to, perhaps he felt that his sacrifices had been for nothing. As a football player, he had believed he was in charge of his own destiny, now he was stripped of his power.[57]

By framing Holtzclaw's actions as the result of football frustrations, Arnold seeks to remove blame for his actions, a decision based on the assumption that the sports-loving audience that makes up the majority of *SB Nation*'s readers would be able to sympathize with Holtzclaw's sports dreams being dashed. Many of his friends and family, though, resisted these alternative explanations because, as his father said of the explanation of brain damage from playing football, doing so "would be to acknowledge his son was capable of committing the crimes he was sentenced to more than 250 years in prison for."[58] While these alternative explanations are intended to absolve Holtzclaw of his crimes, they also involve some degree of culpability beyond complete innocence.

The Turners also engage in this search for alternative explanations, laying the blame solely at the feet of campus drinking and party culture. Brock's identification of raising awareness about the dangers of drinking for college students as one way he could give back to society if he was given probation or a lighter sentence places the culpability for his actions solely on drinking and out of his control.

> I want to take what I can from who I was before this situation happened and use it to the best of my abilities moving forward. I know I can show people who were like me the dangers of assuming what college life can be like without thinking about the consequences one would potentially have to make if one were to make the same decisions that I made. I want to show that people's lives can be destroyed by drinking and making poor decisions while doing so. One needs to recognize the influence that peer pressure and the attitude of having to fit in can have on someone. One decision has the potential to change your entire life.[59]

The only negative action Brock took according to his statement was giving into the belief that drinking was a fundamental part of the college experience and the peer pressure that sought to reinforce that belief, not sexually assaulting a young woman behind a dumpster. By identifying drinking and "making poor decisions while doing so" as the true culprit, Brock's intention is to absolve himself of all responsibility. Brock describes himself as "shattered" by his experiences with drinking culture at Stanford and continues his argument about wanting to contribute to society by speaking out against the dangers of drinking by stating his desire to be a "voice of reason in a time where people's attitudes and preconceived notions about partying and drinking have already been established."[60] Brock refigures his crime as a moment of awakening when he was able to see college culture for what it really is rather than continuing to be naïve like most Americans. His sexual assault of a young woman revealed a truth to him that he now feels compelled to share with others. As rape apologia, this shifting of his crime as a personal failing to the product of external forces that provide him the opportunity to better society is intended to prevent any sense of blame from sticking to Brock himself. Jeff Arnold's search for alternative explanations for Holtzclaw's crimes seeks to accomplish the same goal.

In trying to accomplish the goal of absolving the individual of blame, the alternative explanations sought in rape apologia lack an emotional response that is expected in such situations: shame. According to Sara Ahmed, "shame is about appearance, about how the subject appears before and to others."[61] The "bad feeling" of shame is focused on the self and cannot be attached to others, as is often the case with feelings of anger, hate, or fear.[62] Searching for alternative explanations, as happens in the rape apologia for Holtzclaw and Turner, denies a sense of shame because disappointment at not making it to the NFL or the peer pressures of campus drinking culture are not internal failings but products of external forces. Shame requires a witness, but the witness does not cause the feeling of shame, serving instead to amplify the feelings.[63] Shame is felt when others make us feel ashamed about our personal failures; even when we are alone, the feelings of shame we experience reflect our expectation of the negative response from others.[64] Nevertheless, shame remains within the self, but the rape apologia for Holtzclaw and Turner locate the causes of their crimes within external forces. The statements supporting them fail to accomplish the goal of absolving them of guilt by not presenting them as ashamed of their actions. Holtzclaw and Turner are presented not as looking within themselves to figure out what is wrong with them that led them to commit these crimes but, instead, as grasping at any external cause, particularly seen in Arnold's long list of possible alternative explanations. An apology should communicate a sense of shame for one's actions, but the rape apologia for Holtzclaw and Turner fail in the goal of redeeming them as individuals by not presenting them as ashamed. "Shame can work as a deterrent: in order to avoid shame, subjects must enter the 'contract' of the social bond, by seeking to approximate a social ideal."[65] Turner almost expresses a recognition of the deterrent function of shame, seen in such statements as "I go to sleep every night having been crippled by these thoughts to the point of exhaustion" and "I am completely consumed by my poor judgement and ill thought actions," but he undermines these statements as expressions of shame by then saying, "At this point in my life, I never want to have a drop of alcohol again."[66] His life may be ruined, he may not be able to sleep, and he may want to change what happened in the past but not because of his own actions. Instead, he is tormented by the effects of alcohol. What could have been a statement of his own shame at what he had done and a desire to do better becomes nothing more than yet another tale of the dangers of alcohol. The lack of a sense of shame in rape apologia is also a product of separating the crime from the character of the individual.

Along with providing alternative explanations for Holtzclaw's and Turner's actions, Arnold's story and the Turners' statements to the court also fulfill a final function of rape apologia by differentiating aspects of their character from the context of their status as convicted rapists. Holtzclaw is described in Arnold's story as "naïve and very gullible," "never been associated with trouble," "as straight-laced as they come," "taught to stay on the straight and narrow," "[n]aturally quiet and reserved," "never the loud life of the party or heavy drinker . . . neither was he a silent wallflower who disappeared from sight," "a team leader," "popular with young women," "someone who had [the] reputation of taking responsibility for his actions," and "taught to respect the police and other authority figures."[67] Many of Holtzclaw's personality traits are connected to playing football, with intensity as his "calling card."[68] Despite his fervent desire to play professional football, Holtzclaw is presented as someone who always put others first with his choice to play football at Eastern Michigan, not known as a powerhouse program and not the kind of place most aspiring professional football players would go, which is framed as a decision meant "to keep his parents from having to foot the bill for his college education. To act so unselfishly, say those who know him best, was just who Holtzclaw was."[69] These descriptions of Holtzclaw's character might be understandable in the context of trying to understand how someone who others believed in so strongly could have committed such heinous acts, but when coupled with the alternative explanations for Holtzclaw's actions, the descriptions present him as the kind of person who could never commit the crimes he was convicted of and even if he did commit them, they must be the result of some external factor. The belief in Holtzclaw persists for his supporters, with his father believing those in his hometown "still consider him to be someone who comes from a good family and who comes from a good town."[70]

Brock Turner opens his court statement by listing the things that have changed about himself since he committed the crime in an attempt to differentiate who he is now from who he was before, not as a way of admitting his culpability in his sexual assault of a young woman but as a way of showing all that he has personally lost.

> The night of January 17th changed my life and the lives of everyone involved forever. I can never go back to being the person I was before that day. I am no longer a swimmer, a student, a resident of California, or the product of the work that I put in to accomplish the goals that I set out in the first nineteen years of my life.[71]

At the start of his statement, Turner places agency for the crime within the night itself. His actions did not change things for those involved; he was just another victim of the "night of January 17." He then lists qualities about himself that he used to value and were valued by others (swimmer, student, California resident) that he has now lost as a victim of this horrible night. Through this differentiation function, Turner seeks to cast himself as a sympathetic figure, one who has already suffered greatly from the loss of a privileged status in society. Further punishment is not required, from his perspective, because society has already punished him through its changed perception of him. Brock's father, Dan Turner, reinforces this differentiation in his own court statement, describing Brock before the assault as having "an easygoing personality that endears him to almost everyone he meets," "a person that people like to be around whether they are male or female," having "a very gentle and quiet nature and a smile that is truly welcoming to those around him," "an extremely dedicated person," and "simply a very humble person who would rather hear about someone else's accomplishments rather than talk about his own."[72] Beyond just the night of January 17, Dan Turner lays the blame for Brock's actions on his struggle to adjust to life at Stanford, even though he and his wife "both felt he was totally prepared for the experience . . . In hindsight, it's clear that Brock was desperately trying to fit in at Stanford and fell into the culture of alcohol consumption and partying."[73] It is the campus culture at Stanford that Dan Turner identifies as leading to the changes in Brock. In doing so, he attempts to differentiate Brock before he went to college from the person he was after committing the crime in the hopes that Brock would be judged as the person he was before instead of as the person he was at the time. Rape and sexual assault, what Dan Turner refers to later in his statement as "20 minutes of action out of his 20 plus years of life,"[74] become anomalies that should not attach to who Brock is as a person. The Turners' argument ultimately fell on sympathetic ears as the judge in the case, Santa Clara County Superior Court Judge Aaron Persky, sentenced Brock to only six months in county jail out of concern that a harsher sentence would "have a severe impact on him."[75]

Jeff Arnold concludes his story on Holtzclaw with a description of his reaction to statements made by his victims.

> As each woman spoke, the former cop, whose demeanor in court to this point — apart from his reaction to the conviction — had been controlled and stoic, reacted differently. As the women spoke, Holtzclaw first stared, then glared at each one, visibly growing angrier by the minute until the look on his face began to portray something approaching rage, giving some observers a brief glimpse — perhaps — of the man and player so many others do not admit to having ever before seen: not the caring cop, not the dedicated teammate, not the dutiful son, but someone who was for so long in control suddenly confronting his loss of power and freedom.[76]

Even this extreme reaction is offered as open to interpretation; for supporters, "his face displayed well-earned, righteous anger" while for opponents, "it seemed the face of a man who [was] fully capable of the crimes he was convicted of committing."[77] To the end, Arnold continues to raise questions and present the possibility of Holtzclaw being innocent. In doing so, he also supports a genderblind system that maintains the privilege of men and oppression of women by offering a false promise of individual responsibility in which women are to blame for their own victimization while men's actions are explained away as not reflective of their personal character and, instead, as the result of external factors.

The purpose of the rape apologia for Holtzclaw and Turner is to separate the individuals from the crimes they committed, whether by restoring a positive image of the individual, providing alternative explanations for the events, and differentiating the person before the crime from the person after. A missing component in rape apologia that is found in many apologies is shame since feeling shame would be admitting that Holtzclaw and Turner bore personal responsibility for their actions. Along with performing certain functions of apologia generally, rape apologia reflect a genderblind ideology that underlies the actions taken in American society to respond to and address rape culture. Rape apologia supports the ideological goals of genderblindness by limiting women's avenues for redress. Women may be reluctant to come forward and press charges out of fear of not being believed and even being blamed for their own rape. The defenses of rapists found in rape apologia make it clear who society is most likely to believe. Rape culture as a whole works to make women feel that they are personally responsible for being raped. Katie Roiphe's *The Morning After* serves as an example of the rhetoric of personal responsibility that supports blaming the victim in rape culture.

CRITIQUE OF FREEDOM: RAPE CULTURE

The rhetoric expressive of genderblind beliefs about rape culture are built on convictions about women's complete and total freedom and power when it comes to relationships and their presence in public space. Women are seen as supremely confident and powerful, holding all of the cards in the interactions with men. Rather than trying to control women by making it clear they will not be believed as in rape apologia, the rhetoric of rape culture uses the slim gains women have made over the years in securing their rights and working toward equality as a means of holding them personally responsible for their own rape or sexual assault. Where men are absolved of any individual responsibility through appeals to character and the search for alternative explanations in rape apologia, women are held personally responsible for rape and sexual assault in order to demonstrate their increasing empowerment.

A turn toward women's individual agency and responsibility in dealing with rape is not only found in rape apologia. It was also a prominent feature of the analysis of rape by feminists and other women in the 1990s, particularly Katie Roiphe's *The Morning After: Sex, Fear, and Feminism on Campus*. In her analysis of date rape on college campuses, Roiphe analyzes Take Back the Night marches at Princeton and concludes that the women participating in the marches find empowerment and "authority" through silence and "self-congratulation."[78] In Roiphe's figuring, being the victim of rape or sexual assault is something college women seek out because of the sense of authority that it gives them. "The marchers seem to accept, even embrace, the mantle of victim status."[79] Roiphe is particularly judgmental of women who use victimhood as a site of bonding and struggle, since it does not "help project strength,"[80] and offers, once again, individual responsibility as the solution for the rape crisis.

> The idea is that women get too drunk to know what they are doing, while men stay sober and lucid. If we assume women are not all helpless and naïve, then shouldn't they be held responsible for their choice to drink or take drugs? If a woman's judgment is impaired, as they say, and she has sex, it isn't necessarily always the man's fault; it isn't necessarily always rape.[81]

Roiphe, in her efforts to constitute a new feminism based solely in women projecting their strength, has no qualms in throwing other women under the bus by denying the reality of rape as just bad or unwanted sex. She also engages in the postfeminist trend of blaming feminism, particularly perceived feminist hang-ups regarding sex,[82] for the problems women face regarding rape and is particularly leery of any conception of rape that "stretches beyond acts of violence or physical force."[83] Roiphe wants to believe in a simplistic conception of rape in order to make her brand of feminism easier to adopt, never mind the consequences for innumerable women of her questioning of the legitimacy of certain kinds of rape.

Roiphe is most concerned with what she describes as "viewing rape as encompassing more than the use or threat of physical violence to coerce someone into sex."[84] The reason for her concern is that including other means of coercion, such as verbal coercion or differences in status and power, positions women as passive.

> This is a portrait of the cowering woman, knocked back by the barest feather of peer pressure. Solidifying this image of women into policy implies an acceptance of the passive role. By protecting women against verbal coercions, these feminists are promoting the view of women as weak-willed, alabaster bodies, whose virtue must be protected from the cunning encroachments of the outside world. The idea that women can't withstand verbal or emotional pressure infantilizes them. The suggestion lurking beneath this definition of rape is that men are not just physically but intellectually and emotionally more powerful than women. Printing pamphlets about verbal coercion institutionalizes an unacceptable female position.[85]

Roiphe is troubled by this expansion of what rape looks like because it does not fit her brand of power feminism. Rather than seeing this expansion in definition as empowering women by recognizing their lived experience of being coerced into sex in ways that do not involve physical force, Roiphe takes the position that anything other than physical force cannot be rape because the woman is passive in those instances. In her attempt to empower women, Roiphe ends up making things more dangerous for women by calling into question any type of coercion that does not fit a very narrow definition of rape. This perception of changes in women's lives as emblematic of a troubling move away from traditional roles and values is also seen in the discussion of crisis pregnancy centers in chapter 2 in their locating of their opposition to abortion in the traditional family. Roiphe even questions the idea of consent itself, saying, "The idea that only an explicit yes means yes proposes that women, like children, have trouble communicating what they want."[86] Active consent is rendered here as infantilizing women while Roiphe herself is searching for a simpler definition of rape because the workings of power have become too complex. Creating a culture of consent actually empowers women by providing them with a greater amount of explicit control over sexual encounters while seeking to simplify the definition of rape puts women in more danger by blaming them for falling for certain tactics and excusing men for using them. Attempting to blame women for being raped because their rape did not involve physical force in the name of individual responsibility is the height of genderblindness.

Roiphe is clear that she believes it is a woman's individual responsibility to prevent rape and to understand the difference between actual rape and just bad sex. "Allowing verbal coercion to constitute rape is a sign of tolerance toward the ultrafeminine stance of passivity . . . Whether or not we feel pressured, regardless of our level of self-esteem, the responsibility for our actions is still our own."[87] Being pressured into sex against your will is not rape, according to Roiphe, just a sign of low self-esteem. You should empower yourself and stop playing the victim so that you can avoid such situations! Power feminism is all that you need! This idea that it is somehow the individual responsibility of women to prevent rape by feeling better about themselves and not being passive is a clear example of personal responsibility being used to blame the victim. Women are being conditioned to believe that they are solely at fault for rape. When they are raped in the future, they will be less likely to report it out of concern that they did not do enough on their own to prevent it. And if it did not involve physical force, it was clearly their fault. What we call rape is not even that bad according to Roiphe. "'Rape' becomes a catchall expression, a word used to define everything that is unpleasant and disturbing about relations between the sexes."[88] To Roiphe, when we talk about rape, all we really mean is that sex is sometimes uncomfortable and that men and women do not get along. Roiphe's purpose has been to muddy the waters on rape in the name of empowerment. Roiphe's purpose is based in the misguided notion that individual responsibility can only be empowering and cannot be used by dominant forces in society to lay blame on people for their own suffering. For Roiphe, simplifying the definition of rape is important because it is easier to conceive of resisting physical force as empowerment than it is to conceive of collective recognition of the myriad ways power works to oppress women as empowering. Fighting back against physical violence can be rendered as an individual act while changing the cultural understanding of rape to better reflect women's shared experiences will always be collective. Individual responsibility, though, can only work in a system in which true equality is not available for all groups. In such a system, individual responsibility is merely a tool for convincing the marginalized and oppressed to excuse their own oppression as the result of their individual actions.

Katie Roiphe is not the only scholar to focus on women's individual agency regarding rape. Sharon Marcus pushes back against the focus on legal remedies for addressing rape, which, in her view, seek to "*persuade men* not to rape" thus "assum[ing] that men simply have the power to rape and conced[ing] this primary power to them."[89] Instead, Marcus argues that women should take rape prevention into their own hands through self-defense.[90] In her efforts to identify the "*gendered grammar of violence*" that underlies the "rape script" in order to empower women to escape the societal conception of women as inevitably victims of men's violence,[91] Marcus comes close to arguing that women are solely responsible for preventing rape. While she does acknowledge that "the ethical burden to prevent rape does not lie with us but with rapists and a society which upholds them,"[92] she still believes that if women would exercise their agency in resisting "a would-be rapist's attempt to place us in a sexualized, gendered position of passivity," then rape could be easily prevented.[93] Rape again is a purely physical expression of violence and power that can be easily prevented if women would just make better individual choices.

Scholars and activists have been critical of this focus on women's individual agency in and responsibility for preventing rape. Jessica Valenti makes the case most passionately, stating clearly that "being responsible has nothing to do with being raped. Women don't get raped because they were drinking or took drugs. Women do not get raped because they weren't careful enough. Women get raped because *someone raped them*."[94] The focus on individual responsibility has also been directly harmful to women, with Courtney Fraser finding that victims of rape are negatively affected in trial by evidence that they had exercised agency.[95] Women are told that preventing rape is their responsibility then punished for taking that responsibility in their own hands. The messages about rape by society in general and specific institutions like colleges also makes it difficult for individuals to determine what constitutes rape and what can be done about it beyond individual responsibility.[96]

The focus on individual agency in responses to rape serves the ideological goal of genderblindness of treating everyone as equals as a sign of gender equality having been achieved. The purpose of pushing women to take individual responsibility for their actions in order to prevent rape (how they dress, how they comport themselves in public, how much they have had to drink) while simultaneously absolving men of their individual responsibility through rape apologia is to ensure conformity to genderblind social control. Masculinity and manhood cannot be identified as causes of rape and sexual assault in a genderblind society since men and women can be judged only on their individual behaviors. Genderblindness also attempts to remove any potential organizing around femininity or womanhood in order to prevent rape. Femininity and womanhood are positioned only as causes of rape, leading women to deny or be suspicious of femininity and to avoid alliances with others as women. Women are left feeling ultimately alone despite efforts to prevent rape and sexual assault because they know they will be held solely responsible for anything that might happen. Men, on the other hand, continue to be empowered since they know on some level that their actions are most likely to be defended in a genderblind system, especially if their masculinity is combined with other forms of privilege in terms of race, class, and sexual orientation. We must begin to change these power dynamics if we are ever going to end rape culture.

CONCLUSION

How can we begin to dismantle the rape culture that holds women solely responsible for their rape while encouraging rape apologia that defend men against punishment and criticism for their actions? We must begin by adapting our strategies in fighting rape culture to reflect the current genderblind context. In the logic of genderblindness, rape is constituted as a failure of women to exercise individual responsibility. Since women are being judged solely as individuals, men and masculinity should be examined for any potential culpability because doing so would be bringing gender into the discussion and not judging them as individuals. Men are then defended by society because too much focus on men and rape might lead to examining the connections between gender and rape. The clear message send to women through the genderblind discourse around rape and sexual assault is that they will not be believed if they come forward, and their rapist will most likely be defended. Women are forced into remaining silent, and the system underlying rape culture continues on unabated.

We must recognize the potential negative impacts of adopting a focus on individualism in addressing rape and sexual assault. Individual stories still have power, and we must continue to give all women a voice in the public sphere to share their experiences of oppression and violence. The power of individual stories, though, lies primarily in building and strengthening bonds of solidarity, not in persuading opponents to support efforts to address violence against and oppression of women. As Roxane Gay says, "Immovable people will not be moved by testimony. Her story becomes an emotional spectacle, something for people to consider, briefly, before moving on to the next sad story. There is no shortage of sad stories when it comes to women and their reproductive lives."[97] When we ask politicians and others in positions of power to think of their sisters, daughters, wives, and mothers in order to help them empathize with victims of rape and sexual assault, it only goes so far. They may feel sympathy for the victims, but this strategy alone will not move them to change their approach to policy decisions since they do not truly believe that their sisters, daughters, wives, and mothers would ever become victims. They do not believe that rape and sexual assault happen to women like the ones in their lives since the women in their lives are understood as exercising the individual responsibility necessary to prevent rape. The continued focus on the individual serves to support the genderblind status quo.

What can be done to address the negative effects of this genderblind focus on individual responsibility? "Making women's behavior and identity the site of rape prevention only mirrors the dominant culture's proclivity to see rape as women's problem, both in the sense of a problem women should solve and one that they caused."[98] We need to move beyond a genderblind assertion that individual responsibility is the only solution to rape by recognizing the complicity of this position in maintaining the status quo. "Hegemonic culture typically represents women as dominated by inner and complicated compulsions that require personalized self-help rather than political transformation. Advocating the microlevel cultivation of female self-knowledge and inwardness as deterrent to rape is bound to compound this slide into therapeutic discourse."[99] Genderblindness has convinced us that any problem can be overcome with increased attention to the self, that if we can just take more responsibility for our own actions then we can successfully resist all forms of violence and oppression. In the context of rape and sexual assault, this perspective is particularly galling for blaming victims for not exerting proper control of their selves and exercising individual agency in preventing their own victimization. By bringing attention to the ways our genderblind society perpetuates the privileging of dominant groups through the celebration of individual success as a way to cultivate a mistrust of women, I seek to answer Carine Mardorossian's call for a "feminist politics that addresses the psychological and individual effects of victimization without, however, locating the solution to victimization in individual or psychological narratives."[100] Genderblindness as a system of social control supports the location of victimhood at the individual level as a way of blaming victims for their own victimization. Individual stories, experiences, and effects of rape and sexual assault are important, but they should be understood within the larger context of gender social control. Victims are not blamed because of their failings as individuals to assert their agency and prevent rape. Victims are blamed because doing so conforms to genderblindness as a system of social control. The offering of apologia for convicted rapists also supports this system. Rape apologia to men like Daniel Holtzclaw and Brock Turner are necessary to preserve the system by offering explanations for their actions that remove gender and power as contributing factors. Holtzclaw is presented as a frustrated former football player who allowed this frustration to drive him to commit heinous acts instead of him simply being a man who used the privilege and power his positions in society as a man and a police officer afforded him to rape and sexually assault thirteen vulnerable women. Turner is presented as a homesick college student who fell victim to the peer pressures of campus drinking culture in his decision to sexually assault a young women behind a dumpster. Both are absolved of any wrongdoing in rape apologia by virtue of the (perceived) external forces motivating them, thus preserving the disconnect between gender and rape.

Reconceptualizing the individual is particularly important in addressing rape because of rape apologia's focus on absolving the individual and rape cuture's focus on individual responsibility. Aimee Carrillo Rowe calls for a conception of the individual as always in relationship to others, not as an independent and stable self.[101] This conception of the individual "would entail unmooring the subject from the individual, framing her becoming as always already structured through the various communal sites into which she is inserted and inserts herself."[102] A radical shift in our conception of the individual is necessary in order to begin to push back against genderblindness. The current system distrusts women in general by encoding that distrust into legislative and legal decisions behind the veil of gender neutrality while simultaneously encouraging women to separate themselves from their undeserving sisters by achieving individual success. As a victim of Holtzclaw's stated during the trial, "I didn't think anyone would believe me. I'm a black female."[103] We must work to dismantle this system that is harmful to women by demanding that legislators, lawyers, judges, and others in positions of power own up to the gender motivations behind their decisions and by avoiding falling into a trap of individuality that preserves the unequal status quo. I end with an excerpt from the court statement made by the victim in Brock Turner's case as a reminder that we all are part of the fight against rape, rape culture, and genderblindness.

> And finally, to girls everywhere, I am with you. On nights when you feel alone, I am with you. When people doubt you or dismiss you, I am with you. I fought everyday for you. So never stop fighting, I believe you.[104]

NOTES

1. Eric Levenson and Aaron Cooper, "Bill Cosby Guilty on All Three Counts in Indecent Assault Trial," *CNN*, April 26, 2018. https://www.cnn.com/2018/04/26/us/bill-cosby-trial/index.html

2. Bobby Allyn, "Camille Cosby Defends Bill Cosby, Says He Was the Victim of 'Lynch Mobs,'" *NPR*, May 3, 2018. https://www.npr.org/2018/05/03/608110663/camille-cosby-defends-bill-cosby-says-he-was-the-victim-of-lynch-mobs

3. Ibid.

4. Kate Harding, *Asking for It: The Alarming Rise of Rape Culture—And What We Can Do about It* (Boston: Da Capo Press, 2015) 12.

5. Brownmiller, Susan. *Against Our Will: Men, Women and Rape* (New York: Simon and Schuster, 1975), 391.

6. Ann J. Cahill, *Rethinking Rape* (Ithaca, NY: Cornell University Press, 2001) 164.

7. Ibid., 160.

8. Christine Helliwell, "'It's Only a Penis': Rape, Feminism, and Difference," *Signs* 25, no. 3 (2000): 793-794.

9. I want to acknowledge that, at times in my past, I have supported the very structures of rape culture I am discussing in this chapter, either through silence or participation in conversation. Recognizing my past complicity in rape culture has been an important part of my development of a feminist identity.

10. Roxane Gay, *Bad Feminist* (New York: Harper Perennial, 2014), 129.

11. Emilie Buchwald, Pamela R. Fletcher and Martha Roth, "Preamble," in *Transforming a Rape Culture* (Minneapolis: Milkweed Editions, 1993), vii.

12. Harding, "Asking for It" 3.

13. Peggy Miller and Nancy Biele. "Twenty Years Later: The Unfinished Revolution," in *Transforming a Rape Culture*, ed. Emilie Buchwald, Pamela R. Fletcher and Martha Roth (Minneapolis: Milkweed Editions, 1993), 53.

14. Ann Burnett, Jody L. Mattern, Liliana L. Herakova, David H. Kahl, Jr., Cloy Tobola and Susan E. Bornsen, "Communicating/Muting Date Rape: A Co-Cultural Theoretical Analysis of Communication Factors Related to Rape Culture on a College Campus," *Journal of Applied Communication Research* 37, no. 4 (2009): 475.

15. Ibid.

16. Ibid., 476.

17. Martín Carcasson and James Arnt Aune. "Klansman on the Court: Justice Hugo Black's 1937 Radio Address to the Nation," *Quarterly Journal of Speech* 89, no. 2 (2003): 156.

18. Halford Ross Ryan, "*Kategoria* and *Apologia*: On Their Rhetorical Criticism as a Speech Set," *Quarterly Journal of Speech* 68, no. 3 (1982): 257.

19. Kevin E. McClearey, "Audience Effects of Apologia," *Communication Quarterly* 31, no. 1 (1983): 18-19.

20. Sharon D. Downey, "The Evolution of the Rhetorical Genre of Apologia," *Western Journal of Communication* 57, no. 1 (1993): 57.

21. B. L. Ware and Wil A. Linkugel, "They Spoke in Defense of Themselves: On the Generic Criticism of Apologia," *Quarterly Journal of Speech* 59, no. 3 (1973): 278.

22. Michelle A. Holling, Dreama G. Moon and Alexandra Jackson Nevis, "Racist Violations and Racializing Apologia in a Post-Racism Era," *Journal of International and Intercultural Communication* 7, no. 4 (2014): 261.

23. Susan Svrluga, "A Six-Month Sentence in Stanford Sexual Assault Case Leads to a Push to Recall the Judge," *The Washington Post*, June 6, 2016. Accessed 26 Apr. 2017. https://www.washingtonpost.com/news/grade-point/wp/2016/06/06/a-six-month-sentence-in-stanford-sexual-assault-case-leads-to-a-push-to-recall-the-judge/?utm_term=.7a0112017bc5

24. Tom Cleary, "Full Letter to the Judge by Dan Turner, Brock's Father," *Heavy*, August 29, 2016. https://heavy.com/news/2016/06/brock-turner-father-dad-dan-turner-full-letter-statement-stanford-rapist/

25. Dave Phillips, "Former Oklahoma City Police Officer Found Guilty of Rapes," *The New York Times*, December 10, 2015. https://www.nytimes.com/2015/12/11/us/former-oklahoma-city-police-officer-found-guilty-of-rapes.html

26. Ibid.

27. Ben Fenwick and Alan Schwarz, "In Rape Case of Oklahoma Officer, Victims Hope Conviction will Aid Cause," *The New York Times*, December 11, 2015. https://www.nytimes.com/2015/12/12/us/daniel-holtzclaw-oklahoma-police-rape-case.html

28. Anna Merlan, "Ex-Cop Daniel Holtzclaw Sentenced to Full 263 Years in Prison for Raping, Assaulting Black Women," *Jezebel*, January 21, 2016. https://jezebel.com/ex-cop-daniel-holtzclaw-sentenced-to-full-263-years-in-1754238842

29. Barry Petchesky, "SB Nation Publishes, Deletes 'Complete Failure' of a Story about Convicted Rapist Cop Daniel Holtzclaw," *Deadspin*, February 17, 2016. https://deadspin.com/sb-nation-publishes-deletes-complete-failure-of-a-st-1759738484

30. Edwin Black. "The Second Persona", in *Readings in Rhetorical Criticism*, 2nd ed., ed. Carl R. Burgchardt (State College, PA: Strata Publishing, 2000), 192.

31. Philip Wander, "The Third Persona: An Ideological Turn in Rhetorical Theory," in *Contemporary Rhetorical Theory: A Reader*, ed. John Louis Lucaites, Celeste Michelle Condit and Sally Caudill (New York: The Guilford Press, 1999), 370.

32. Robin DiAngelo, "White Fragility," *International Journal of Critical Pedagogy* 3, no. 3 (2011): 57. See also Shefali Chandra, "'India Will Change You Forever': Hinduism, Islam, and Whiteness in the American Empire," *Signs* 40, no. 2 (2015): 508-509; Raka Shome, "Outing Whiteness," *Critical Studies in Media Communication* 17, no. 3 (2000): 368.

33. Cleary, "Full Letter."

34. Michael Planty, Lynn Langton, Christopher Krebs, Marcus Berzofsky and Hope Smiley-McDonald, "Female Victims of Sexual Violence, 1994-2010," *U.S. Department of Justice, Office of Justice Programs, Bureau of Justice Statistics*, (2013): 3.

35. Gay, "Bad Feminist" 128-129.

36. Rebecca Shapiro, "Poppy Harlow, CNN Reporter, 'Outraged' over Steubenville Rape Coverage Criticism: Report," *The Huffington Post*, March 20, 2013. https://www.huffingtonpost.com/2013/03/20/poppy-harlow-cnn-steubenville-rape-coverage-criticism_n_2914853.html

37. Deevia Bhana and Emmanuel Mayeza, "We Don't Play with Gays, They're Not Real Boys . . . They Can't Fight: Hegemonic Masculinity and (Homophobic) Violence in the Primary Years of Schooling," *International Journal of Educational Development* 51 (2016): 39.

38. Syed Haider, "The Shooting in Orlando, Terrorism or Toxic Masculinity (or Both?)," *Men and Masculinities* 19, no. 5 (2016): 559.

39. Pierre Bourdieu, *Masculine Domination*, trans. Richard Nice (Stanford: Stanford University Press, 2001), 35.

40. Sam Levin and Julia Carrie Wong, "Brock Turner's Statement Blames Sexual Assault on Stanford 'Party Culture,'" *The Guardian*, June 7, 2016. https://www.theguardian.com/us-news/2016/jun/07/brock-turner-statement-stanford-rape-case-campus-culture

41. Devon W. Carbado, "Colorblind Intersectionality," *Signs* 38, no. 4 (2013): 817.

42. Aimée Lutkin, "Daniel Holtzclaw Says His Accusers Saw Joining the Case against Him as a 'Lottery Ticket,'" *Jezebel*, May 24, 2016. https://jezebel.com/daniel-holtzclaw-says-his-accusers-saw-joining-the-case-1778003140

43. Ibid.

44. Marian Meyers, "African American Women and Violence: Gender, Race, and Class in the News," *Critical Studies in Media Communication* 21, no. 2 (2004): 111.

45. Jeff Arnold, "Who Is Daniel Holtzclaw?," *SB Nation*, February 17, 2016. http://www.sbnation.com/longform/2016/2/17/10989296/who-is-daniel-holtzclaw

46. Harding, "Asking for It" 3.

47. Arnold, "Who Is."

48. Levin and Wong, "Brock Turner's Statement."

49. Ibid.

50. Cleary, "Full Letter."

51. Arnold, "Who Is."

52. Ibid.
53. Ibid.
54. Ibid.
55. Ibid.
56. Ibid.
57. Ibid.
58. Ibid.
59. Levin and Wong, "Brock Turner's Statement."
60. Ibid.
61. Sara Ahmed, *The Cultural Politics of Emotion*, 2nd ed. (New York: Routledge, 2015), 104-105.
62. Ibid., 104.
63. Ibid., 103.
64. Ibid., 103-105.
65. Ibid., 106-107.
66. Levin and Wong, "Brock Turner's Statement."
67. Arnold, "Who Is."
68. Ibid.
69. Ibid.
70. Ibid.
71. Levin and Wong, "Brock Turner's Statement."
72. Cleary, "Full Letter."
73. Ibid.
74. Ibid.
75. Nick Martin, "Former Stanford Swimmer Gets Six Months in Jail for Sexual Assault of Unconscious Woman," *The Washington Post*, June 3, 2016. https://www.washingtonpost.com/news/early-lead/wp/2016/06/03/former-stanford-swimmer-gets-six-months-in-jail-for-sexual-assault-of-unconscious-woman/?utm_term=.436f1a7bf95f
76. Arnold, "Who Is."
77. Ibid.
78. Katie Roiphe, *The Morning After: Sex, Fear, and Feminism on Campus*, (Boston: Little, Brown and Company, 1993), 35-36.
79. Ibid., 43-44.
80. Ibid., 44.
81. Ibid., 53-54.
82. Ibid., 56-60.
83. Ibid., 66-67.
84. Ibid.
85. Ibid., 67-68.
86. Ibid., 62-63.
87. Ibid., 68.
88. Ibid., 80.
89. Sharon Marcus, "Fighting Bodies, Fighting Words: A Theory and Politics of Rape Prevention," in *Feminists Theorize the Political*, ed. Judith Butler and Joan W. Scott (New York: Routledge, 1992), 388.
90. Ibid., 389.
91. Ibid., 392.
92. Ibid., 400.
93. Ibid., 397.
94. Jessica Valenti, *The Purity Myth: How America's Obsession with Virginity Is Hurting Young Women* (Berkeley: Seal Press, 2010), 150-151.
95. Courtney Fraser, "From 'Ladies First' to 'Asking for It': Benevolent Sexism in the Maintenance of Rape Culture," *California Law Review* 103, no. 1 (2015): 158.
96. Ann Burnett et al., "Communicating/Muting Date Rape" 472.
97. Gay, "Bad Feminist" 191.

98. Carine M. Mardorossian, "Toward a New Feminist Theory of Rape," *Signs* 27, no. 3 (2002): pp. 755-756.

99. Ibid., 758.

100. Ibid., 772.

101. Aimee Carrillo Rowe, *Power Lines: On the Subject of Feminist Alliances* (Durham, NC: Duke University Press, 2008), 26-27.

102. Ibid. 27.

103. Treva Lindsey, "A Serial Rapist is in Jail, but the Healing for Victims Has Just Begun," *Cosmopolitan*, January 26, 2016. https://www.cosmopolitan.com/politics/news/a52708/daniel-holtzclaw-is-in-jail-but-the-healing-has-just-begun/

104. Katie J.M. Baker, "Here's the Powerful Letter the Stanford Victim Read to Her Attacker," *Buzzfeed News*, June 3, 2016. https://www.buzzfeednews.com/article/katiejmbaker/heres-the-powerful-letter-the-stanford-victim-read-to-her-ra

Chapter Four

Genderblindness and Tech Culture

Naomi Wu is a tech engineer, innovator, and maker from Shenzhen, China, who publishes popular YouTube videos of her various creations that often focus on wearable tech like LED-lit skirts and boots with projectors in them.[1] Wu's physical attractiveness and status as a female maker have often attracted negative online attention and harassment. A prominent example of this harassment came in November 2017 when Dale Dougherty, founder of *MAKE Magazine* and considered the father of the maker movement, published tweets accusing Wu of not being who she claims to be. He claimed in a tweet that was later deleted: "I am questioning who she really is. Naomi is a persona, not a person. She is several or many people."[2] Dougherty later apologized for his insinuation that Wu does not actually make her creations herself and is instead the public face for a team of engineers, but Wu says that her reputation in the tech community was damaged by the accusations and that she has lost business as a result.[3] Wu also had a public dispute with *VICE News* over an article they published about her in which she claims that the journalist wanted to discuss the accusations in an article Wu says had been pitched to her as focused on her work as a maker; the dispute led to Wu's Patreon account being suspended after she discussed information about the journalist writing the story.[4]

Wu's experiences of harassment reflect the continuing sexism, misogyny, and genderblindness that are present in the tech industry. Failing to recognize the sexism inherent in accusing a female tech creator of just being a pretty face for the people who do the real work or that giving undue coverage to a female creator's private life implies that relationship drama is more interesting than a woman's actual skills demonstrate the continuing bias against women that exists in tech culture. This bias also feeds a genderblind rhetoric that actively avoids discussion of gender issues in the tech industry and culture since results from the work supposedly level the playing field. Women are unable to achieve all that they could as a result of these attitudes and are unable to address them publicly because any efforts to do so will be dismissed as nothing but whining. The genderblind rhetoric found in tech culture not only denies continued disparities women face but also women's place in the history of tech.

Women have played an important role in the history of tech since the very beginning. Ada Lovelace, for example, is widely recognized as the progenitor of modern coding.[5] During World War II, the "computers" calculating artillery trajectories and decoding enemy communications were young women with a background in mathematics.[6] Wendy Chun observes that "programming became programming and software became software when the command structure shifted from commanding a 'girl' to commanding a machine."[7] Coding itself became masculine when men deemed it a skill worth having and "began to apply scientific epistemologies to describe software and programming as practices" thus transforming the programmer into "a figure of knowledge, expertise, and mastery."[8] Where coding before had been a feminine activity built around just entering numbers and performing calculations, it, and the tech field as a whole, became masculinized by refiguring it as a serious practice that demands a certain level of expertise that is made inaccessible to women. As coding became more professionalized, women were excluded from the very field they originated.

Despite the important place of women in the history of tech, the contemporary tech industry and culture treat women as if they do not belong. The current climate makes women feel "excluded and out-of-place."[9] According to Karla Mantilla, the harassment and exclusion of women from tech culture "is a kind of mass cultural response to women asserting themselves into previously male-dominated areas and that it functions to impede and penalize women for fully occupying places of authority online and from publicly promoting equality for women."[10] Some of the characteristics of the discourse in the tech industry and culture that exclude women include "that such discourse relies on hyperbolic and sexualised derision; that e-bile amplification often follows e-bile exposure and the electronic venom directed at one woman is all but indistinguishable from that directed at another."[11] Encountering this discourse everyday online and at work leaves women drained and hesitant to engage in the future.

Women do not just face interpersonal exclusion but a system designed to favor men. Shira Chess and Adrienne Shaw argue in regards to the video game industry that

> In referring to the video game industry's patriarchal undercurrent, we do not mean to imply that all men working in the game industry or who are involved in gaming culture are personally guided by sexism—but rather that systemic

sexism structures the industry and gaming culture as a whole to the extent that the very idea of integrating elements of feminism into video games is read as actual evidence of a conspiracy.[12]

It does not matter if an individual man is sexist or not if the system as a whole continues to exclude women and treat them as somehow at fault for trying to address their exclusion. This systemic exclusion is especially nefarious for treating any efforts to address the exclusion of women as evidence that women are not actually excluded or that they are somehow being favored over men. Participation by women thus decreases out of a lack of desire to continue fighting this battle. Men also do not recognize that the system harms them by presenting limiting stereotypes of what it means to be a man in tech.

Existing stereotypes of what it means to be in the tech industry center men and masculine qualities.[13] Women are more receptive to the idea of a career in tech when it was communicated to them that the existing stereotypes were no longer dominant.[14] Straight, white men, though, are more likely to self-identify as gamers than other groups.[15] Existing stereotypes continue at least in terms of self-identification even if the realities of the makeup of tech culture is changing.

One of the dominant stereotypes is of the programmer achieving mastery over the code which "is rendered masculine because of its historical nature and because of its epistemological assumptions—the productivity of individual realization through erasure of shared labor. Mastery is the erasure of the intermediary, the investment of creative and productive authority in the articulated individual of code."[16] Mastery implies complete control over the code while ignoring the processes being performed by the computer behind the scenes.[17] Mastery as a means of conceiving of coding as a practice feeds into existing masculine stereotypes of the tech industry and culture by conceiving of industry practices as achieving dominance by exerting power and control.

Men in the tech industry and culture also assert their dominance through a practice Brandee Easter terms "digital manspreading" in which men talk more in order to push out women's voices and impersonate women in order to control women's presence in online spaces.[18] In the specific example Easter provides, a code was released in response to a woman's question about what feminist coding would look like that was much longer than it needed to be to perform its function and parodied feminist discourse. Releasing this code in response to a question about feminist coding claims the space for men by taking up more space than is necessary and excludes women through the mocking of what women's talk in an online space would consist of.[19] By taking up more digital space, men push women even further out of the industry and culture.

It is not just the culture of the industry that is not welcoming to women and those who do not conform to traditional gender norms but the design of tech products themselves, such as Facebook's coding of individuals as occupying one of two gender options in the database even if no gender is selected or other options have been made available.[20] Women must contend not only with industrial and cultural exclusion but also with technological exclusion. The effect of this culture of exclusion is "to inhibit women from pursuing interests, and even careers, in what have been male-dominated arenas, many of which have now moved online."[21]

In spite of this concerted effort to exclude women, research has shown that women can succeed in the tech field and desire careers in tech. Research by Michal Armoni and Judith Gal-Elzer on computer science education in Israel has shown that young women who pursue an education and career in computer science typically do well.[22] Wilfred Lau and Allan Yuen also found no difference in the performance of men and women in performance in computer science education.[23] Men and women do not differ in their career goals or motivations for pursuing education in computer science, but they do differ in their expectations for the future, with women having lower expectations for success than men and a significantly lower sense of self-efficacy for their ability to affect the situation.[24] Differences have also been seen in the perception by men that coding is easier and their higher intention to code in the future as compared to women.[25] Even though women may have the same desire to pursue a career in the tech industry, they have internalized the message that such a career will be difficult to achieve and may be beyond their personal efforts to affect.

In order to increase the possibility for success for girls and women in the tech field, efforts have been made to increase the quality of education girls and women receive in computer science and other aspects of tech. One method that has had some success is designing courses around computational thinking that encourage students to work out problems using the principles of computer science rather than focusing specifically on programming.[26] Doing so "can shift both how learners view the field of CS and, more importantly, how they view their own position relative to computing and participation in computing culture."[27] Beyond just teaching girls competency in specific programs, Carolyn Cunningham argues that computer science education should focus on increasing "technological literacy" that would lead to a fluency on how to translate skills to a variety of contexts.[28] Pair programming has also been found to increase girls' interest in programming because it "affords the opportunity for increased socialization, improved comprehension and immediate help and support."[29] In spite of these efforts to improve tech education for girls and women, one problem that holds back these efforts is that instructors do not feel they need to take an active role in promoting gender diversity in tech; the feeling is that making the programs available to all is enough even if they continue to be dominated by boys and men.[30]

The efforts to improve tech education for girls and women is a good first step to increasing women's representation, participation, and success in the tech industry and culture, but these efforts will not be enough so long as the culture is hostile to women's presence in tech. The hostile culture that confronts women and other marginalized groups continues to push them out of tech. A feminist approach provides avenues for addressing this continued exclusion of women because it recognizes that those arguing that feminism and considerations of gender have no place in the tech industry and culture "are making the assumption that men have no gender and no connection to feminism."[31] "Feminist theory reminds us that white, able-bodied, cisgendered male bodies are intersectional bodies too, and that critiques from the margins are not just about marginalized bodies."[32] In this chapter, I use a feminist approach to analyze the rhetoric around gender diversity in the tech industry itself and harassment of women in online spaces to show how this hostile culture that excludes women continues to perpetuate itself.

I begin with a critique of domination of James Damore's Google memo that aims to control women by working to prevent their success in the tech industry. Damore makes four claims to support his argument: differences between men and women are the result of biology, men and women are suited for different roles in tech, efforts to diversify the workforce are harmful to business, and diversity programs are discriminatory toward conservative white men. His argument has an impact on women's lives as it reduces their financial opportunities and other related benefits. Damore's memo also reflects a genderblind ideology in its reduction of women's lack of success in the tech industry to biological differences as a means of preventing women from using gender to address how they are prevented from achieving success based on their gender.

I then conduct a critique of freedom of online harassment of women that seeks to make women feel unwelcome online. Online spaces have been conceived of as egalitarian and open to all. Instead of online harassment of women serving as an example of the limitations of this openness, the harassment is offered as a sign of the true openness of the internet. Harassment is rendered through a genderblind ideology as a test of the true strength of an idea; an individual's ideas must be able to withstand harsh criticism from others if they are to hold any value. The genderblindness of the idea of harassment as an individual's price of entry into online spaces is revealed through the disproportionate amount and scope of harassment directed at women and other marginalized groups online. The reduction of harassment to an individualized experience that everyone must go through in order to fully express themselves online is used to obscure the fact that most of the online harassment of women is based in gender. If harassment is just an individual experiences that everyone goes through, women will have no need to organize around their shared experience of harassment.

The ideological goal of genderblindness served by online harassment is making women feel uncomfortable, unwelcome, and unsafe in public life. Online spaces are an important part of contemporary public life, and the inability for many women to access online spaces free of harassment for their gender is a clear limitation of their ability to be full and equal participants in public life. Online harassment as a form of rhetoric is intended to remind women and other marginalized groups of their unwelcome status in online spaces. I identify four themes in the online harassment of women: explicit death threats, comments on women's appearance, framing women as only attention-seeking, and framing women as the truly repressive ones. Together, the genderblind rhetoric found in the tech industry and culture sends the message to women that they should feel uncomfortable and unwelcome.

CRITIQUE OF DOMINATION: JAMES DAMORE'S GOOGLE MEMO

On August 5, 2017, ex-Google employee James Damore released a ten-page memo titled "Google's Ideological Echo Chamber" in which he railed against the company's efforts to increase diversity, especially efforts to recruit more women.[33] While Damore's argument may not have persuaded his immediate audience as he was fired from Google soon after publishing the memo,[34] the rhetoric within it is concerning because of how it reflects dominant attitudes within the tech industry that men's success relative to women is a product of natural differences. The tech industry views itself as the ultimate meritocracy in which skill at programming determines whether or not you are successful. Nothing else is supposed to matter, so the fact that women and other marginalized groups continue to find limited success within the industry is merely a result of the fact that they are not as skilled as the dominant group. Damore's memo reveals the ideological worldview that underlies this belief. It is a worldview grounded in biological determinism in which the differences of women and men are a product of biology, and these differences lead women and men to have different dominant traits that make them better suited for certain positions. The fact that the positions occupied by men lead to greater chances for success and advancement are just a product of other biological traits, like men's higher drive for status. The existing hierarchy within the industry should be preserved, according to Damore, because any discomfort that might result from having to interact with those who hold different beliefs from you will lead those at the top of the hierarchy to be less productive which will ultimately hurt the company's bottom line. In this worldview, diversity programs are discriminatory toward men in general and conservative white men specifically because they threaten the position these men think is owed to them and increase the potential for discomfort once they are in those positions.

While Damore addresses his memo toward diversity efforts in general, he focuses exclusively on gender when making his argument. His argument works to limit women's chances for success within the tech industry and the financial security and other benefits that come from that success. It accomplishes this by ensuring that women will not be judged based on their individual merit but rather according to their gender. It is also genderblind in its attempts to remove gender from public discussion of the tech industry and its continued lack of representation and success for women. Any attempt to bring gender into the discussion will just be dismissed as ideologically biased while completely ignoring the biases of the current dominant worldview. Damore's memo is worth analyzing for the way an argument from this worldview is constructed to ensure the continuation of the current hierarchical system and position the dominant group as the true victims.

Damore opens his memo with an attempt to deflect criticism by claiming that his criticisms are not motivated by animus toward the project of diversity.

> I value diversity and inclusion, am not denying that sexism exists, and don't endorse using stereotypes. When addressing the gap in representation in the population, we need to look at population level differences in distributions. If we can't have an honest discussion about this, then we can never truly solve the problem. Psychological safety is built on mutual respect and acceptance, but unfortunately our culture of shaming and misrepresentation is disrespectful and unaccepting of anyone outside its echo chamber. Despite what the public response seems to have been, I've gotten many personal messages from fellow Googler's expressing their gratitude for bringing up these very important issues which they agree with but would never have the courage to say or defend because of our shaming culture and the possibility of being fired. This needs to change.[35]

The real problem in Damore's figuring is that those who support diversity efforts are not interested in hearing other perspectives. He refers to this side as an "echo chamber" that makes use of "shaming" to prevent those with different opinions from having their opinions heard in public. This idea of dominant members of society being silenced in expressing their opinions is key to Damore's rhetoric on diversity in tech. He views the tech world as dominated by those who are politically liberal and supportive of racial and gender diversity, and their disinterest in listening to those who critique efforts to increase diversity is the truly discriminatory action.

> At Google, we talk so much about unconscious bias as it applies to race and gender, but we rarely discuss our moral biases. Political orientation is actually

a result of deep moral preferences and thus biases. Considering that the overwhelming majority of the social sciences, media, and Google lean left, we should critically examine these prejudices.[36]

Damore views himself as speaking up for the truly marginalized in American society (conservative white men), and he must speak up before diversity efforts destroy the potential of the tech industry. In order to accomplish his rhetorical goals while maintaining his stance that he is not anti-diversity, Damore first attempts to establish that his viewpoint is back up by scientific fact.

Differences between Men and Women Are Framed as the Result of Biology

Damore grounds his argument in the indisputable facts (from his perspective) of biological differences between men and women. He takes particular issue with the idea of social constructionism, rhetorically setting it up as in opposition to biological reality.

> On average, men and women biologically differ in many ways. These differences aren't just socially constructed because:
>
> - They're universal across human cultures.
> - They often have clear biological causes and links to prenatal testosterone.
> - Biological males that were castrated at birth and raised as females often still identify and act like males.
> - The underlying traits are highly heritable.
> - They're exactly what we would predict from an evolutionary psychology perspective.[37]

Damore does not provide any evidence to support this broad claim about the fact of biological differences, though he does attempt to link to some studies for specific traits later, because the fact of biological difference is not in dispute for him. This claim is important for Damore's argument because establishing that difference is the result of biology means that the differences found in men and women's experiences and achievements in the tech industry are merely the result of these differences. Damore's argument is built on the idea that you cannot argue with biology so any attempt to dispute his claims must mean that the person doing so is just a "social constructionist." (Damore uses social constructionism as a bogeyman throughout the memo without every really demonstrating an understanding of what it means.) Establishing this is an important part of his deflection: he is not saying that women and other marginalized groups should have a reduced role in the tech industry, but biology demands it. Damore probably truly believes in a biological determinist viewpoint, but this viewpoint also serves his rhetorical goals well too.

After stating that differences between men and women are biologically determined, Damore then makes his use of this argument to deflect criticism that he is anti-diversity.

> Note, I'm not saying that all men differ from women in the following ways or that these differences are "just." I'm simply stating that the distribution of preferences and abilities of men and women differ in part due to biological causes and that these differences may explain why we don't see equal representation of women in tech and leadership. Many of these differences are small and there's significant overlap between men and women, so you can't say anything about an individual given these population level distributions.[38]

This again is an attempt to justify the existing disparities between men and women while deflecting criticism for supporting those disparities. Damore claims to not be making value judgments ("I'm not saying . . . these differences are 'just,'") and that he merely wants to discuss the facts of the issue, but as will be shown in later sections, his purpose is to primarily maintain the status quo in which men are able to achieve greater success in the tech industry. He views diversity as harmful to the tech industry because people who are not biologically suited for certain positions are supposedly advanced over those who are. Biology is being used in this case for its air of objectivity that allows Damore to present his argument against women's advancement as merely a statement of fact. A major component of his argument is that men and women are suited for different roles in the tech industry that have different levels of success.

Men and Women Are Better Suited to Different Roles in Tech

Having made the argument that the differences between men and women are biological, Damore moves to identifying the traits associated with each gender. This identification of inherent differences between men and women is similar to the argument denying the wage gap as discussed in chapter 1. First for women, Damore claims that they on average are more inclined to openness and an interest in people. "Openness directed toward feelings and aesthetics rather than ideas. Women generally also have a stronger interest in people than things, relative to men (also interpreted as empathizing and systematizing)."[39] This distinction between empathizing and systematizing is a key part of Damore's argument because empathizing means that someone is better suited to working with people while systematizing means that someone is better suited to the strictures demanded of coding. Women's lack of success in the tech industry is natural, according to Damore, because tech is a place of systems which goes against women's natural talents for working with people. As Damore puts it, "More men like coding because it requires systemizing and even within SWEs [software engineers], comparatively more women work on front end, which deals with both people and aesthetics."[40] At most, women can work in programming only if they are working on the parts of the project that people directly access, not the behind the scenes parts where the actual functions are located that are of more interest to men. It is only a coincidence, of course, that the aspects of coding that interest men lead to higher-paying jobs with more respect in the industry. It could not be that we have socially constructed organizations to favor certain behaviors we have ascribed to men over those attributed to women.

Damore then identifies gregariousness and agreeableness as traits associated with women as compared to assertiveness with men. "This leads to women generally having a harder time negotiating salary, asking for raises, speaking up, and leading. Note that these are just average differences and there's overlap between men and women, but this is seen solely as a women's issue. This leads to exclusory programs like Stretch and swaths of men without support."[41] It is ironic that Damore feels the need to specify that these are just average traits and do not apply to all individuals since making connections between the traits and gender is his entire purpose in this section. It makes sense when you remember that Damore's larger purpose is to argue that men are actually the one's facing discrimination. The point here is just intended to serve as ammunition for the larger battle to come later.

Damore then attributes to men a higher drive for status.

> We always ask why we don't see women in top leadership positions, but we never ask why we see so many men in these jobs. These positions often require long, stressful hours that may not be worth it if you want a balanced and fulfilling life. Status is the primary metric that men are judged on, pushing many men into these higher paying, less satisfying jobs for the status they entail.[42]

By Damore's reasoning, men are only more successful in the industry because of this higher drive for status, implying that women are uninterested in status so industry leaders should not waste time investing in women's advancement since they do not really care about the rewards that come with it. Once again, Damore cannot see the social construction that underlies his claims since we have built a society that rewards a trait that is attributed to men rather than men just responding to an internal drive for status. There is also the issue that men's traits just happen to lead to better paying jobs that also come with industry respect and other perks. If men are truly only driven by a desire for status, let us see how many men would still want to strive for the highest position if there was not the attendant pay raise and benefits. Men can have a title that attests to their high status while the increase in pay and cost of the other benefits can be used to improve the company. If men would not be satisfied with this arrangement, a drive for status then is not a built-in trait that men pursue regardless of material benefit and, instead, our society has just been built around encouraging that behavior instead of responding to it.

Damore's purpose is to identify traits associated with women that decrease their chances for success and increase the chances for men. When paired with a biological determinist worldview, the current structure of the tech industry is just the natural order, and any attempts to increase diversity risk destroying the natural order. Damore's next step in making his argument is to identify the specific ways in which Google's current diversity efforts are harming the company by going against the natural order.

Efforts to Diversify the Workforce Are Harmful to Business

Damore first argues that women's jobs at Google should be focused on their greater interest in people.

> We can make software engineering more people-oriented with pair programming and more collaboration. Unfortunately, there may be limits to how people-orientated some roles and Google can be and we shouldn't deceive ourselves or students into thinking otherwise (some of our programs to get female students into coding might be doing this).[43]

While research has shown that pair programming does help with increasing girls' interest in computer science,[44] this is not the same as saying that women can only succeed in areas focused on working with people. Based on his biological determinist worldview, Damore equates encouraging women to pursue careers in programming with lying since all positions cannot be made collaborative and people-oriented. Damore believes that women's potential for success in the tech field is so limited that efforts to increase diversity are actively harming the company and women themselves. Since success is tied to jobs that women are not biologically suited for, any effort to actively recruit them is the same as lying to them.

By implying that women are incapable of succeeding in certain jobs because these jobs are not people-oriented, Damore is actively harming the potential for success for women in the tech industry. Women who are seeking to advance in their careers within the industry will face increased scrutiny and barriers based on rhetoric like Damore's. They also should not bother trying to advance too far since, as Damore claims, "as long as tech and leadership remain high status, lucrative careers, men may disproportionately want them. Allowing and truly endorsing (as part of our culture) part time work though can keep more women in tech."[45] This is tied to Damore's claim that men have a higher drive for status; men will always want the higher status jobs so there will not be any available for women. Not only are women not suited for the jobs that lead to advancement, but they should not even try to get them and should content themselves with part-time positions instead. As a result of such rhetoric, women may be moved from career tracks that offer greater opportunities for success and advancement onto other career tracks that do not offer the same opportunities based on the assumption that they are better suited for these people-oriented positions. Women who are interested in people-oriented careers will also have their prospects further diminished as they will continue to be assumed to not be interested in advancement. Damore's worldview allows him to see the positions that lead to advancement being occupied by men and those that do not being occupied by women as the result of inherent biological differences rather than as reflective of ideological biases against women. By claiming that women's natural traits lead them to lesser positions, Damore helps to ensure that women's opportunities in the industry will continue to be limited.

While Damore claims repeatedly to not be opposed to diversity itself, he dismisses any attempts to increase diversity as a social experiment.

> Philosophically, I don't think we should do arbitrary social engineering of tech just to make it appealing to equal proportions of both men and women. For each of these changes, we need principled reasons for why it helps Google; that is, we should be optimizing for Google – with Google's diversity being a component of that. For example currently those trying to work extra hours or take extra stress will inevitably get ahead and if we try to change that too much, it may have disastrous consequences. Also, when considering the costs and benefits, we should keep in mind that Google's funding is finite so its allocation is more zero-sum than is generally acknowledged.[46]

Through his rhetoric, Damore presents his concern as not maintaining men's place of dominance in the social hierarchy but the company's bottom line. Diversity should not be pursued not because it is unimportant but because such efforts actually harm the company. Instead of finding the best employees, Google's diversity efforts will lead them to hire subpar people just because of the groups they belong to. A business's decisions, from Damore's point of view, must always be guided by concern for the bottom line, and increasing diversity does not do anything to specifically improve the company's profits. The status quo should be maintained because it is what is best for the company. It's just a coincidence, of course, that Damore and people like him benefit from the status quo.

Damore ends this part of his argument by claiming that Google's efforts to increase diversity are ideologically driven and discriminatory.

> These practices are based on false assumptions generated by biases and can actually increase race and gender tensions. We're told by senior leadership that what we're doing is both the morally and economically correct thing to do, but

without evidence this is just veiled left ideology that can irreparably harm Google.[47]

I doubt Damore would be convinced by any evidence showing the benefits of diversity. Based on his worldview, women and other marginalized groups are biologically unsuited to certain positions. Any efforts to actively recruit members of these groups is discriminatory because such efforts must mean an individual more suited for the position is being passed over. Individuals may be able to buck the trend and succeed, but Damore is more than willing to miss out on talented individuals who may be found through diversity programs. Diversity programs, by their very nature for Damore, mean that the people hired are not talented. Damore claims later that he is only interested in individuals and not in group identity. "I'm also not saying that we should restrict people to certain gender roles; I'm advocating for quite the opposite: treat people as individuals, not as just another member of their group (tribalism)."[48] This is a recent argument from the Right: we value individual freedom and seeing people as unique individuals while the Left wants to group everyone together. What this argument obscures, of course, is that conservatives like Damore believe that all of our behaviors are the result of biological differences so you can value the individual confident that they will adhere to traditional norms and values. Despite his claims to not care about group identity, Damore ends his argument by making his ultimate point that his group of conservative white men are the ones actually facing discrimination.

Diversity Programs Are Discriminatory toward Conservative White Men

After articulating his worldview in regards to diversity, Damore then makes the major point of his argument: diversity efforts are discriminatory toward conservative white men. He says that conservatives have been alienated at Google for holding different viewpoints. "Viewpoint diversity is arguably the more important type of diversity and political orientation is one of the most fundamental and significant ways in which people view things differently. . . . In highly progressive environments, conservatives are a minority that feel like they need to stay in the closet to avoid open hostility."[49] Damore's co-opting of the language of the LGBTQ+ movement, conservatives feeling pressure to stay "in the closet," is meant to position viewpoint diversity as the equivalent to other forms of discrimination and marginalization. Not liking someone because of their political beliefs and ideology are rendered in Damore's thinking as the same as hating someone because of their gender, race, ethnicity, socioeconomic class, religion, gender identity, or sexual orientation. He even claims that it is more important to support someone's right to express intolerance toward other groups than it is to protect those groups from discrimination and marginalization. This rhetorical strategy is intended to make Damore and those who support his views seem like the victim so that his larger point will be more easily accepted by those who do not want to seem intolerant themselves.

Everything he has said has been building to this point, from the biological differences between men and women and the traits associated with those differences to the need to make decisions in regards to diversity that are in line with the company's bottom line. If there are inherent differences between men and women that lead them to have different traits that make them better suited for certain positions, the decision that makes the most business sense is to continue to hire people in line with these differences. Any efforts to increase diversity that go against this line of reasoning are discriminatory to conservative white men who, being biologically superior to other groups, will be disadvantaged by not being able to get the high-paying jobs that they so rightly deserve. Damore makes his argument by questioning the morality of diversity, questioning the benefits of diversity programs, emphasizing psychological safety for those with differing viewpoints, and prioritizing intention over outcome. These points, along with others like accepting the science of human nature and de-emphasizing empathy, work together to support Damore's belief that conservative white men are the true victims.

Damore first argues for de-moralizing diversity efforts. "As soon as we start to moralize an issue, we stop thinking about it in terms of costs and benefits, dismiss anyone that disagrees, and harshly punish those we see as villains to protect the 'victims.'"[50] This is part of Damore's earlier claim that businesses should consider diversity efforts within the context of the bottom line. It is interesting, though, that he argues against the morality of diversity rather than arguing for the morality of viewpoint diversity. He does this because his purpose is to tear down diversity efforts rather than promoting the morality of his own position. His focus on costs and benefits also reveals that he is attempting to take a pragmatic approach (diversity efforts lead to less talented people being hired which leads to decreased profits for the company) which fits his overall goal. It does not matter to Damore to establish that his position is a moral good. Instead, morality interferes with business by leading people to make decisions as driven by the belief that increasing diversity is morally correct even though it hurts the business. Removing morality from the equation, in Damore's view, allows for purely cost/benefit analyses that will benefit conservative white men because they bring the least costs and highest benefits. Viewpoint diversity does not have to be moral so long as it does not add costs to the business. Morality clouds your judgment by leading you to hire someone less qualified in the name of diversity. Hiring someone like Damore will always be the better decision, according to his worldview, so he does not feel compelled to make a moral argument in favor of his position.

Damore then returns to his argument that we should focus on the costs and benefits of diversity programs. "Discriminating just to increase the representation of women in tech is as misguided and biased as mandating increases in women's representation in the homeless, work-related and violent deaths, prisons, and school dropouts."[51] Any efforts to increase diversity are framed as discrimination against the dominant group. Damore also argues that an interest in increasing women's representation in one area of life must necessitate a demand for women's equality in all areas of life. It never occurs to Damore that efforts might be made to decrease the number of men suffering violent deaths, incarceration, or dropping out of school; the only way he can conceive of to balance those figures is to increase the number of women who suffer these outcomes. Connecting back to his previous point about morality, Damore also argues that these efforts are alienating for those who do not support them. "These programs are highly politicized which further alienates non-progressives."[52] Damore's costs and benefits here are not actually focused on the company's bottom line (he is not pointing out the amount of money spent on the programs as compared either to the company's profits or the increased productivity of those involved), so what are the actual costs of the programs according to Damore? The costs are all ideological. Having diversity programs makes conservatives feel upset which might mean that they will be less interested in working for the company. And since Damore has tried to establish that conservative white men are superior workers in the tech industry, losing them in favor of having diversity programs means losing out on the best workers. No company would be able to survive without having the best workers (conservative white men), so companies should ditch their diversity programs in order to appease this group.

Damore continues this line of reasoning with his next point about the need for psychological safety.

> We should focus on psychological safety, which has shown positive effects and should (hopefully) not lead to unfair discrimination. We need psychological safety and shared values to gain the benefits of diversity. Having representative viewpoints is important for those designing and testing products, but those benefits are less clear for those more removed from UX [user experience].[53]

Psychological safety for Damore means the comfort in knowing that those around you share your worldview. You do not have to worry about those around you being upset by your beliefs since they share them. Productivity can only result from the safety of never having your beliefs challenged. He does concede that diverse viewpoints might benefit those working more directly with users, since users will have diverse viewpoints themselves, but

Damore has already relegated more people-oriented positions to women so the group he is defending (conservative white men) is not involved with the user experience and diverse viewpoints will not help them in doing their jobs. They will only be able to do their jobs with the safety that will come from everyone around them sharing their worldview. Diversity programs are threatening to those like Damore because they increase the likelihood that they will have to work with people who have differing beliefs. Damore is trying to shut down diversity programs to ensure that his beliefs are never challenged. He uses the language of cost/benefit analysis to make his demands seem like they are driven by a concern for the company rather than by sexism and racism. Damore wants to see his group protected while simultaneously arguing that others are too biased toward group identity. It is only through a worldview that views your group as biologically superior that these contradictory ideas could be sustained.

Damore's last major argument in this section is to focus on intention.

> Our focus on microaggressions and other unintentional transgressions increases our sensitivity, which is not universally positive: sensitivity increases both our tendency to take offense and our self censorship, leading to authoritarian policies. Speaking up without the fear of being harshly judged is central to psychological safety, but these practices can remove that safety by judging unintentional transgressions.[54]

This is a continuation of his argument for psychological safety. People need to be protected from accusations that their actions are harmful. They need the freedom to take harmful actions with impunity so long as they did not intend any harm. This is again an effort to protect people from having to interact with those whose beliefs differ from their own. Instead of reassessing your own behavior after having someone point out the harmful effects of it, Damore believes that people should be free to remain unaware of that harm. It is only then that they will be able to work in comfort. Diversity programs are once again a challenge to this comfort because they bring in more people with different beliefs. The only way to ensure that people are able to work in comfort, according to Damore, is to ensure that they are only working with those who are similar to them. Diversity efforts are particularly discriminatory to conservative white men because, from Damore's point of view, they cannot help being harmful and are also unable to recognize the ways their actions cause harm and change them. Rather than expecting more from conservative white men, we should protect them from ever having to interact with someone who differs from them.

Damore's argument was unsuccessful with his immediate audience, as he was fired by Google on August 7, 2017, for creating a hostile work environment.[55] On February 16, 2018, the National Labor Relations Board ruled that Google's firing of Damore was legal after Damore accused the company of discrimination.[56] While Damore's memo may have not had its intended effect at Google, the worldview presented within it needs to continue to be challenged. It is not sufficient to remove one bad actor if the argument they made continues to dominate the industry. One particular concern is that Damore's firing could be pointed to as removing the need to discuss gender in the tech industry anymore. "The one bad actor is gone so can women please shut up about gender?" We should not sit back comfortably and feel content with having addressed sexism and misogyny in the tech industry. The current genderblind system will persist so long as women do not feel free to include gender in their efforts to persuade people to address the gender imbalance in the industry and society as a whole, and Damore's firing can potentially be used as a means of perpetuating the system. We need to continue to push for gender equality and justice and not stop after one victory. Outside of the tech industry, women also experience attempts to prevent their use of gender in public persuasive appeals as a result of online harassment.

CRITIQUE OF FREEDOM: ONLINE HARASSMENT OF WOMEN

Online harassment has negatively impacted the lives of many women and members of other marginalized groups. However, we often do not take online harassment very seriously. "Commentators trivialize the harassment of women online by arguing that: (1) it constitutes innocuous teasing, (2) women can address the harassment on their own, and (3) cyber harassment coheres with the internet's unique norms."[57] This dismissive attitude toward online harassment often leaves many women to fend off harassers on their own. This attitude is also built on the genderblind belief that online spaces are already egalitarian and open to all, so everyone is judged solely as an individual. Any harassment that does occur must be dealt with at an individual level according to this worldview.

Our perception of online harassment is influenced by our worldview and group membership. Kurt Borchard argues that online forms of harassment "are delivered anonymously and virtually" and are seen by perpetrators as "a form of inconsequential 'virtual harm' from which the perpetrator gains pleasure."[58] This perception of online harassment as "virtual harm" allows the individual to distance themselves from responsibility for the harassment because it is not real, whether they harass people individually or harassment is common in their community. Everyone, though, does not distance themselves from harassment and treat it as different from their behavior in real life. Research by Jobi Biber and colleagues found that people do "not hold more relaxed standards for online behavior, but seemingly held similar or even more stringent standards for online behaviors."[59] Women were particularly stringent in their assessment of others' online behavior.[60] When interacting online, people do not view the behavior of others as inconsequential but watch their behavior the same or more closely as they would in real life. This goes against assumptions that we excuse online harassment and other negative behaviors because they take place online. The findings may also represent a shift in perception of online behavior given recent histories of increased online harassment and abuse.

Online harassment affects women mentally and emotionally. Women report greater levels of anxiety and depression as a result of harassment.[61] Online harassment also leads to greater feelings of fear for women based on their relationship to the harasser and whether they had asked for the harassment to stop.[62] Adrienne Massanari terms the spaces in which online harassment occurs as toxic technocultures that "demonstrate retrograde ideas of gender, sexual identity, sexuality, and race and push against issues of diversity, multiculturalism, and progressivism" and "often rely heavily on implicit or explicit harassment of others."[63] She is not claiming that everyone involved in a toxic technoculture holds exactly the same views or engages in the same behavior. "However, the larger discourse which characterizes a 'toxic technoculture' often relies an Othering of those perceived as outside the culture, reliance on outmoded and poorly understood applications of evolutionary psychology, and a valorization of masculinity masquerading as a peculiar form of 'rationality.'"[64] Individuals within the community often "champion the power of the community as a way to effect change or voice displeasure with others they view as being adversaries" while "distancing themselves from what they perceive as the more ethically dubious (and illegal) actions of others."[65] These actions are intended to allow individuals to support the actions of the community while preserving their self-image as a good person. Massanari's research on toxic technocultures, however, reveals how harassment is able to persist online when no one does anything to stop it, even when it is being done in their name. The tolerance for harassment as a tactic of silencing opponents implicates all members of a community even if they have not engaged in the harassment themselves.

Recent events allow us to examine online harassment's function as genderblind rhetoric in making women feel unwelcome in online spaces and in preventing gender from being used in public persuasive appeals around tech culture. I analyze five cases of online harassment of women in the section: Zoë Quinn, Anita Sarkeesian, Leslie Jones, Kelly Marie Tran, and Jessica Valenti. I begin with brief descriptions of the events surrounding each woman's harassment. Zoë Quinn is a game developer best known for a narrative game titled *Depression Quest*. Quinn became the target of harassment after an ex-boyfriend claimed in a blog post that she had cheated on him by sleeping with video game reviewers in exchange for positive reviews of her game. The harassers rallied under the hashtag #GamerGate to harass Quinn and other women involved in the video game industry. In September 2014, a chat log of users planning how they would harass Quinn was released.[66] Anita Sarkeesian is a feminist media critic who releases videos on YouTube as part of the channel *Feminist Frequency*. She became the target of online harassers after launching a Kickstarter campaign in 2012 to raise money for a series analyzing gender representation in video games called "Tropes vs. Women in Video Games." In January 2015, Sarkeesian posted on Tumblr a week's worth of the harassment she had received.[67] Leslie Jones is a well-known comedian and actress. She was the subject of a harassment campaign led by conservative troll Milo Yiannopoulos in July 2016 as a way of expressing anger at her role in the female-led remake of *Ghostbusters*. The harassment led Jones to briefly leave Twitter.[68] Kelly Marie Tran is an actress best known for her role as Rose Tico in *Star Wars: The Last Jedi*. Tran was harassed off of Instagram in June 2018 by fans expressing their misogynistic anger at the film.[69] Finally, Jessica Valenti is a feminist activist and one of the founders of the blog Feministing. She documented some of the harassment she received in her book *Sex Object*.[70]

I want to mention that while I highlight individual examples of harassment in this section, each woman has suffered hundreds more. I also have chosen to not include usernames for the harassers in order to not give them more attention; usernames can be found in the sources for those interested. Finally, while these may seem like individual instances of harassment, these women were often the targets of organized campaigns in which hundreds, if not thousands, of messages would be sent in a short amount of time. While it may seem easy to ignore an individual instance of harassment, it is much harder to ignore hundreds all at once.

Online harassment of women works to make women feel unwelcome online. When women are told to just suck it up in response to death threats and other forms of harassment or to leave if they cannot handle it, the message is being sent that online spaces are not intended for women. The genderblindness of online harassment manifests in claims that harassment is just part of online culture. The claim is made that everyone suffers harassment online, but this claim ignores that fact that women are disproportionately more likely to suffer harassment.[71] Rather than being a claim that is intended to be verified, the purpose of this claim is to frame online harassment as having no connection to gender so any attempts to base arguments against harassment in women's experiences are out of place and are examples of women looking for special treatment since everyone is harassed online. This blasé attitude toward harassment would be troubling (why would anyone put up with harassment?), but then you remember its purpose in silencing women. The rhetoric of online harassment of women exhibits four themes: explicit death threats, comments on women's appearance, framing women as only seeking attention, and framing women as the truly repressive ones. Death threats are the first theme found in online harassment of women, and they have led many women to flee their homes out of fear that they might come true.⁷²

Explicit Death Threats

Death threats are, in many ways, the most troubling form of online harassment, particularly for those who receive them. They are also the clearest form of harassment. The message that you need to leave the online space is clearly communicated. The messages are also almost savage in their bizarre specificity in the imagined ways they want the other person to die. Death threats are often excused as nothing more than venting of anger and frustration that no one would ever actually follow through on. Anyone who takes them seriously is mocked for not understanding online discursive norms. Even if we do not take the actual threats seriously, though, the purpose behind the threats is clear. They are intended to provoke a visceral response of fear and anxiety for the receiver's safety. The messages are also often sent en masse so while it may seem easy to dismiss one message, it is harder to dismiss hundreds received on a regular basis. The person receiving the messages may feel that they should just leave the online space in order to stop having to put up with the constant threats. Once that possibility is considered or pursued, the harassment has achieved its goals. The harassers have maintained control over the space by putting the harassed in their place. A message is also sent to other members of the group to expect similar treatment should they venture into online space.

On January 20, 2015, Anita Sarkeesian received this message on Twitter: "I hope every feminist has their head severed from their shoulders." This is just the first of dozens of death threats she would receive over the course of the following week. Later that day, she received this message: "I Hope you fucking Kill yourself Get Ice Skates Split your throat And drink bleach." A final death threat for Sarkeesian on January 20: "kill yourself you piece of garbage. You shouldn't be able to breathe. Such a waste of oxygen." On January 23, 2015, she received this message: "I'm gonna beat you with a sock of quarters and your supporters if you come to my town."

Jessica Valenti also received many direct death threats, including this email from April 11, 2012. "I think you need to be gagged. All we do is fuck and chuck women nowadays because of the rhetoric of cunts like you. I hope you perish in a gasoline explosion induced by car crash."⁷³ In Zoë Quinn's case, discussion in the chat focused primarily on harassing her to the point that she would kill herself. On August 12, 2014, one user asks another if they have a reason for harassing Quinn. "You need a reason . . ." "Well I don't have a legitimate reason." "Nothing?" "I just want to see her die horribly." By August 25, 2014, a group of users is concerned about whether or not getting Quinn to kill herself is the right thing to do, not morally, or course, but for the advancement of their cause. "If she commits suicide we lose everything . . ." "If you can't see how driving Zoe to suicide would fuck this entire thing up then you're a fucking idiot" "Imagine the kotaku article . . ." . . . "not the right PR play." Harassing Quinn is decided against by this group not because it is wrong to harass someone to the point of suicide but because it would make them look bad. The chat discussions about harassing Quinn reveal that there are legitimate hopes by the harassers that their efforts will have the stated result. This is not just harmless venting but messages intended to inflict severe mental and emotional distress. Regardless of whether the messages actually prompt someone to kill themselves or if the harasser actually makes an attempt at violence, the constant threats of violence have the intended effect on the harassed woman and those who see the harassment take place that she is not welcome in online spaces.

Another aspect of the general death threats is that harassed women also receive messages telling them that everyone receives similar threats. On January 21, 2015, Anita Sarkeesian received this message on Twitter: "Stop. You do not understand about gaming. Death Threats are made daily, as well as rape threats. guess what? It's not only women!" Another message followed the same day: "you're a fucking bitch, EVERYSINGLE FKN PERSON who play online gets DEATH THREAT!, and NO one cares, its NOT a big deal." The purpose of these messages is to normalize death threats in order to take away any power that might come from women bringing attention to them. The normalization of the threats also establishes a barrier to entry into the online space. If women truly want to participate online, then death threats and other forms of harassment are the price of entry. The gendered aspects of the amount and severity of the threats directed at women are neutralized by an acceptance of the threats as normal. Preserving a dominant place within the online space is shown to be more important than actually confronting the negative behavior within that space.

Beyond just basic death threats, many of the messages take on a more clearly gendered tone by being combined with threats of rape. On June 4, 2011, Jessica Valenti received the following email from a self-identified feminist critical of her activism around rape and sexual assault.

> So you pple do slut walk? Look at yourself, fat elephant, you and the likes of you don't need to worry about getting raped. In LA, you'd have to pay for that, dumb broads. Hope your children will get violently, brutally raped. And yes, I'm a feminist and female. Just the trash like you and your website is polluting the movement and doing disservice, ugly fat pig.[74]

It is ironic, of course, that a message identified as a critique of rape activism would include rape threats in it. This self-identified feminist takes issue with Valenti's mode of activism and decides to perpetuate rape culture in order to express her disdain. Gender and ideology do not make a difference when it comes to making women feel unwelcome in online spaces.

Anita Sarkeesian received less ideologically complex threats of rape on Twitter. One such message came on January 20, 2015: "BITCH WERE NOT TALKING ABOUT THAT SO I HOPE YOU GET FUCKING RAPED U FUCKING WHORE." Another similar message came on January 21, 2015: "I hope you get raped by 4 men with 9 inch cocks." Jessica Valenti also received this more straightforward threat of rape in a Facebook message on June 30, 2014. "You're one heck of a disgusting ugly looking hag. What you need is a big fat dick inside you to set you straight. Thankfully, you're nowhere near being my type. I hope some mack truck crashes head into you."[75]

Along with clear intersections with gender through rape threats, many death threats also include a racial component. On January 21, 2015, Anita Sarkeesian received the following message: "kill yourself paki." The use of an ethnic slur implies that Sarkeesian's ascribed ethnic identity should make her want to kill herself more. Sarkeesian is frequently ascribed a wide range of racial and ethnic identities that are not actually accurate in an attempt to further marginalize her. The fact that these ascribed identities are not accurate does not excuse the implications of the use of race in such messages. A racial component can also be seen in the type of violence directed at women online. On January 25, 2015, Sarkeesian received this message: "hope you get raped by a wild pack of niggers." This message contains multiple racist layers, including the stereotype that black men are inherently violent, that black people as a whole are less civilized, and that being violated by a black man is somehow even more demeaning for a white woman than just being raped. Race tends to be invoked in these threats as a means of amplification. When a death threat may not be harmful enough, adding in some racism will help. This use of racist slurs and stereotypes reveals the depths of the bigotry of those who would employ death threats in defense of an online space. Along with death threats, another major theme in online harassment of women is a focus on personal appearance.

Comments on Women's Appearance

Unwanted attention to personal appearance is a form of harassment familiar to women even outside of online spaces. Many of the harassing messages have the same tenor as the street harassment women often have to endure when moving through public space. Comments on women's appearance is a particularly feminized form of attack based on the perception that women are especially sensitive to critiques of their attractiveness. Constantly criticizing a woman's appearance online is intended to make women feel uncomfortable in online spaces, just as the wolf whistles and catcalls make women feel uncomfortable when moving through public space. Just as many women take precautions when moving through public space in order to avoid harassment, such as avoiding certain areas or wearing headphones, they may also take precautions in online spaces, such as not posting photos of themselves or not making comments about current events involving rape and sexual assault. This self-policing of behavior demonstrates how harassment shapes the experiences of women in online and public spaces.

A lot of the harassment that focuses on women's appearance mirrors the types of comments women receive from street harassers. In an email from November 19, 2009, Jessica Valenti was told, "Don't look so serious next time you post your picture. I bet you have a beautiful smile :)."[76] The demand that a woman smile more will be familiar to anyone who has experienced harassment in public space. Harassers also often combine demands for access to women's bodies with other forms of abuse. Anita Sarkeesian received the following message on January 20, 2015: "oi fuck you mother fucker slut bitch female ass hoe slut fuck you show me your tits." The demand to see Sarkeesian's breasts coming at the end of a string of invective against her demonstrates how most of the comments around women's appearance and bodies reflects a disdain for women and a desire to control them. None of these comments, even those framed as positive, are meant as legitimate advice to improve a woman's public perception. Instead, they reflect the belief that women should do whatever someone (usually a man) demands of them.

A final example of the general use of comments on women's appearance comes from an email Jessica Valenti received on February 18, 2010. The harasser expressed disbelief at Valenti's attractiveness based on her politics and activism. "Never thought that a feminist could have such a charming smile and appear that friendly."[77] This comment reflects popular attitudes that feminists are angry because they are unattractive and cannot get a man. It is a backhanded compliment that Valenti does not conform to this perception of feminists. It is intended as the other messages are to make Valenti feel uncomfortable when appearing in online spaces because of the additional scrutiny she is receiving for her personal appearance rather than her ideas. This is another goal of comments on women's appearance: reducing women's presence online to just their appearance rather than engaging with their ideas. Flooding the space with comments on their appearance ensures that women's ideas will receive even less attention.

Comments on women's appearance also intersect with race. On January 21, 2015, Anita Sarkeesian receive the following message: "uh boohoo stop crying you selfish faking bitch and get over it who would rape you your fucking ugly you Arab bitch." The harasser claims that Sarkeesian would never be raped because she is not attractive enough and then connects that unattractiveness to her perceived ethnic identity as Arab. As with death threats, this combination of attacks on appearance and racism is used for amplification. The racism is intended to make what would be a mere attack on appearance even worse. On December 19, 2017, Kelly Marie Tran was the target of a message on Instagram that said, "Battlestar Galactica Asian vs. #LastJedi Asian. Obviously, The First Order failed to cut off the #Resistance supply line of food." The message was accompanied by a picture of Grace Park on the left as her character Boomer from *Battlestar Galactica* and Tran on the right as her character Rose Tico from *The Last Jedi*.[78] The purpose of comparing the two is to fat-shame Tran for her appearance, and the specific choice of Park is to focus on another Asian actress in a sci-fi franchise for comparison. The racist comparison of two Asian actresses is also based in perceptions of Asian women as erotic because of their daintiness. A final purpose behind this specific attack on Tran is that the recent Star Wars films have received praise for their increased gender and racial diversity as compared to the original trilogy. By comparing Tran to another Asian actress, the harasser is arguing that Tran should still be expected to conform to racist and misogynistic standards of attractiveness in order to deserve the praise that she and the franchise are receiving. The fact that she is perceived as failing to live up to that standard as compared to another Asian actress from an older sci-fi franchise implies that neither she nor the franchise deserve the praise they have received.

Among all of the racist attacks on women's appearance I have analyzed, no one endured more vicious attacks than Leslie Jones. During the wave of harassment against her that was stirred up by Milo Yiannopoulos, much of it focused on her appearance. In a Twitter message Jones received on July 18, 2016, a harasser tells Jones, "If we have the technology, we can revive your brother." This comment is accompanied by a picture of a cyborg gorilla with a rifle in reference to Harambe, the gorilla killed at the Cincinnati Zoo in 2016 after a three-year-old boy fell into the gorilla enclosure and officials were concerned for the boy's life.[79] The comparison of a black person to a gorilla has a well-known racist history, and this comparison dominated the harassment of Jones. On the same day, Jones received another message connecting her to Harambe that said, "I know you only wanted to protect that kid"; the message was accompanied by a picture of Harambe.[80] Other messages harassing Jones made more general reference to Jones being an ape, saying,

> SHE HAS NO STYLE
> SHE HAS NO GRACE
> THIS LESLIE (KONG)
> HAS A FUNNY FACE.[81]

Kong, of course, refers to *King Kong*. The choice of a giant ape as a comparison to Jones is intentional since Jones has often been attacked for her height.

Harassers also made connections between gorillas and Jones's film *Ghostbusters* that inspired the harassment. One harasser says to Jones on July 18, 2016, "Your Ghostbusters isn't the first to have an ape in it." The message is accompanied by a picture from the 1970s TV show *The Ghostbusters*, no relation to the movie franchise, that included a gorilla among its team of mystery solvers.[82] Comparing Jones to an ape was not the only racist way she was harassed as one harasser sent her a message on July 18, 2016, that just included the phrase "big lipped coon" eight times.[83]

The fact that the vicious attacks on Jones concentrate on her race shows how online harassers do not know how to interact with black people in general and black women more specifically except through racism. The intersection of gender and race in these messages amplifies the experience of the harassment since the processing of this harassment cannot be separated into messages only about gender and messages only about race. The harassment is experienced at the intersection of those identities which may increase the power of the messages, which is why it is such a common tactic of the harassers. The full context of racist comments on women's appearance must be examined in order to fully understand the impact of these messages on the individual.

Death threats and comments on women's appearance are two forms that online harassment often takes when directed at women. These messages reveal some of the purposes behind the harassment, but they do not show how the harassers understand their actions. The final two themes of online harassment of women reveal some of the thinking of harassers in how they frame their attacks.

Framing Women as Only Seeking Attention

Part of the reasoning for why these women deserve to be harassed is that they are just seeking attention and are not actually invested in their public statements. When Anita Sarkeesian critiques video games or Zoë Quinn calls attention to harassment she has received, they are just doing this to get attention. Attention is the primary way to demonstrate status and engagement in online spaces so the attention women receive must be what really motivates them rather than the critical analysis they are engaged in or the reality of the attacks they have endured. Harassment is justified by this framing because the women being harassed are not being honest in their motivations. They do not truly believe what they have said and even make up attacks for more attention so harassing them in turn is okay. Women who think they can express their ideas in public and then discuss those ideas with others find themselves harassed by people who do not believe the statements that they made were made in good faith. If you can frame your opponents as always acting in bad faith, then any bad faith actions you take, like death threats, are justified. Framing women as only interested in attention allows the harassers to present themselves as right while taking reprehensible actions themselves. If you present your opponents as nothing but liars, they deserve whatever treatment they receive since it is the result of their own actions.

The harassment of Zoë Quinn was framed in this way when discussing attempts to harass her into killing herself. On August 21, 2014, a user made the following argument on the downsides to harassing Quinn: "The more you try to attack her directly, the more she gets to play the victim card and make a bunch of friends who will support her because, since she has a vagina, any attack is misgony." Even in a chat discussion about harassing Quinn, the harassers claim that she will benefit from it by playing the victim. This argument is revealing because usually this framing of harassment is used to claim that the victim is just making up the harassment for attention. In this case, the people actively harassing Quinn are worried that she will still receive positive attention as a result of their harassment. Rather than attacking her for making up the harassment, the harassers are worried about continuing their harassment out of concern that Quinn might still benefit. It is also important to recognize that even though the larger chat discussion reveals that Quinn is a victim of harassment, the harasser here argues that she will still be playing the victim. Quinn is still framed as taking action on her own part to benefit from her status as a victim. Playing the victim in this case does not mean that nothing happened to you but that you will use what has happened to your advantage. Framing Quinn as taking deliberate action to use her victim status to her own benefit allows the harassers to justify their harassment. Quinn is positioned as an active participant in the exchange by publicizing her harassment so she has to put up with it because she benefits as well. Since both sides are framed as benefitting, the harassers can feel that they have done nothing wrong.

Anita Sarkeesian is a primary target for this argument that women only claim to be harassed online in order to get attention. She has been harassed relentlessly since she began her critiques of video games. Since video games are generally constructed as a masculine interest, Sarkeesian's interest in games, especially critiquing them from a feminist perspective, are framed as illegitimate. Because her interest in games is seen as not real, she must be critiquing them for the attention that comes from being controversial. Her harassment is framed as being her own fault for daring to venture into an online space where she is not welcome.

On January 20, 2015, Sarkeesian received a message accusing her of using the harassment within the message itself to generate more content: "please shut the fuck up but wait you'll make a article about how I threatened you and act like I'm satan well bitch u r." A similar message followed on January 23, 2015: "Threats ARE an accepted part of gamin, except in non-cunt lingo its called *trash talk*. But sure, Keep milkin it." Harassers also accused her of seeking attention for money, with the attendant accusation that she was a whore. One user told her on January 23, 2015, "keep on scamming your followers. threats are a part of gaming, always has been. Stop trying to victimize yourself for money!" A similar message followed on January 26, 2015: "you deserve every single threat you get, what a stupid bitch, most people already understand that all you want is money.whore." A final line of argument is to attack her presence in the gaming community. One user said to her on January 22, 2015, "Let me ask you kindly, anita: Get the fuck out of the gaming community, you are like a parasite, would you?" A message sent the previous day said, "if you were a real gamer you would know this happens to men + women also I think ur just a whore looking for daddys attention."

This framing of harassment as the result of women seeking attention works to silence women by making sure their voices are not heard. If a woman tries to bring attention to the harassment she is experiencing, she is nothing but an attention whore looking to profit from her victimization. If she does not discuss her harassment publicly, she has to endure it alone. The results of this framing may make some women cautious in expressing themselves online. Their very participation in the discussion may also be framed as motivated only by attention-seeking, removing the ability of women to make claims to their interest in and experience with the subject as a defense against the harassment. Such evidence is just used by harassers as further proof of the harassed woman's attention-seeking behavior. Both their discussion of the harassment and claims of interest in the subject become justifications for more harassment. Along with framing women as only seeking attention, harassers also frame their behavior as justified because of women's repressive actions against them.

Framing Women as the Truly Repressive Ones

A final theme in the harassment of women online is the framing of women as truly repressive as compared to the harassers. Whether it be starring in a movie, making a video game, or critiquing video games, these actions are framed by the harassers as repressive for taking the harasser's enjoyment out of a pastime, which is used to justify harassment of the women responsible. Just being women is also framed as a repressive action. Women are presented as not intelligent enough to function in society or as ideologically driven feminists whose every action will soon lead to the downfall of society. Framing online harassment of women in this way allows the harassment to continue as a noble action in defense of a cherished media text or society itself. The harassers also seek to reduce sympathy for the women harassed as not deserving of it. As with being attention-seeking whores, the harassed women are presented as reaping the consequences of their own actions. If they were not prepared for the harassment, they should have never had the nerve to do something as outrageous as critique video games or star in a movie. These nefarious actions obviously necessitate almost constant harassment of these women. It is this framing that allows harassers to find redeeming qualities in their actions.

One important aspect of this framing is treating women as if they are not intelligent enough to participate in society. Jessica Valenti received an email on June 8, 2008, in which the harasser told her, "GET BAK IN THE KITCHEN AND MAKE ME DINNER, BITCH. Tiny brained women, why did we ever let them think they are someone?"[84] Another email she received on August 8, 2012, infantilized Valenti as a feminist: "Feminists remind me of little girls who cry because they didn't get their way. If you wanted to be important, you should have been born with a penis. (:"[85] Anita Sarkeesian received a similar message on January 25, 2015, in which the harasser claimed that she deserved the harassment because of her lack of intelligence, saying, "you're not being abused, don't act like a victim you bitch. Your being rebelled. Your views are close-minded and ignorant." This diminishment of women as public individuals is intended to justify the harassment they receive as stepping in to stop someone dangerous from influencing society with their misguided views. The harasser presents themselves as a defender of society from the threat of women expressing themselves in public. Women may be reluctant to express themselves online in the face of such harassment.

Harassers also attack women on the basis that their feminist worldviews are dangerous. Anita Sarkeesian received a message on January 21, 2015, telling her that being a feminist means she should not have rights, saying, "fucking bitch you dont deserve rights feminist need to go to jail for existing #MeninistTwitter." A similar message followed on January 26, 2015, claiming that her analysis of the gender representation in video games was propaganda, saying, "Just kill yourself dumb whore, stop feeding the media with all this fake feminist propaganda. you're worse than pat robertson." Jessica Valenti received an email on May 1, 2010, questioning her announcement that she was having a baby since she is pro-choice, saying, "Jessica you are having a baby? I thought you didn't believe in having babies . . . just killing them. I feel sorry for your child who will learn to devalue human life."[86] An email Valenti received on May 31, 2008, informs her that as a feminist, she is at fault for her harassment for leading men on, saying, "You and your cult are the majority of the reason that women are hated. You can't tease the poor men and then yell at them for drooling."[87] Feminism receives specific attention because the harassers believe it is the greatest threat to society. In order to counter this threat, they argue that constant harassment of women until they leave online spaces is necessary. A user in the chat discussion of the harassment of Zoë Quinn, though, reveals that all of these attempts to justify harassment as part of a noble effort to defend the public good are nothing more than pretense when a user is asked why they want to harass Quinn, and they respond, "i couldnt care less about vidya, i just want to see zoe receive her comeuppance." Harassing women is revealed to be what it really is: an effort to keep women in their perceived place for daring to act like men's equals in public.

One other specific aspect of this framing is demands and pleas that the harassed woman leave some aspect of online culture, such as video games or sci-fi films, alone. In December 2017, Kelly Marie Tran's character Rose Tico's entry on Wookiepedia, a Wikipedia-like website for information about Star Wars, was changed to the following: "Ching Chong Wing Tong is a dumbass fucking character Disney made and is a stupid, retarded, and autistic love interest for Finn. She better die in the coma because she is a dumbass bitch."[88] This harassment of Tran, using a racist nickname for her and hoping her character dies, is intended to push her out of the franchise. The fans view her as someone who does not belong so they use harassment to send that message to her so she will leave. Anita Sarkeesian generally receives more directly pleas to stop talking about video games, such as a message on January 21, 2015, saying, "Fuck you and fuck everything you stand for. You are the shit stain of the gaming community, just leave games the fuck alone." Sarkeesian's discussion of video games is framed as invalid and the demand is made that she leave gaming alone. The presence of women in communities around pastimes generally framed as masculine, like sci-fi films and video games, is unwanted by many in those communities, especially those who hold conservative worldviews on gender and race, so harassing them is justified as a means of reclaiming control of those communities and spaces. By refusing to leave, the harassed women are framed as bringing the harassment on themselves by preventing the members of the community from freely enjoying their media texts. Rather than the harassment silencing women, the harassers view themselves as the ones truly silenced and their harassment as a means of remedying the situation.

The online harassment of women works to make women feel uncomfortable in online spaces and reluctant to express themselves online out of fear of harassment. The intention of harassers to silence women and drive them out of online spaces is clear from the forms their harassment takes and the framing used to justify their actions. Many harassers celebrate the use of harassment and pledge to continue. Anita Sarkeesian received a message on January 26, 2015, saying, "'harassing' will continue and accelerate. We're not going to stop until no one will openly admit to being feminist." The harasser makes it clear that the intention of the harassment is to drive women out of online spaces and away from a worldview seeking to advance the cause of gender equality and justice. Another user responded to the news of Kelly Marie Tran leaving Instagram by posting a GIF of Anakin Skywalker from *Star Wars: Episode I—The Phantom Menace* saying, "It's working, It's working!"[89] The rhetoric of online harassment is also genderblind in its attempts to prevent women from using gender in order to make public persuasive appeals. If a woman has to endure constant death threats, comments about her appearance, and other forms of harassment and that harassment is going to be framed as justified because of her attempts to speak up, women are not only going to be less likely to discuss their experiences in online spaces, but they are also going to be even less inclined to bring attention to the gendered nature of the harassment. The harassers will be able to continue to frame their actions and those of the harassed women as equivalent, as two sides of an exchange where all involved benefit. We must not only call out harassment when it happens but also work to develop strategies of how to resist the framing of the harassment in ways that benefit the harassers. We must stop letting harassers dictate the form that discourse online will take or women will never feel welcome in online spaces.

CONCLUSION

The rhetoric of the tech industry and culture works to make women feel uncomfortable and unwelcome. These feelings of being unwelcome serve the goals of a genderblind ideology by making women less likely to center gender in their efforts to bring attention to and fight harassment. Genderblindness argues that the tech industry and culture are egalitarian and open to everyone, so any critiques of tech should focus solely on the individual. Any attempts to bring gender or other marginalized identities into the discussion is portrayed as a betrayal of the true values of tech culture. The rhetoric seen in biological determinist defenses of women's lack of success in the tech industry and online harassment of women support the ideological goals of genderblindness. James Damore's Google memo reduces the changes for women's success in the industry and prevents them from seeking redress based on gender. Online harassment of women silences women from speaking in online spaces and prevents them from critiquing harassment from their experiences as women. In order to resist this rhetoric, what are some ways to improve women's experiences in tech?

One suggestion is to ground responses to harassment in the community, either by involving community members in adjudicating misbehavior or through the use of technology like blockbots that are created by the community and allow individuals to block entire groups of people on social media so that they never have to interact with them.[90] One issue with this community-based approach is that many harassers are active members of the community. While it was found that community members tended to judge actions by others very stringently,[91] it is not inconceivable that bad faith actors could hijack such efforts and lead to the harassed individuals being punished rather than the harassers. Another issue is that blocking harassers only prevents people from having to interact with them. It does not change their behavior or make online spaces more welcoming to all. A community-based approach will have to ensure that efforts to curb harassment cannot be taken over by the harassers and that efforts are made to actually change behavior rather than just reducing exposure to it.

Another suggestion is to encourage people to engage in digital citizenship, which was found to be related to less experience with and perpetration of online harassment.[92] Digital citizenship was found to decrease with age, though, so efforts would need to be made to ensure that it is sustainable.[93] Digital citizenship does address the need to try to change behavior, but it may be too optimistic to pin our hopes on people acting better in online spaces out of a sense of investment in other members of the community.

A third suggestion is to raise awareness of institutional responses to the treatment of people, primarily on social media.[94] We need to push for institutions to be more vocal and open in their support for those enduring harassment. We also need institutions to demonstrate a stronger commitment to women's representation in the tech industry. A recent case illustrates problems at the intersection of these two aspects of institutional response. On July 6, 2018, a game designer named Jessica Price was fired by her employer ArenaNet after she had a negative interaction with a fan on Twitter.[95] When Price was dismissive of the fan's attempts to explain her job to her, a harassment campaign seeking to get her fired was launched. The campaign worked as Price and Peter Fries, a fellow designer at the company who defended Price online, were quickly fired. Not only did the company take the side of the harassers in this case, but they also fired a woman from a job in the tech industry as a result of harassment when representation of women in the industry is already so low. We need to hold institutions accountable for siding with harassers and make it clear that women need support if they are ever going to feel welcome in the tech industry and culture.

A final suggestion is to create a "feminist social media toolbox, comprising more familiar tactics, such as how to mobilize and be heard via Facebook, Twitter, or Tumblr, as well as other approaches that users have found productive."[96] This is a more practical response to the experiences women have in the tech industry and culture. While this suggestion does place a lot of the responsibility to respond on the individual woman, most women often find themselves alone when dealing with mistreatment either in the form of not being supported in the workplace or being harassed online. Providing women with suggestions on how best to respond is a good first step. I hope this chapter will become part of some women's toolboxes in the future.

NOTES

1. Emily Gaudette, "Meet Naomi Wu, Target of an American Tech Bro Witchhunt," *Newsweek*, November 7, 2017. https://www.newsweek.com/naomi-wu-sexy-cyborg-misogyny-silicon-valley-704372
2. Kassy Cho, "A Male CEO has Apologized after Saying That This Female Tech Designer Wasn't Real," *BuzzFeed*, November 20, 2017. https://www.buzzfeednews.com/article/kassycho/a-male-ceo-has-apologized-after-saying-that-this-female#.kbvYvz5gW
3. Ibid.
4. Josh Feola, "Shenzhen Maker Naomi Wu on Twitter Wars, Chinese Tech, and Her Growing Profile," *Radii*, April 12, 2018. https://radiichina.com/shenzhen-maker-naomi-wu-on-twitter-wars-chinese-tech-and-her-growing-profile/
5. Walter Isaacson, *The Innovators: How a Group of Hackers, Geniuses, and Geeks Created the Digital Revolution* (New York: Simon & Schuster, 2014), 28-29.
6. Wendy Hui Kyong Chun, *Programmed Visions: Software and Memory* (Cambridge, MA: The MIT Press, 2011), 29.
7. Ibid.
8. Gerald Stephen Jackson, "Transcoding Sexuality: Computational Performativity and Queer Code Practices," *QED: A Journal in GLBTQ Worldmaking* 4, no. 2 (2017): 17.
9. Cherie Todd, "GamerGate and Resistance to the Diversification of Gaming Culture," *Women's Studies Journal* 29, no. 1 (2015): 66.
10. Karla Mantilla, *#Gendertrolling: How Misogyny Went Viral* (Santa Barbara: Praeger Press, 2015), 134-135.
11. Emma Alice Jane, "'Back to the Kitchen, Cunt': Speaking the Unspeakable about Online Misogyny," *Continuum: Journal of Media & Cultural Studies* 28, no. 4 (2014): 566.
12. Shira Chess and Adrienne Shaw, "A Conspiracy of Fishes, or, How We Learned to Stop Worrying About #GamerGate and Embrace Hegemonic Masculinity," *Journal of Broadcasting & Electronic Media* 59, no. 1 (2015): 208-209.
13. Sapna Cheryan, Victoria C. Plaut, Caitlin Handron and Lauren Hudson, "The Stereotypical Computer Scientist: Gendered Media Representations as a Barrier to Inclusion for Women," *Sex Roles* 69, no. 1-2 (2013): 63.
14. Ibid., 67.
15. Adrienne Shaw, "Do You Identify as a Gamer? Gender, Race, Sexuality, and Gamer Identity," *New Media & Society* 14, no. 1 (2011): 34-37.
16. Jackson, "Transcoding Sexuality" 17-18.
17. Ibid.
18. Brandee Easter, "'Feminist Brevity in Light of Masculine Long-Windedness': Codes, Space, and Online Misogyny," *Feminist Media Studies* 18, no. 4 (2018): 679.
19. Ibid., 676.
20. Rena Bivens, "The Gender Binary Will Not Be Deprogrammed: Ten Years of Coding Gender on Facebook," *New Media & Society* 19, no. 6 (2017): 888.
21. Mantilla, "#Gendertrolling" 134-135.
22. Michal Armoni and Judith Gal-Elzer, "High School Computer Science Education Paves the Way for Higher Education: The Israeli Case," *Computer Science Education* 24, no. 2-3 (2014): 112.
23. Wilfred W. F. Lau and Allan H. K. Yuen, "Exploring the Effects of Gender and Learning Styles on Computer Programming Performance: Implications for Programming Pedagogy," *British Journal of Educational Technology* 40, no. 4 (2009): 701.
24. Wendy Doubé and Catherine Lang, "Gender and Stereotypes in Motivation to Study Computer Programming for Careers in Multimedia," *Computer Science Education* 22, no. 1 (2012): 71.
25. Miguel Angel Rubio, Rocio Romero-Zaliz, Carolina Mañoso and Angel P. de Madrid, "Closing the Gender Gap in an Introductory Programming Course," *Computers & Education* 82 (2015): 416.
26. Corey Brady, Kai Orton, David Weintrop, Gabriella Anton, Sebastian Rodriguez and Uri Wilensky, "All Roads Lead to Computing: Making, Participatory Simulations, and Social

Computing as Pathways to Computer Science," *IEEE Transactions on Education* 60, no. 1 (2017): 62.

27. Ibid., 64.

28. Carolyn Cunningham, "Girl Game Designers," *New Media & Society* 13, no. 1 (2011): 1373-1384.

29. Janet Liebenberg, Elsa Mentz and Betty Breed, "Pair Programming and Secondary School Girls' Enjoyment of Programming and the Subject Information Technology (IT)," *Computer Science Education* 22, no. 3 (2012): 232.

30. Hilde G. Corneliussen & Lin Prøitz, "*Kids Code* in a Rural Village in Norway: Could Code Clubs be a New Arena for Increasing Girls' Digital Interest and Competence?," *Information, Communication & Society* 19, no. 1 (2016): 104.

31. Adrienne Shaw, "The Internet Is Full of Jerks, Because the World Is Full of Jerks: What Feminist Theory Teaches Us about the Internet," *Communication and Critical/Cultural Studies* 11, no. 3 (2014): 273.

32. Ibid., 276.

33. Kate Conger, "Exclusive: Here's the Full 10-Page Anti-Diversity Screed Circulating Internally at Google," *Gizmodo*, August 5, 2017. https://gizmodo.com/exclusive-heres-the-full-10-page-anti-diversity-screed-1797564320

34. Matt Weinberger and Steve Kovach, "The Google Employee Who Wrote the Controversial Google Memo Was Fired After CEO Sundar Pichai Called It 'Not Okay,'" *Business Insider*, August 7, 2017. https://www.businessinsider.com/google-sundar-pichai-anti-diversity-manifesto-fired-2017-8

35. Conger, "Exclusive."

36. Ibid.

37. Ibid.

38. Ibid.

39. Ibid.

40. Ibid.

41. Ibid.

42. Ibid.

43. Ibid.

44. Liebenberg et al., "Pair Programming" 232.

45. Conger, "Exclusive."

46. Ibid.

47. Ibid.

48. Ibid.

49. Ibid.

50. Ibid.

51. Ibid.

52. Ibid.

53. Ibid.

54. Ibid.

55. Weingberger and Kovach, "The Google Employee."

56. Louise Matsakis, "Labor Board Rules Google's Firing of James Damore Was Legal," *Wired*, February 16, 2018. https://www.wired.com/story/labor-board-rules-google-firing-james-damore-was-legal/

57. Danielle Keats Citron, "Law's Expressive Value in Combating Cyber Gender Harassment," *Michigan Law Review* 108, no.3 (2009): 395.

58. Kurt Borchard, "Super Columbine Massacre RPG! and Grand Theft Autoethnography," *Cultural Studies/Critical Methodologies* 15, no. 6 (2015): 449.

59. Jodi K. Biber, Dennis Doverspike, Daniel Baznik, Alana Cober and Barbara A. Ritter, "Sexual Harassment in Online Communications: Effects of Gender and Discourse Medium," *CyberPsychology & Behavior* 5, no. 1 (2002): 36-38.

60. Ibid., 38.

61. Megan Lindsay, Jaime M. Booth, Jill T. Messing and Jonel Thaller, "Experiences of Online Harassment among Emerging Adults: Emotional Reactions and the Mediating Role of Fear," *Journal of Interpersonal Violence* 31, no. 19 (2016): 3182.

62. Ibid., 3185.

63. Adrienne Massanari, "#Gamergate and The Fappening: How Reddit's Algorithm, Governance, and Culture Support Toxic Technocultures," *New Media & Society* 19, no. 3 (2017): 333.

64. Ibid.

65. Ibid.

66. David Futrelle, "Zoe Quinn's Screenshots of 4chan's Dirty Tricks Were Just the Appetizer. Here's the First Course of the Dinner, Directly from the IRC Log," *We Hunted the Mammoth*, September 8, 2014. http://www.wehuntedthemammoth.com/2014/09/08/zoe-quinns-screenshots-of-4chans-dirty-tricks-were-just-the-appetizer-heres-the-first-course-of-the-dinner-directly-from-the-irc-log/

67. Feminist Frequency, "One Week of Harassment on Twitter," January 27, 2015. https://femfreq.tumblr.com/post/109319269825/one-week-of-harassment-on-twitter

68. Erin Donnelly, "Update: Twitter Bans Top Leslie Jones Troll, Pledges to Fight Harassment," *Refinery29*, last modified July 19, 2016. https://www.refinery29.com/2016/07/117216/leslie-jones-racist-trolls

69. Constance Grady, "Star Wars Fans Harassed Kelly Marie Tran for Months. She Just Deleted Her Instagram Posts," *Vox*, June 5, 2018. https://www.vox.com/culture/2018/6/5/17429196/kelly-marie-tran-instagram-deleted-harassment-star-wars-rose-last-jedi

70. Jessica Valenti, *Sex Object* (New York: Dey Street, 2016), 193-204.

71. Lindsay et al., "Experiences of Online Harassment," 3182.

72. Nicole Arce, "Gamergate Continues: Female Video Game Developer Flees Home After Receiving Chilling Death Threats on Twitter," *Tech Times*, October 15, 2014. https://www.techtimes.com/articles/17901/20141015/gamergate-continues-female-video-game-developer-flees-home-after-receiving-chilling-death-threats-on-twitter.htm

73. Valenti, "Sex Object" 199.

74. Ibid., 198.

75. Ibid., 201.

76. Ibid., 196.

77. Ibid.

78. David Moye, "Kelly Marie Tran of 'Last Jedi' Facing Racist, Sexist Comments Online," *The Huffington Post*, last modified December 28, 2017. https://www.huffingtonpost.com/entry/kelly-marie-tran-racists-last-jedi_us_5a4400fee4b06d1621b6b2bb

79. Erin Donnelly, "Update: Twitter Bans."

80. Ibid.

81. Ibid.

82. Abby Ohlheiser, "Just How Offensive Did Milo Yiannopoulos Have to Be to Get Banned from Twitter?," *The Washington Post*, July 21, 2016. https://www.washingtonpost.com/news/the-intersect/wp/2016/07/21/what-it-takes-to-get-banned-from-twitter/?noredirect=on&utm_term=.964313b6c241

83. Kristen V. Brown, "How a Racist, Sexist Hate Mob Forced Leslie Jones off Twitter," *Splinter*, July 19, 2016. https://splinternews.com/how-a-racist-sexist-hate-mob-forced-leslie-jones-off-t-1793860398

84. Valenti, "Sex Object" 193.

85. Ibid., 199.

86. Ibid., 197.

87. Ibid., 193.

88. Moye, "Kelly Marie Tran."

89. Constance Grady, "Star Wars Fans."

90. John S. Ehrett, "E-Judiciaries: A Model for Community Policing in Cyberspace," *Information & Communications Technology Law* 25, no. 3 (2016): 288; R. Stuart Geiger, "Bot-Based Collective Blocklists in Twitter: The Counterpublic Moderation of Harassment in a Networked Public Space," *Information, Communication & Society* 19, no. 6 (2016): 795.

91. Ehrett, "E-Judiciaries" 288.
92. Lisa M. Jones and Kimberly J. Mitchell, "Defining and Measuring Youth Digital Citizenship," *New Media & Society* 18, no. 9 (2016): 2072.
93. Ibid.
94. Eve Ng, "Structural Approaches to Feminist Social Media Strategies: Institutional Governance and a Social Media Toolbox," *Feminist Media Studies* 15, no. 4 (2015): 719.
95. Owen S. Good and Michael McWhertor, "Guild Wars Developers Fired after Social Media Argument Roils Community," *Polygon*, July 6, 2018. https://www.polygon.com/2018/7/6/17540382/guild-wars-2-developers-fired-arenanet
96. Ng, "Structural Approaches" 720.

Conclusion

In *Genderblindness in American Society*, my purpose has been to analyze the rhetoric of genderblindness. Genderblindness is the current ideology that guides social control of women in American society. It is built on the principles that gender no longer matters in issues of relevance to public life and that since men and women are already equal in society, people should be judged only as individuals. This ideology has the material effects of reducing women's life chances by restricting their access to the full benefits of an equal ability to participate in public life and compelling them to monitor their individual behavior in order to ensure that it fits within a system in which gender and other forms of discrimination are no longer in effect. Genderblind rhetoric supports these ideological goals by seeking to remove gender as a means of public persuasive appeal. In a genderblind system, gender is no longer relevant in public life or people's lived experiences so efforts to organize around gender are deemed illegitimate. When gender is raised or seems relevant in public life, genderblind rhetoric is employed to show that the issue is not really about gender, to take a neutral, objective stance that makes decisions about women's lives without directly addressing their actual needs, or aggressively working to shape their behavior in ways that fit the current dominant ideology. Genderblind rhetoric does not create the material effects of the ideology, but it does work to encourage them.

In order to analyze the rhetoric of genderblindness, I employed a critical rhetoric approach. Critical rhetoric analyzes discourse as the tactical dimension of reinforcing existing power relations and creating new ones. As a means of analyzing discourse, critical rhetoric utilizes the critique of domination and critique of freedom. A critique of domination focuses on how discourse is used to control the lives of marginalized and oppressed groups in accordance with the ideologies of the dominant groups in society. In analyzing genderblind rhetoric, I conducted critiques of domination of denials of the gender wage gap, rhetoric in support of TRAP laws that restrict abortion access, rape apologia intended to defend and recuperate the images of rapists, and biologically determinist conceptions of the skills of women and men in the tech industry. These examples of genderblind rhetoric seek to control the life chances of women by working to restrict their equal access to public life. The rhetoric here is often grounded in the character of the speaker or writer, arguing that they should be believed because of who they are as individuals. Ben Shapiro and Jordan Peterson want the audience to just accept their claims about the wage gap as self-evident fact, Brock Turner and Daniel Holtzclaw want the audience to know that they are not the kind of people who would ever disobey authority so they can be trusted even though they committed heinous acts, and James Damore wants the audience to know that he does not have a problem with diversity—he just wants everyone to receive equal treatment, including conservative white men. This focus on the individual's ethos downplays the negative effects of their rhetoric by keeping the focus on them rather on what they are saying.

This rhetoric is also grounded in the idea that the speaker has the best interests of those involved at heart. Scott Keller in defending Texas's TRAP laws wants the audience to believe that the state is guided by protecting women's safety even though he cannot provide adequate evidence that women are actually at risk, Shapiro and Peterson just want to ensure that the benefits of the current workplace structure are not lost in our efforts to achieve equality, Damore wants to make sure that Google does not lose money by hiring less qualified individuals in an effort to increase diversity, and Turner and Holtzclaw just want to help others avoid the mistakes they made, like drinking too much and trying too hard to be professional athletes. The focus on the ethos of the individual and the belief that they have the best interests of others at heart helps to achieve the ideological goals of genderblindness by casting its proponents as just concerned individuals trying their best to find workable solutions to society's problems. Women find their ability to access public life to be more restricted while those working to limit their access are seen as upstanding individuals with only the best intentions. Reducing the effectiveness of the ethos of those who seek to control women's lives is paramount to resisting the rhetoric of genderblindness.

Along with a critique of domination, I also conducted critiques of freedom of the different areas of genderblind rhetoric. A critique of freedom focuses on the creative uses of power in which a new status quo is created in response to shifts in social relations. Even in creating a new status quo, power still constrains people's abilities to live their lives. Critiques of freedom were conducted through analyses of self-help books for women in the workplace, the rhetoric of crisis pregnancy centers, manifestations of rape culture in the resistance to changing conceptions of rape and women's status as victims, and online harassment of women that seeks to make women feel unwelcome in online spaces. The main purpose of this rhetoric is to make women change their behavior in order to conform to existing norms. Self-help writers encourage women to conform to existing standards in the workplace if they want to succeed; crisis pregnancy centers work to prevent women from having abortions by presenting the procedure as unsafe, unhealthy, and immoral; Katie Roiphe wants women to police their own behavior in order to avoid confusing rape with just bad sex; and online harassers want women to remove themselves entirely from online spaces in order to avoid continued harassment. The effects of this rhetoric is that women are less free to be active participants in public life because they must be always on guard so that their behavior does not lead to attacks and harassment. All of the energy that women could be devoting to improving their lives and the world around them is instead direct inward to make sure their behavior does not draw unwanted attention.

Another major aspect of this rhetoric is to present men and women as already equal so any appeals to gender are illegitimate. Genderblind rhetoric in these areas accepts that some progress has taken place but argues that the progress that has been made is far enough to consider men and women equal. This new status quo is then used against women who push for greater change. Roiphe wants women to avoid identifying with each other as victims and instead embrace their own power, crisis pregnancy centers want their anti-abortion positions to be accepted as a legitimate choice, self-help writers make some acknowledgment of the continuing systemic issues affecting women in the workplace but believe that becoming leaders within the existing system without changing it is all that is need to achieve equality, and online harassers conceive of online spaces as egalitarian and open to all so any women who bring attention to their harassment are just looking for special treatment beyond what is available to everyone else. By conceiving of the fight for gender equality as already won, genderblind rhetoric leads to further attacks on any woman who is continuing to fight.

A final aspect of this rhetoric are the appeals made to some higher value that goes beyond mere gender equality. Crisis pregnancy centers present their work as God's calling to preserve the traditional family; online harassers conceive of online spaces as driven by merit while women who exist in these spaces and bring attention to their harassment are doing so for special treatment or personal financial gain; self-help writers view individual success as the true sign of empowerment rather than changing the system to benefit all women; and Roiphe wants women to embrace her form of individualized empowerment rather than the sense of community that comes from shared lived experiences. Through their appeals to what are perceived as higher values, the speakers and writers using genderblind rhetoric present themselves as devoted to the benefit of everyone while those women still fighting for gender equality are positioned as interested in only their own advancement. The new status quo of perceived equality allows these speakers and writers to look beyond the quotidian issues of gender to what is truly important.

In both a critique of domination and a critique of freedom, it is obvious that the rhetoric of genderblindness makes it more difficult for women to speak out on the gendered nature of their experiences and organize to end discrimination because other explanations are privileged instead. These explanations downplay the systemic nature of the marginalization and discrimination women currently experience in American society in favor of an ideology of personal responsibility and individual freedom. The privileging of this perspective will continue to stifle efforts to achieve gender equality and justice by keeping women isolated in their efforts to seek change by the belief that what they are experiencing is unique to them as individuals. In order to counter this ideology, we need to search for solutions that benefit all women, all who operate under the sign "woman," as Sara Ahmed argues,[1] rather than hoping that enough advancement for individual women will eventually lead to the betterment of all.

Genderblindness as an ideology works to limit women's ability to achieve equality in all aspects of life. Before things seem too bleak, I want to offer some examples of women organizing and speaking out against genderblindness. The main way to resist genderblind rhetoric is to shift the discourse so that gender is made central to the discussion of relevant issues and so that women are addressed as a united, diverse group. These efforts must recognize how gender intersects with other identities rather than arguing for a universal experience for all women while also avoiding cultural pressures to isolate women as individuals who share no common bonds. The Women's March on Washington and the #MeToo movement offer examples for what a resistance to genderblindness might look like.

The Women's March on Washington took place on January 21, 2017, the day after President Donald Trump's inauguration, and was organized by a diverse group of women, led by national co-chairs Bob Bland, Tamika D. Mallory, Carmen Perez, and Linda Sarsour.[2] While the main march in Washington attracted hundreds of thousands of protestors, millions more women and their allies marched in similar events across the country.[3] While the main purpose of the March was to protest the election of a misogynist like Donald Trump as president, the March also served as a show of solidarity among a wide group of women, sought to bring women's issues to national attention, and connected gender to other identities and prominent issues in the country. In her speech to the March on Washington, national co-chair Carmen Perez centers her approach to the fight for gender justice in her identity as "a Chicana Mexican-American woman" and her work fighting for prison reform.[4] She then identifies the need for collective effort, saying,

> We know what the problems are. We know who our enemy is. We know what the injustices have done to us and those we love. But to overcome them we have to stand in solidarity. We have to listen to each other and know that we always have more to learn. To protect each other, we don't always have to agree with one another. But we *have* to organize and stand together. We must remember that unity of action does not mean we have to be unanimous in thought, but that an injury to one is an injury to all.[5]

Perez recognizes that everyone involved in the March will not agree on every issue, but she also stresses to her audience that none of their issues will be addressed without collective effort. Resisting genderblindness does not demand universal agreement on all issues, but it does depend on a united effort to re-center gender in public discourse.

Perez also makes it clear that the March recognizes the intersectional nature of gender justice by highlighting other issues that must be addressed if true justice is ever to be achieved, saying,

> We will hold all officials—whether elected or appointed—accountable. There are some in this country who say we should work with and adjust to hatred. But Dr. Martin Luther King spoke of the power of being maladjusted to an unjust society. We will *not* adjust to hatred and bigotry. We will resist islamophobia, xenophobia, white supremacy, sexism, racism, misogyny, and ableism. We will be brave, intentional, and unapologetic in addressing the intersections of our identities. And collectively we will stand up for the most marginalized among us—because *they* are us.[6]

Perez's argument that the Women's March should represent an intersectional approach to gender is echoed in the speech given in Washington by civil rights activist Angela Davis, saying, "This is a women's march and this women's march represents the promise of feminism as against the pernicious powers of state violence. And inclusive and intersectional feminism that calls upon all of us to join the resistance to racism, to Islamophobia, to anti-Semitism, to misogyny, to capitalist exploitation."[7] The vision put forward by Perez and Davis is also echoed by trans rights activist Janet Mock in her speech in Washington, saying,

> Our approach to freedom need not be identical but it must be intersectional and inclusive. It must extend beyond ourselves. I know with surpassing certainty that my liberation is directly linked to the liberation of the undocumented trans Latina yearning for refuge. The disabled student seeking unequivocal access. The sex worker fighting to make her living safely.[8]

The Women's March on Washington serves as an excellent example of how to resist genderblindness by seeking to mobilize a collective effort to fight for an intersectional gender justice that places women's voices at the forefront and recognizes that gender's connections to other identities and issues increases the relevancy of gender in our public discourse rather than pushing it to the side as unimportant. The #MeToo movement to bring attention to the prevalence of rape and sexual assault in America and to hold the perpetrators accountable also exhibits these qualities.

In 2006, Tarana Burke began the Me Too campaign to let survivors of sexual violence know that they were heard,[9] and the movement gained more attention in 2017 when #MeToo began being used on Twitter by women to acknowledge their own status as survivors of rape and sexual assault in light of the accusations of sexual assault against powerful Hollywood producer Harvey Weinstein by numerous women.[10] While most of the attention given to the #MeToo movement has focused on the naming of perpetrators of sexual violence, Burke, in an April 2018 speech at the *Variety* Power of Women event, sought to bring the focus back to survivors, saying, "With two words, folks that have been wearing the fear and shame that sexual violence leaves you with like a scarlet letter, are able to come out into the sunlight and see that we are a global community."[11] Burke's statement as a leader of the #MeToo movement reminds us of the importance of the collective community that must develop around the resistance to genderblindness. Being part of such a community and recognizing that you are not alone in your experiences can be a profound, transforming experience for many women and should not be ignored in our efforts to fight for gender justice.

Actress Rose McGowan, a vocal member of the #MeToo movement who has spoken frequently about being sexually assaulted by Harvey Weinstein, encourages women to continue their efforts to speak up about their experiences of being raped or sexually assaulted at the Women's Convention in Detroit in October 2017, saying, "No more. Name it. Shame it. Call it out. Join me, join all of us as we amplify each other's voices and we do what is right for us and for our sisters and for this planet, mother Earth."[12] While McGowan is more focused on calling public attention to the perpetrators of sexual violence, she, like Burke, also clearly recognizes the collective nature of her efforts, saying,

> I want to thank you for being here, for giving me wings during this very difficult time. The triggering has been insane. The monster's face everywhere, my nightmare. But I know I'm not alone because I'm just the same as the girl in the tiny little town who was raped by the football squad, and they have full dominance and control over the little town newspaper. There really is no actual difference. It's the same situation, and that situation must end because it is not our shame. The scarlet letter is theirs. It is not ours. We are pure, we are strong, we are brave and we will fight. Pussies grab back. Women grab back. We speak, we yell, we march, we are here, we will not go away.[13]

McGowan is intentional here in here decision to draw an analogy between herself and an unknown young woman in a small town because the easiest way to push back against McGowan would be to claim that she is only being listened to because of her status as a celebrity. Instead, McGowan argues that her voice is relevant because of the experience she shares with many other women, and she will use the platform available to her to continue to bring attention to that shared experience of sexual violence. The continued focus by national figures on the collective nature of the fight for gender justice should give all of us hope for the success of the cause.

While the Women's March and the #MeToo movement serve as hopeful examples for resisting the rhetoric of genderblindness, we should also be concerned that genderblindness could end as a system of social control of women not as a result of efforts to achieve gender justice but as a result of a coarsening of our discourse that reflects efforts to move back to previous systems of control. This is most clearly seen in statements made by President Donald Trump. In the infamous *Access Hollywood* tape that was released in October 2016 ahead of the 2016 presidential election, Trump is heard talking about his efforts to seduce a married woman, saying, "I moved on her like a bitch, but I couldn't get there."[14] Trump then describes himself as unable to control himself around women, saying, "You know I'm automatically attracted to beautiful—I just start kissing them. It's like a magnet. Just kiss. I don't even wait."[15] Trump ends by talking about using his celebrity status to hit on women, saying, "And when you're a star, they let you do it. You can do anything . . . Grab them by the pussy. You can do anything."[16] When combined with Trump's other statements publicly demeaning women, such as his assertion in August 2015 that then-*Fox News* host Megyn Kelly could not objectively moderate a debate because she had "[b]lood coming out of her wherever,"[17] a misogynistic and sexist attitude that women should not be equal participants in public life is revealed. Should Trump's attitude toward women become dominant, the era of genderblindness will come to an end but not because women have achieved a share of gender justice but because the public discourse will have become even more marginalizing and discriminatory against women.

The Women's March on Washington and the #MeToo movement offer models for how to resist the rhetoric of genderblindness by centering women's voices and drawing clear connections between gender and other relevant identities and issues. These efforts should offer us hope for ending the current era of genderblindness, but Donald Trump's demeaning public statements remind us that forward progress is not a given. Genderblindness as a system of social control of women will only end once true gender equality and justice have been achieved. Hopefully, this book has offered some help in achieving this goal by showing how genderblindness dominates the current public discourse and limits the persuasive appeals available for addressing gender marginalization and discrimination.

NOTES

1. Sara Ahmed, *Living a Feminist Life* (Durham, NC: Duke University Press, 2017), 14-15.

2. Emily Crockett, "The 'Women's March on Washington,' Explained," *Vox*, last updated January 21, 2017. https://www.vox.com/identities/2016/11/21/13651804/women-march-washington-trump-inauguration

3. Sarah Frostenson, "The Women's Marches May Have Been the Largest Demonstration in US History," *Vox*, last updated January 31, 2017. https://www.vox.com/2017/1/22/14350808/womens-marches-largest-demonstration-us-history-map

4. Perez, Carmen, "Women's March on Washington Speech," 1, Last accessed March 12, 2019. https://static1.squarespace.com/static/55ddb058e4b07360409f7c32/t/5893ba55893fc09b19ce5b20/1486076502311/CP_WM_Speech.pdf

5. Ibid.

6. Ibid., 2.

7. Lyndsey Matthews, "Here's the Full Transcript of Angela Davis's Women's March Speech," *Elle*, January 21, 2017. https://www.elle.com/culture/career-politics/a42337/angela-davis-womens-march-speech-full-transcript/

8. Catie L'Heureux, "Read Janet Mock's Empowering Speech on Trans Women of Color and Sex Workers," *The Cut*, January 21, 2017. https://www.thecut.com/2017/01/read-janet-mocks-speech-at-the-womens-march-on-washington-trans-women-of-color-sex-workers.html

9. Tara Bitran, "Tarana Burke on Me Too: 'It's a Mistake to Think of This as a Moment," *Variety*, April 13, 2018. https://variety.com/2018/biz/news/viola-davis-tarana-burke-power-of-women-1202751993/

10. Anna North, "'For Every Harvey Weinstein, There's a Hundred More Men in the Neighborhood who are Doing the Exact Same Thing,'" *Vox*, October 28, 2017. https://www.vox.com/2017/10/28/16563668/me-too-tarana-burke-harvey-weinstein-harassment-assault

11. Bitran, "Tarana Burke."

12. Katie Reilly, "'No More.' Read Rose McGowan's First Public Remarks since Accusing Harvey Weinstein of Rape," *Time*, October 27, 2017. http://time.com/5000381/rose-mcgowan-harvey-weinstein-speech-transcript/

13. Ibid.

14. David A. Fahrenthold, "Trump Recorded Having Extremely Lewd Conversation about Women in 2005," *The Washington Post*, October 8, 2016. https://www.washingtonpost.com/politics/trump-recorded-having-extremely-lewd-conversation-about-women-in-2005/2016/10/07/3b9ce776-8cb4-11e6-bf8a-3d26847eeed4_story.html?utm_term=.9c997791d29b

15. Ibid.

16. Ibid.

17. Holly Yan, "Donald Trump's 'Blood' Comment about Megyn Kelly Draws Outrage," *CNN*, last updated August 8, 2015. https://www.cnn.com/2015/08/08/politics/donald-trump-cnn-megyn-kelly-comment/index.html

Index

1st Way Life Center, 69, 72, 76
20/20, 92
2016 presidential election, 1, 153

ableism, 151
abortion, 16, 53, 55, 57, 58, 60, 65, 67, 68–69, 72, 73, 76, 77, 78, 79, 80, 148; access, 53, 54, 55, 57, 58, 59, 60, 64, 66, 67, 70, 73, 75, 76, 78, 79, 147; admitting privileges, 58, 64, 65, 81n32; ambulatory surgical center (ASC), 58, 61, 64–65; choice, 6, 16, 53, 54, 55, 57, 68, 69, 70, 75, 76, 77, 78, 79, 149; civil rights, 54; clinics, 58, 61, 63, 64, 73; complications, 60, 62, 65; discrimination, 54; health, 53, 57, 69, 78, 80, 148; legal position, 55; legal status, 67, 68, 78–79; medically-induced, 60, 65; moral position, 55, 68, 70, 73, 78, 148; narrative, 54; normalization, 54; personhood amendments, 6, 55, 58; politics, 55, 58, 63, 70, 73, 78; pro-choice, 54, 55, 68, 77, 78; pro-life, 54, 67, 77, 138; providers, 58, 64, 81n32; public opinion, 59, 61, 62, 63; rights, 6, 53, 63, 66, 68, 80; risk, 148; safety, 59, 60, 61, 62, 63, 64, 65, 66, 148; social disapproval, 53; state regulations, 53, 54, 55, 58, 59, 60, 62, 64, 65, 66, 68, 79, 148; stigma, 54; storytelling, 54; stress, 53; surgery, 60, 63; Targeted Regulation of Abortion Providers (TRAP) laws, 6, 16, 53, 58, 59, 60, 61, 62, 63, 66, 68, 79, 147; undue burden, 64
acceptance, 117
Access Hollywood, 153
advice, 23, 30, 31, 32, 34, 36, 37, 38, 40, 43, 46
ageism, 40
agency, 9, 31, 98, 100, 103, 104, 105
Ahmed, Sara, 13, 97, 150
Alexander, Michelle, 5
Alito, Samuel, 63
All the Money in the World, 21
Amoruso, Sophia, 15, 23, 32, 39, 45
anger, 69, 76, 128, 130
anti-abortion activism/movement, 53, 54, 55, 56, 57, 63, 67, 71, 75, 76, 77, 78, 79; apocalyptic, 55; over-weighing, 54; rhetoric, 53, 54, 55, 68, 79; testimony, 72, 73, 74, 75
anti-Semitism, 151
anxiety, 130
apologia, 88, 90, 94, 95, 100
ArenaNet, 141
Arnold, Jeff, 87, 90, 91, 94, 95, 96, 97, 99
ascribed identity, 132
audience, 12, 13, 24, 28, 29, 46, 77, 94, 126, 147, 151
authority, 14, 31, 36, 100, 112, 113

Index

baby, 68, 70, 72, 73, 74, 75, 77, 78, 138
backlash, 6
Battlestar Galactica, 133
Bennett, Jessica, 15, 23, 32, 36, 47
Bethany Christian Services, 69, 70, 71, 74, 75
bigotry, 132, 151
biological determinism, 16, 115, 116, 118, 119, 121, 123, 124, 140, 147; traits, 119, 120, 121, 124
biopolitics, 8, 9, 22, 24, 30, 55, 57
Birthright, 69, 70, 73, 74
blame, 33, 85, 87, 88, 89, 95, 97, 102
Bland, Bob, 150
bodily autonomy, 80
Bonilla-Silva, Eduardo, 5
Bourdieu, Pierre, 92
Breitbart, 22
Breyer, Stephen, 60, 61, 66
Brownmiller, Susan, 86
Burke, Tarana, 152

Care Net, 69, 70, 71, 75, 77, 78
Channel 4, 24, 25
character, 147
Charland, Maurice, 12
children, 53, 55, 69, 71, 78, 80, 92, 101, 131
Christian, 14, 68, 71, 72, 74; Evangelical, 71, 72
class, 2, 14, 55, 66, 89, 90, 92, 93, 95, 104, 123
Clinton, Hillary, 1
Cloud, Dana, 8, 11, 30
CNN, 91
colorblindness, 5; considerations of race, 5; individual success, 5, 6; mass incarceration, 6
community, 152
compassion, 77
computer, 112, 113
computer science, 114; education, 114, 115
confidence, 42, 43, 45, 47
conformity, 8, 22, 30, 31, 34, 36, 37, 38, 41, 43, 46, 57, 148
control, 1, 3, 5, 9, 12, 13, 16, 22, 30, 57, 59, 64, 66, 79, 80, 86, 87, 88, 100, 104, 105, 113, 115, 130, 133, 147, 153; system of control, 5, 6

Cosby, Bill, 85
Cosby, Camille, 85, 87
crisis pregnancy center, 16, 53, 57, 67, 68, 69, 70, 71, 72, 73, 74, 75, 76, 77, 78, 79, 101, 148, 149
critic, 13
critical race theory, 5
critical rhetoric, 11, 12, 26, 147; critique of domination, 11, 12, 15, 16, 22, 57, 58, 87, 88, 115, 147, 150; critique of freedom, 11, 12, 15, 16, 23, 57, 67, 87, 100, 115, 127, 147, 148, 150; *telos*, 12

The Daily Wire, 22, 24
Damore, James, 16, 115, 116–127, 140, 148
Davis, Angela, 151
de Beauvoir, Simone, 13
Depression Quest, 128
DiAngelo, Robin, 91
difference, 5
digital citizenship, 141
disciplinary power, 8, 9, 22, 31, 57
discourse, 2–3, 4, 8, 11, 12, 54, 55–57, 104, 112, 147, 150, 151, 152, 153
Disney, 139
diversity, 22, 114, 115, 133
doubt, 76
Dougherty, Dale, 111
Douglas, Susan, 10
Duke lacrosse case, 91

Eastern Michigan University, 97
echo chamber, 116, 117
emotional appeal, 69, 70, 76
empathy, 104, 119, 124
empowerment, 1, 9, 31, 43, 100, 101, 102, 103, 149
Enid, Oklahoma, 95
equality, 1, 3, 6, 9, 12, 22, 24, 27, 28, 45, 47, 59, 86, 100, 102, 104, 112, 125, 126, 139, 149, 150, 153
ethnicity, 132, 133
ethos, 25, 26, 28, 29, 44, 94, 147

Facebook, 32, 114, 132, 141
family planning, 54
fat shaming, 131, 133

Index

fear, 42, 43, 69, 70, 78, 86, 87, 100, 126, 128, 130
feminine, 13, 14, 40, 43, 50n100, 54, 67, 102, 104, 112, 132
feminism/feminist, 9, 13, 28, 86, 100, 101, 112, 113, 115, 128, 130, 131, 133, 136, 137, 138, 139, 151; second wave, 9; third wave, 9
Feminist Frequency, 128
feminist social media toolbox, 141
Feministing, 128
fetus, 6, 16, 54, 55, 57
Fifth Amendment, 85
First Amendment, 68, 85
football, 87, 94, 95, 97, 105
Fox News, 153
Foucault, Michel, 8
Fourteenth Amendment, 85
framing, 2, 3, 5, 6, 8, 9, 16, 22, 30, 37, 39, 43, 46, 53, 55, 66, 68, 69, 70, 71, 75, 76, 77, 78, 94, 95, 97, 106, 116, 118, 125, 129, 133, 135, 136, 137, 138, 139
Frankel, Lois, 23, 32, 35, 36, 37, 40
freedom, 1, 3, 10, 16, 59, 66, 68, 75, 76, 78, 79, 99, 100, 126, 151
Fries, Peter, 141
frustration, 130

Gay, Roxane, 104
gamer, 113, 136
GamerGate, 128
gaming culture, 112, 131, 136
gender, 1, 2, 12, 13, 17, 24, 43, 53, 89, 92, 104, 105, 114, 115, 116, 117, 126, 128, 129, 131, 139, 140, 147, 149, 150, 151, 153; binary, 114; discrimination, 3, 10, 19n42, 27, 32, 34, 36, 37, 120, 125; essentialism, 13; gender roles, 7, 123; socialization, 35, 42
gender identity, 13, 19n42, 123
gender non-conforming, 6, 80
gender pay equity, 45
gender representation, 128, 138
gender wage gap, 3, 6, 11, 15, 21, 25, 28, 31, 33, 41, 46, 147; age, 21; class, 21; competition, 22; denial, 22, 24, 26, 29, 30, 46, 147; education, 21; ideal worker norm, 43, 50n100; mothers, 22; race, 21; risk taking, 42, 43; statistics, 21;

sticky floor, 22
genderblindness, 1, 2, 3, 9, 10, 12, 15, 17, 24, 30, 31, 34, 43, 46, 50n100, 56, 57, 59, 61, 62, 66, 69, 79, 80, 86, 87, 88, 91, 93, 99, 100, 101, 104, 105, 111, 115, 116, 117, 126, 127, 128, 129, 139, 140, 147, 148, 149, 150, 151, 153; axes of control, 6; and colorblindness, 6; framing, 3
Ghostbusters, 128, 134
The Ghostbusters (TV series), 134
Ginsburg, Ruth Bader, 60, 62, 64, 65
#GIRLBOSS, 15, 23
glass ceiling, 22
glass cliff, 42
God, 67, 69, 71, 74, 76, 77, 78, 149
Google, 47, 115, 116, 117, 121, 122, 123, 126, 140, 148
Google memo, 16, 115, 116–127
Gosnell, Kermit, 61, 62, 63
governmentality, 9
guilt, 43, 75, 97

Hall, Stuart, 2
happiness, 31
Harambe, 134
harassment, 32, 47, 132
hard work, 95
Hariman, Robert, 12
Harlow, Poppy, 92
hatred, 151
Heartbeat International, 69, 71, 75, 77
hegemony, 105
heteronormative, 15, 30, 67, 68, 70, 71
hierarchy, 29, 116, 117, 122
Hill, Sharday, 90
Holtzclaw, Daniel, 16, 87, 89, 90, 91, 92–95, 97–98, 99–100, 105–106, 148
hope, 70, 77
hostile environment, 126
Hunt, Darryl, 85
Hyde Amendment, 55

ideograph, 54
ideology, 1–2, 2, 4–5, 6, 8, 11, 12–13, 17, 30, 43, 46, 50n100, 54, 57, 59, 63, 78, 79, 87–88, 91, 100, 104, 115, 116, 125, 137, 140, 147–148, 150; critique, 8, 13; definition, 2; goals, 1, 104, 116, 147,

148; material effects, 8, 10, 11, 22, 24, 30, 31, 55, 57, 66, 79, 87, 147
in the closet, 123
individual, 1, 9, 24, 29, 31, 68, 70, 73, 80, 86, 88, 89, 91, 94, 97, 100, 104, 106, 115, 123, 127, 128, 140, 141, 147, 150; choice, 9; freedom, 9, 11, 15, 17, 55, 78, 123, 150; merit, 7, 31, 117; relationship to others, 106; responsibility, 2, 7, 30, 32, 33, 34, 45, 86, 87, 91, 96, 97, 99, 100, 102, 103, 104, 106, 150; success, 9, 10, 15, 29, 31, 32, 33, 35, 38, 42, 43, 44, 45, 105, 106, 149
Instagram, 16, 128, 139
Internet, 16
intersectionality, 13, 21, 43, 53, 55, 89, 90, 92, 93, 115, 132, 135, 150, 151
Islamophobia, 151
isolation, 15, 70, 78, 150

Jesus Christ, 71, 72, 77
Jones, Leslie, 16, 128–129, 134–135
justice, 9, 47, 126, 139, 150, 151, 152, 153

Kagan, Elena, 61
Kavanagh, Brett, 53, 79
Keller, Scott, 58, 60, 61, 62, 63, 64, 65, 148
Kelly, Megyn, 153
Kennedy, Anthony, 53, 60, 79
Kickstarter, 128
King Kong, 134
King, Martin Luther, 151
Kotaku, 130

leadership, 15, 22, 31, 35, 36, 45, 46, 47, 120, 121, 149
Lean In, 15, 23
Ledbetter, Lily, 7
LGBTQ+, 123
Ligons, Jannie, 90
loneliness, 69, 70, 76, 78
Lorde, Audre, 47
love, 69, 70, 71
Lovelace, Ada, 112
Lublin, Joann, 15, 23, 32, 35, 38, 40, 41, 42, 45, 47

maker, 111
male fragility, 91, 92
Mallory, Tameka, 150
Marcus, Sharon, 103
marginalization, 3, 4, 8, 11, 12, 13, 22, 31, 43, 102, 115, 116, 123, 132, 147, 150, 151, 153
masculine, 1, 14, 16, 91, 92, 104, 112, 113, 128, 136
McCrory, Pat, 6
McGee, Michael, 3
McGowan, Rose, 152, 153
McKerrow, Raymie, 11, 12
McRobbie, Angela, 10
media, 8, 55, 77, 85, 91, 92, 137, 138
#MeToo movement, 17, 150, 151, 153
microaggressions, 126
misogyny, 6, 9, 17, 111, 126, 128, 133, 136, 150, 151, 153
Mock, Janet, 151
The Morning After, 16, 87, 100

Nasty Gal, 32
National Football League (NFL), 90, 91, 95, 97
national identity, 55
National Institute of Family and Life Advocates v. Becerra, 68
National Labor Relations Board, 126
neoliberal, 9
New Mexico, 64
The New York Times, 32, 91
Newman, Cathy, 26, 28, 29
North Carolina House Bill 2, 6
The Nurturing Network, 69, 75

Oklahoma City, 90, 92, 95
online harassment, 16, 111, 115–116, 126–140, 148–149; acting in bad faith, 135, 140; amplification, 132, 133, 135; anonymous, 127; blocking, 141; death threats, 129, 130, 131, 132, 133, 135, 139; discursive norms, 130, 140; dismissal of, 127, 130, 131; disproportionate, 129; en masse, 129, 130; group membership, 127; institutional responses, 141; mental and emotional effects, 128, 130; normalization, 131; Othering, 128;

playing the victim, 136; pleasure, 127; rite of passage, 115, 131; seeking attention, 129, 135, 136, 137, 149; special treatment, 129, 149; status and engagement, 135; toxic technocultures, 128; violence, 130, 132; virtual harm, 127; women as repressive, 129, 137; women's appearance, 129, 132, 133, 135, 139
online space, 16, 113, 115–116, 127, 128, 129, 130, 131, 132, 136, 138, 139, 140–141, 149
Ono, Kent, 12
oppression, 6, 7, 8, 9, 11, 12, 13, 31, 43, 99, 102, 104, 105, 147
Option Line, 69, 76

Park, Grace, 133
partisanship, 58
Patreon, 111
patriarchy, 10, 14, 15, 29, 59, 112
peer pressure, 96, 97, 101, 105
Perez, Carmen, 150, 151
performance-enhancing drugs, 87, 95
Persky, Aaron, 91, 98
persona, 89, 90, 111; first persona, 90; second persona, 90; third persona, 90
persuasive appeal, 1, 12, 17, 30, 46, 72, 74, 76, 79, 126, 128, 139, 147, 153
Peterson, Jordan, 15, 23, 24, 25–27, 28–29, 36, 148
Planned Parenthood, 61, 63
Planned Parenthood v. Casey, 64, 65
Plummer, Christopher, 21
police/law enforcement, 90, 91, 92, 94, 95, 98, 99, 105
police brutality, 95
policy, 6, 10, 11, 62, 64, 66, 101, 104, 126
politician, 14, 63, 104
postfeminist, 9, 101
power, 1, 11, 12, 36, 47, 77, 86, 87, 90, 92, 94, 95, 99, 100, 101, 103, 104, 105, 106, 113, 147, 148
power feminism, 101–102
president, 1, 17, 150; masculinity, 1
Price, Jessica, 141
Princeton University, 100
prison, 89
prison reform, 150

privilege, 9, 14, 28, 40, 47, 56, 86, 88, 98, 99, 105, 150
propaganda, 138
public life, 1, 12, 79, 87, 89, 116, 138, 147, 148, 153
public space, 1, 16, 80, 100, 132, 133
public sphere, 9, 15, 54, 104
Pulse nightclub shooting, 92

Quinn, Zoë, 16, 128, 130, 135, 136, 138

race, 5, 6, 55, 89, 90, 92, 93, 95, 104, 123, 128, 132, 133, 134, 135
racism, 5, 88, 125, 132, 133, 134, 139, 151
rage, 99
rape, 11, 16, 85, 87, 88, 89, 91, 92, 94, 96, 98, 100, 101, 102, 103, 104, 105, 131, 132, 133, 148, 151; alcohol, 87, 89, 94, 96, 97, 98, 101, 104, 105, 148; blaming the victim, 85, 91, 94, 100, 102, 105; bodily comportment, 86, 104; coercion, 101, 102; college, 87, 96, 98, 100, 103, 105; consent, 101; date rape, 86, 87, 100; false allegations, 91; individualization, 86, 87; legitimacy, 101; potential, 91; power, 86, 87, 89, 90, 92, 94, 95, 99, 100, 101, 103; prevention, 86, 103, 104, 105; self-defense, 103; shadowboxing, 86; stress, 87; victimization, 87, 91, 99, 100, 102, 105; victims, 85, 90, 100, 103, 104, 106, 148, 149; violence, 86, 91, 92, 93, 101, 103, 104, 153
rape apologia, 16, 87, 88, 90, 91, 92, 93, 94, 95, 96, 97, 100, 104, 105, 106; alternative explanation, 95, 96, 97, 100; character, 97, 99, 100; differentiation, 98, 100; external cause, 94, 96, 97, 99, 105
rape culture, 3, 16, 85, 86, 87, 88, 89, 91, 92, 100, 104, 106, 131, 148
Reagan, Ronald, 53
reflexivity, 13
regret, 76, 91
religion, 53, 67, 75, 77, 81n32, 123
religious freedom, 6
respect, 78, 117
Roberts, John, 63
Robertson, Pat, 138

Roe v. Wade, 53, 54, 57
Roiphe, Katie, 16, 87, 100, 102, 103, 148
Rolling Stone, 91
Rose, Nikolas, 9
Rowe, Aimee Carillo, 106

sadness, 76
Sandberg, Sheryl, 15, 23, 32, 33, 36, 40, 42, 43, 45, 47
Sanger, Margaret, 54
Sarkeesian, Anita, 16, 128, 130, 131, 132, 133, 135, 136, 138, 139
Sarsour, Linda, 150
SB Nation, 90, 94, 95
Scott, Ridley, 21
self-fulfilling prophecy, 40
self-help, 23, 30, 31, 32, 33, 34, 36, 38, 43, 45, 46, 105, 148, 149
self-police, 9, 10, 16, 19n42, 23, 38, 43, 44, 45, 46, 132
Selman, Cortland, 94
sensitivity, 126
Serano, Julia, 14
Sex Object, 128
sex worker, 151
sexism, 3, 9, 17, 32, 111, 112, 117, 125, 126, 151, 153
sexual assault. *See* rape
sexual harassment, 34, 38, 41
sexuality/sexual orientation, 14, 71, 104, 123, 128
shame, 91, 97, 100, 152
shaming, 117
Shapiro, Ben, 15, 22, 24, 26, 28, 147
Shenzhen, China, 111
silence, 5, 47, 78, 90, 91, 93, 100, 104
silencing, 117, 128, 129, 137, 140
Sloop, John, 12
SlutWalk, 131
smile, 133
social constructionism, 13, 118, 119
social contract, 97
solidarity, 104, 150, 151
Sotomayor, Sonia, 60, 62, 64, 65
Spacey, Kevin, 21
St. John v. General Motors, 21
Stanford University, 89, 94, 96, 98
state violence, 151

status quo, 2, 9, 15, 27, 29, 31, 33, 57, 67, 68, 75, 78, 87, 104, 106, 119, 122, 148, 149
Star Wars, 16, 133, 139
Star Wars: Episode 1 – The Phantom Menace, 139
Star Wars: The Last Jedi, 128, 133
Steubenville, Ohio, 91
suicide, 127, 130, 132, 136, 138
Supreme Court, 53, 57, 58, 66, 68, 79
symbolic violence, 92
sympathy, 98, 104, 137

Take Back the Night, 100
tech culture, 16, 111, 112, 113, 115, 128, 129, 139, 140, 141; bias against women, 111, 117, 121; community, 127, 128, 136, 140; digital manspreading, 113; egalitarian, 115, 127, 140, 149; exclusion, 112, 113, 115, 116, 120, 128; merit, 149; stereotypes, 113, 117, 132
tech industry, 3, 16, 111, 112, 113, 114, 115, 116, 117, 118, 119, 121, 125, 126, 140, 141, 147; business practices, 115, 121, 122, 124, 125, 148; coding/programming, 112, 113, 114, 116, 119, 121; conservatives, 115, 116, 123, 124, 125, 126, 147; diversity, 115, 116, 117, 119, 121, 122, 123, 124, 126, 147; diversity programs, 115, 116, 117, 118, 121, 123, 124, 125, 126; gender representation, 117, 119, 125, 141; history, 112; liberals, 117; meritocracy, 116; pair programming, 114, 121; people, 119, 121, 125; productivity, 116, 125; psychological safety, 117, 124, 125, 126; rules, 115, 119; software engineering, 119, 121; status, 120, 121; success, 114, 115, 116, 117, 119, 121, 140; systems, 119; user experience, 125
technological literacy, 114
Texas, 60, 61, 62, 63, 64, 66, 148
Texas House Bill 2, 58, 63, 66
therapeutic discourse, 30, 105
Till, Emmett, 85
toxic masculinity, 89, 92
traditional family, 30, 50n100, 67, 69, 70, 71, 75, 78, 79, 101, 149

Index 161

traditional marriage, 30, 68, 71
traditional values, 1, 8, 22, 30, 50n100, 67, 70, 74, 78, 101, 123
Tran, Kelly Marie, 16, 128, 133, 139
transgender, 6, 13, 14, 19n42, 80, 151; restroom access, 6
Trump, Donald, 1, 17, 53, 150, 153
Tumblr, 128, 141
Turner, Brock, 16, 87, 89, 91, 92, 93, 94, 96, 97, 98, 100, 105, 106, 147
Turner, Dan, 87, 89, 91, 94, 98
Twitter, 16, 128, 130, 132, 141, 152

unconscious bias, 117
University of Virginia, 91

Valenti, Jessica, 7, 103, 128, 130, 131, 132, 133, 138
VICE News, 111
video game industry, 112
video games, 131, 135, 136, 138
viewpoint diversity, 123, 124, 125
virtue, 101

Wahlberg, Mark, 21
The Wall Street Journal, 32
Weinstein, Harvey, 152
white fragility, 91, 92
white supremacy, 151
whiteness, 92, 123, 124
"Who is Daniel Holtzclaw?", 87, 90
Whole Woman's Health v. Hellerstedt, 57
Williams, Michelle, 21

woman/women, 13, 14, 43, 79, 104, 106, 150; caretakers, 43; dangerous, 138; family, 15, 25, 30, 43, 50n100, 67, 104; health, 53, 54, 55, 58, 59, 65; infantilization, 101; intelligence, 138; life chances, 1, 8, 9, 16, 19n42, 22, 24, 30, 46, 57, 91, 93, 147; life choices, 25, 28, 79; lived experience, 1, 6, 13, 55, 57, 101, 147, 149; mothers, 22, 42, 67, 69, 73, 74, 78, 104; passivity, 14, 101, 102, 103; rights, 3, 6, 9, 14, 45; self-esteem, 102; shared experiences, 8, 16, 43, 54, 87, 153; voice, 1, 14, 37, 87, 104, 113, 137, 151, 152, 153; wife, 42, 67, 69, 104
Women's March on Washington, 17, 150, 151, 153
Wookiepedia, 139
work-life balance, 6, 30, 120
workplace, 6, 15, 22, 23, 24, 25, 26, 28, 29, 30, 31, 32, 33, 34, 35, 36, 37, 38, 40, 42, 43, 45, 46, 50n100, 141, 148, 149; expectations, 22, 23, 30, 36, 38, 40, 41, 43
World War II, 112
worldview, 13, 16, 116, 117, 121, 123, 124, 125, 126, 127, 138, 139
Wu, Naomi, 111

xenophobia, 151

Yiannopoulos, Milo, 16, 128, 134
YouTube, 111, 128

About the Author

Lucy J. Miller (PhD, Texas A&M University) is lecturer in the Department of Communication at Texas A&M University. Her work appears in *Women & Language*, *Spectator*, and *Participations: Journal of Audience and Reception Studies*. She is also co-editor with Amanda R. Martinez of *Gender in a Transitional Era: Changes and Challenges* (Lexington Books, 2015).